Literary LONDON
AN ILLUSTRATED GUIDE

EDWIN WEBB

SPELLMOUNT LTD
Tunbridge Wells, Kent

In preparation in this same illustrated London Guide series:
LAWYERS' LONDON
MUSICAL LONDON
LONDON'S ART & ARTISTS
CEREMONIAL LONDON

First published in U.K. in 1990 by
SPELLMOUNT LIMITED
12 Dene Way, Speldhurst
Tunbridge Wells, Kent TN3 0NX

© Edwin Webb 1990

British Library Cataloguing in Publication Data
Webb, Edwin
  Literary London – (London Literary guides)
  1. London. Literary associations – visitors' guides
  I. Title
  914.210859

ISBN 0-946771-64-2

Title page illustration by courtesy of The Witch Ball Antiquarian Print Shop.

All rights reserved. No part of this publication may be reproduced, stored in a retrieval system or transmitted in any form or by any other means, electronic, mechanical, photocopying, recording or otherwise, without prior permission in writing from Spellmount Limited, Publishers.

Designed by Words & Images, Speldhurst, Tunbridge Wells, Kent
Printed in Great Britain by the KPC Group Ltd, Ashford, Kent
Typeset by Vitaset, Paddock Wood, Kent

CONTENTS

Acknowledgements	7
Introduction	8

CITY OF LONDON

Fleet Street	13
The Temple	23
Ludgate, St Paul's and Aldersgate	30
Charterhouse and Smithfield	39
City Road (Islington)	50
Moorgate to the Bank	57
The Bank to London Bridge	65
Eastcheap and the Tower	74

SOUTHWARK

The Borough and Bankside	87

CITY OF WESTMINSTER

Whitehall and Westminster	104
The Strand	113
Covent Garden	121
Soho	132
Marylebone I	144
Marylebone II	151

CAMDEN

Holborn	159
Bloomsbury I	170
Bloomsbury II	180
Hampstead	189
Bibliography	201
Index of Persons	203

THIS BOOK IS FOR
MATTHEW
RICHARD
AND
ROBERT

ACKNOWLEDGEMENTS

My own first introduction to the literary associations of London was through George Williams's *Guide to Literary London* (1973). Though the construction of tours in the following pages has been assembled to a different design, I am considerably indebted to Professor Williams's book; and despite the fact that much has changed in London since his book was first published, it remains still the most comprehensive listing of London locations and literary associations.

Anyone who takes London as a theme for writing will be indebted to *The London Encyclopaedia* (1983) edited by Ben Weinreb and Christopher Hibbert, and I am happy to add my acknowledgement too to this invaluable resource.

I owe a special debt of gratitude to Simon McCudden and Julian Bousher, Senior Archaeologists within the Museum of London's Department of Greater London Archaeology, and Site Directors of the Globe and Rose theatre excavations respectively. Both gave me generously of their time and specialised knowledge, and made their findings available to me. To Julian Bousher I am additionally indebted for supplying me with copies of scale site-plans of the Rose theatre on which further work could be conducted, as below. Other members of the DGLA, Harvey Sheldon, Gavin Evans, and Michael Hammerson, have each, at different times, responded to my requests for help and information, and I thank them for their courtesy.

I thank Christine Eccles for permitting me to use the findings of an experiment, conducted on her behalf by Julian Bousher, in advance of the publication of her own book *The Rose Theatre*. To my colleague Keith Wood I extend my thanks for the detailed calculation of pit and stage areas for both phases of the Rose theatre; from which, by an extrapolation from the estimates resulting from Christine Eccles's experiment, I have arrived at my own calculations of the standing capacity for that Elizabethan theatre.

I owe thanks to the Librarians of Thames Polytechnic (Roehampton branch) for their unfailing help, as always, in locating copies of books which I required. The ready assistance offered me by Elinor Stewart, Slide Curator within the School of Architecture and Landscape, Thames Polytechnic, proved most useful in the conduct of picture research. To Nina Tranter I am indebted for tracing texts through the second-hand book market, as well as for her help in constructing the Hampstead tour.

From his own extensive knowledge of London and its literary and artistic associations Vincent Whitcombe offered me several suggestions to follow up, for which I thank him. For his enthusiasm and encouragement on this, as with many of my projects, I thank also Edward Lee.

Richard Meier of the Shakespeare Globe Museum, Southwark, was most helpful to me, whilst Jennifer Jones, Public Relations Officer of the Shakespeare Globe Project, kindly responded to my enquiries about the project in the light of the discoveries at Bankside. I thank them both.

I am grateful to Peter Joslin for the care and time he devoted to working with me on the picture research, and for some of the original photographs which he made at my request. I am indebted, too, to Mike Abrahams who generously made available to me illustrations in his possession. Annabel Elton, of the Federation of British Artists, helped me in trying to trace an item of copyright.

Various groups of my students at Thames Polytechnic have accompanied me on some of the tours as described in these pages. Their responses, as well as their questions, have enabled me to be clearer as to what the reader is likely to find of interest – as well as prompting me to search further information. On my many personal wanderings whilst constructing the shape of the sections of this book I have been helped by many persons – all of whom must remain anonymous, since we did not exchange names. Clergymen, gardeners, curators, doormen, caretakers, and passers-by have all volunteered information to me – not all of it on all occasions either relevant or accurate, it must be said – but I thank them all for their interest and their desire to be helpful.

Finally I should like to thank my publisher, Ian Morley-Clarke, for extending to me a privilege rarely offered to an author – of making this book with a free hand. Though I am grateful for his lack of interference, it means therefore that the sins of omission or commission remain mine entirely.

Edwin Webb
January 1990

INTRODUCTION

Three of the old Gateway entrances to the City of London: left to right, Aldersgate, Newgate, Moorgate.

Within the accumulated and rich heritage which is English literature, London features repeatedly and prominently; through its associations with people, events, places, and the works and lives of numerous authors. From Chaucer's day on, writers have chosen to live and work in London all because there – in degree larger than anywhere else in the British Isles – were to be found the opportunities they needed or desired: of patronage, of employment, of publication, of performance. Even well into the eighteenth century, writers who were not themselves either aristocratic, or eminent, or rich, regularly sought and often needed patronage and the protection which it afforded. In earlier periods, certainly through to the Tudor, the consumers of literature were its 'begetters' – an educated, noble élite who wrote for their own small society. Those not of noble birth sought the sponsorship of those who were; and were rewarded with money and with advancement. Rich and powerful patrons tended to be at court or connected with court; thus many writers were where the court was. The economy of English literature was therefore for some centuries almost of a feudal nature.

The 'democratisation' of literature probably emerges from a confluence of influences. First, there was the invention of the technology of moveable-type printing – which made possible the (comparatively) speedy and cheap production of books in large numbers. Circulation was no longer dependent upon the handing on, or copying out, of manuscript copy. And as London grew, both spatially and in the numbers of its citizens, so the demand for writings of all kinds enlarged. Bookseller entrepreneurs readily satisfied, and additionally stimulated, the demand. Then there was, as I see it, the great impetus supplied by the Elizabethan-Jacobean theatre, a phenomenon started in the fourth quarter of the sixteenth century. For here, on the stage, was presented 'active literature', the drama of events enacted to large crowds of people – ordinary folk, artisans, apprentices, shopkeepers, suddenly the majority consumers of the art, the wealthy in the audience now a minority. The transition can be seen in the case of Shakespeare: his poems (*Venus and Adonis*, *The Rape of Lucrece*, the *Sonnets*) dedicated to his patron, Henry Wriothesley, Earl of Southampton, and the majority of his plays 'sponsored', as it were, by an eager play-going public. In this new arrangement of things the 'public' became the patrons of literature, and the economy of literature a mixed one. Printed literature of a whole variety of kinds, of course, could also be offered directly to the public – many of them unedited by the need for patronage, and hence the sweeteners of dedication. Though, clearly, the writer who could ingratiate himself might still hope for advantage, the arbitrator of taste became increasingly the bookseller, the publisher whose tastes in the main and for the majority of them were derived from market forces: what would sell, to satisfy a demand, and what might be promoted in order to create a demand. Alongside all of these forces must be put, too, the fact of an enlargingly literate society to which the publication trade must itself somehow have contributed – since the sheer volume of works produced, of 'high' and 'low' literature alike, can not be accounted for by an equation with the small numbers of citizens with the benefit of formal schooling.

The growth of a city, and London more than most cities, establishes a differently organised economy: where the rich and powerful set up there will be opportunities for employment, gathering more people to the same place; the level of wants consequently increases, and more tradespeople and others are required to service those needs – and because the services are there and the labour is available in numbers, even more of the rich and the fashionable are attracted to the place in increasing numbers. New trades and services can be offered, specialisation and sophistication develop, and some citizens achieve new wealth. The old and the newly wealthy alike establish themselves in the city, because that is the place to be or to be seen to be, and the city stratifies its population – from the noble, through its ranked classes of citizenry, to its underworld of footpads, murderers, cheats and rogues. The sheer variety of humanity thus congregated becomes its own spectacle, and thereby itself a source of inspiration to its writers. The eighteenth century, for example, though looking back to classical models of literature, increasingly freed itself of the need for imitation: it is *contemporary* sense-impression which fills the novels of Defoe, Fielding, Richardson. The city becomes its own subject in literature, supplying its own texture of events, people, places. The city grows, its population increases, the range and variety of its buildings, its institutions, its entertainments, all expand.

Reasons such as these to which I have very briefly pointed all contribute to the important gravitational pull which London exerted upon writers. Of course, there are other reasons, of a different character.

A great city, by its compression of people – persons so many and so various and all sharing the same comparatively small space – can also generate its own energies. Ideas spark in the electricity of a city's activities, and in the current of conversation (even competition) with other communities of writers, artists, intellectuals. Where the city itself does not supply its own theme to the writer there is nonetheless the stimulation of the company of like-minded people, practitioners in the arts. The London of Shakespeare and his contemporaries, and their gatherings, shows this clearly; as, in like measure, do the coteries grouped around Dryden and then Johnson; and, in more recent times, so does the Bloomsbury Group illustrate the point. Clearly writers have been attracted to London because it became a 'centre' for their operations. Many stayed, and made London their permanent base. Others were attracted to the city, or found it unavoidable, or were required to make short or extended visits, but made their home elsewhere. Such writers often left their impressions of the city. Johnson loved his London, as did Dickens (though with many particular reservations) to whom the city was a major source of inspiration. Wordsworth's responses, however, were very much mixed – attraction and repulse often a simultaneous reaction. The detailed account is in Book Seventh of *The Prelude*; and, as here, it is clear that Wordsworth both delighted in the profusion of activity, colour, and movement which he saw and heard everywhere in London, and was at the same time disenchanted, glad to be free of such sensuous assaults:

> Thou endless stream of men and moving things!
> Thy everyday appearance, as it strikes –
> With wonder heightened, or sublimed by awe –
> On strangers, of all ages; the quick dance
> Of colours, lights and forms; the deafening din;
> The comers and the goers face to face,
> Face after face; the string of dazzling wares,
> Shop after shop, with symbols, blazoned names,
> All the tradesman's honours overhead . . .
> . . . the roar continues, till at length,
> Escaped as from an enemy, we turn
> Abruptly into some sequestered nook,
> Still as a sheltered place when winds blow loud!

Many visitors to London will undoubtedly share something of Wordsworth's reaction: the profusion of sights and sounds, the busyness of the city's bustle, and the sometimes overwhelming density of people – workers, tourists, residents. Yet the 'sequestered nook' remains, too; and will be encountered throughout all parts of the city, as those who follow the itineraries of this guide will perhaps surprisingly discover. For in some important respects London projects not a single but a more various *persona*, one with several histories.

The evolution of London, its acquisitive outgrowing from the original cities of London and of Westminster, has suffered from three major catastrophies: the Great Fire of 1666 which burned out the medieval heartland of the City of London; the Blitz of the 2nd World War which laid waste whole tracts of land and buildings; and the post-war blight of much of the 'development' which ensued. Much has been razed, obliterated, or drastically altered. Yet there is a very great deal more which remains than one might at first suspect; and there are compensations.

There are the glories of Wren's churches to replace those lost in the Great Fire; there is the fact that a great deal of faithful restoration and preservation of buildings has followed the 2nd World War. And there is the compensation that without the speculative development of land some important discoveries would have remained undisclosed. Most significant among these are the recent discoveries, at Bankside in Southwark, of the remains of the foundations of the Rose theatre, followed months later by those of the Globe, the theatre of Shakespeare. And in the fact that without public pressure and campaigning the Rose foundations would have been covered over, buried again within just months of their finding, there is another sign of the consciousness (shared by many of its guardians also) that London is not private property. It belongs not to its speculators and entrepreneurs. London belongs to its nation, and is an irreplaceable repository of the history of a nation and its culture.

***

In preparing this book, in visiting (in many instances, several times over) every location cited, I have tried to make accessible the sense of discovery, or rediscovery, which awaits the visitor and the armchair-tourist alike: to animate verbally and visually a sense of the spirit of place and time which illustrates the connection of author, works, and location.

The tours have been designed, first, as intrinsically interesting in themselves, incorporating established places of pilgrimage with lesser-known locations. Whole areas of the capital which, given 'world enough and time', I would have wished to map out have had to be excluded from this book – whilst those which are incorporated will ensure that the reader is presented with most of the important references, and will be provided with something of that variety in the character of London to which I referred earlier.

The areas covered occupy discrete, if occasionally flexible, geographical zones. Most tours have been designed to occupy a leisurely half-day or so, though the Hampstead tour is an exception and would require a whole day. Other tours may readily expand in duration with the inclination of the tourist; and it is perhaps worth stating that all of these tours will take the visitor past places which, though not having a specifically literary connection, one might very well wish to inspect. Within the text will also be found suggestions as to how to combine some of these tours, for those with limited time (or limitless energy).

Because, from personal experience, I have found that many guide books are adequate in the directions they give only if you already know where to find the place mentioned, I have tried to give full and precise instructions as to location, directions, and distances or walking-times. Even without a map the user of this book should therefore encounter little difficulty in locating each place referred to.

Though it may be – as one philosopher noted – that the point of a journey is not to arrive but to travel with a different view, it remains nonetheless true, I think, that it helps to have specific places to visit on the way. It is in that spirit which this book is offered.

Finally, one of the great personal joys of the several years spent researching, collating, and presenting this guide has been to send me back to a re-reading of literary works and, on even more occasions, to propel me to a first reading of many others. I hope that this book will induce in turn the same response in its readers.

***

FLEET STREET

CITY OF LONDON

From the time of the first newspaper published here towards the end of the eighteenth century, Fleet Street's most prominent associations through to the present have been with the newspaper-publishing industry, though the 'new technology' of news-gathering and printing has in recent years promoted a movement away from this centre of most of the leading presses. The history of literary publications within the vicinity, however, considerably pre-dates the newspaper empire. From the mid sixteenth century onwards, in printing-houses located both in the small courts leading off, and in Fleet Street itself, was sited a succession of presses. Close to the entrance to Middle Temple Lane, for example, Richard Tottel published the translation of *The Aeneid* made by Henry Howard, Earl of Surrey (1517-1547), and the *Book of Songs and Sonnets* (1557) which included Howard's other poetry together with the work of Sir Thomas Wyatt. From the same site a later publisher issued work by Sir John Vanbrugh, John Gay, Sir Richard Steele and Alexander Pope. From Falcon Court, a little further east along Fleet Street, was issued *Gorboduc* (1565), established as the first tragedy in English, written by Thomas Sackville (1536-1608) and Thomas Norton (1532-1608). And around the site of a former church where the present St Dunstan's now stands a number of booksellers congregated. Most notably, from here were sold the first quarto of Shakespeare's *Hamlet* (1604) and Milton's *Paradise Lost* (1667).

* * *

Fleet Street takes its name from the old Fleet River which used to run from Hampstead to join the Hole Bourne (from which derives Holborn), to enter the Thames at Blackfriars. From the Blackfriars tube station subway exit No. 8 leads into New Bridge Street, heading towards Fleet Street. Shortly before the turning into Fleet Street itself, however, will be found a narrow entrance to the left, Bride Lane, which leads around St Bride's Church. St Bride – a corruption of Bridget – was a 6th-century Irish saint, popular with the Vikings, who founded the first church here. Following an air raid of December 1940 archaeological investigations revealed the foundations of seven previous churches on this site, dating from the earliest and original sixth-century Saxon building to a church of the seventeenth century. Excavations revealed, too, that the site had also once been a pagan Roman cemetery; and among the finds was that of the skeleton of a Roman woman who had been given a Christian burial. The present church, to replace the one burnt down in the Great Fire of 1666, was built to a design of Sir Christopher Wren, between the years 1671-8.

In the font, which still survives, of the preceding church Samuel Pepys was baptised. The font, surmounted by a wooden model of Wren's design for the 'wedding-cake' spire (added to the church in 1703), will be found in the far aisle directly facing the entrance.

John Milton (1608-1674) lived at one time in a house in the church yard of St Bride's. And John Dryden (1631-1700) composed 'Alexander's Feast' for the fourth Annual Society of St Cecilia's Festival held at St Bride's in 1689.

Richard Lovelace (1628-57), Cavalier poet, was buried in the church. Lovelace had died, in extreme poverty, in the garret of a house in nearby Gunpowder Alley – which was at that time an extension of Wine Office Court, on the opposite side of Fleet Street, connecting with Shoe Lane.

Lovelace's poems were published posthumously in 1659. Though some appear contrived and can be over-elaborated, many of the simpler lyrics contain a memorable directness. Ranging across subject (and including emblem poems such as 'The Snail'), most of the poems centre upon the conditions of love. Among these are the famous lines from 'To Lucasta, on Going to the Warres': 'I could not love thee (Deare) so much, Lov'd I not Honour more'; and the impressive dignity of the poem 'To Althea, from Prison' (see Whitehall and Westminster section).

Also buried in the former church were Thomas Sackville (see above) and Samuel Richardson.

Richardson (1689-1761), one of the earliest of English novelists, had lived for some years at Salisbury Square, almost adjacent to the church, during which time he had produced both *Pamela* (1740) and *Clarissa Harlowe* (1747-48) – both of which were composed in letter-form, and the first of which seems to echo recollections from the youthful stage of Richardson's own life-story.

Richardson had been born in Devon where, as a young boy, he had acquired the nickname 'Serious' – and, for the rest of his life he would be regarded as somewhat solemn, even priggish. From early youth he helped local servant-girls to write their love-letters; at seventeen he became apprenticed to a printer, whose daughter he married in 1721, and developed a prosperous printing business. So much so that he was appointed printer to the House of Commons and Master of the Stationers' Company.

In middle age he undertook to produce a collection of model letters to serve as a manual on the art of letter-writing. And it was this project which suggested to him the possibility of fictional work structured as a series of letters. Within two months of composition he had produced *Pamela; or Virtue Rewarded*. The story-line is simple: Mr B, the son of the household where Pamela is employed, tries to seduce her. He uses all his charm and persuasion – but she, with the good sense and strength which her innate virtue lends her, is able to repel all his advances. Eventually the son, recognising her true value, offers her his hand in marriage.

The novel was an immediate success, and was even treated as a text worthy of sermons preached from the pulpit. There were critics, though, who questioned the nature of this particular virtue – seeing a certain degree of artful manipulation in the

St. Bride's church.

innocent maid. Richardson was thus also satirised (most notably by Henry Fielding in *Shamela*, 1741) as well as being received with excessive praise.

Clarissa Harlowe, a huge novel, was accorded an equally great reception, and Richardson's influence upon the English novel has been immense. Among the critical claims still made for him the most significant is that he was perhaps the first English novelist to introduce a true sense of the psychology of character where the inner realities of motive and reflection become visible.

When the present St Bride's was built by Sir Christopher Wren in 1670-84 the locations of the graves of Lovelace and Sackville were lost, though it is known that Richardson's grave was in the centre aisle. During the blitz of 1940, however, much of the Wren building was demolished, with the exception of the steeple and most of the outer walling. Richardson's gravestone also survived. In 1956-57 the church was restored to Wren's design.

George Williams recounts the following 'macabre but well-authenticated story':

> . . . an American scholar, specializing in Richardson, rushed over to London immediately after the Second World War, and visited St Bride's. He found the coffins and corpses that had been exposed by the bombings

now stacked to one side, waiting for reinterment, and rebuilding of the church. The scholar found the body of Richardson, and touched him on the nose!

The Richardson gravestone will be found today set against the left-hand corner of the outside back wall of the church. The top half of the stone is now badly worn, though the inscriptions for both Richardson and his wife are clearly readable.

The crypt of St Bride's should certainly be visited. There the fascinating history of St Bride's can be traced through the whole series of its churches. Among the exposed Roman and Norman stoneworks there is mounted a fine display of the church's history and its connections with Fleet Street, and thus with printing. There will be found also a facsimile volume of Caxton's translation of the first nine books of Ovid's *Metamorphoses* made in 1480.

* * *

The passageway around St Bride's leads out into Fleet Street itself where a little distance on, on the left-hand side, will be found Whitefriars Street (known formerly as Water Lane). Here, about fifty or so yards along on the right-hand side, stood the Black Lion Inn where James Boswell (1740-95) spent his first night in London on Friday 19 November 1762. It was later, in the following January, the house to which he triumphantly returned with Mrs Lewis, an actress at Covent Garden Theatre, the Louisa of his *London Journal* (1762-63). Arrived there, they heard the bells of St Bride's ring out 'their merry chimes' – at which sound Boswell remarked to his Louisa that 'the bells in Cupid's court would be this night set a-ringing for joy at [their] union'. The *Journal* goes on to record the young man's self-congratulatory 'godlike vigour' with which he enjoyed the 'most luscious feast' of that 'voluptuous night'. Now a self-styled 'Man of Pleasure' he records with evident satisfaction:

> I really conducted this affair with a manliness and prudence that pleased me very much. The whole expense was just eighteen shillings.

* * *

A few steps beyond Whitefriars Street, Bouverie Street opens to the left. At No 3, on the right-hand side of the street, will be found a plaque commemorating the fact that 'In a house on this site lived William Hazlitt 1829'. Hazlitt (1778-1830), critic and essayist, had not resided long in lodgings at this address before moving to Soho where he died shortly afterwards. (See Soho section.)

* * *

Continuing along Fleet Street, about 25 yards or so beyond the opening to Old Mitre Court, will be found another plaque (at what is now No 37) recording the site of the Mitre Tavern. The Mitre was a favourite of Dr Johnson, where he and his company frequently met. It was also a highly respectable tavern – one at the least, according to Johnson himself, where if a man led in a wench both parties had to be well dressed.

The present Olde Cock Tavern where T. S. Eliot held regular editorial meetings for the Criterion *in the 1920s.*

Further along Fleet Street, at No 22, there is the Old Cock Tavern, not the original, but a reminder of the former which stood on the opposite side of the street, facing the opening to Middle Temple Lane. Samuel Pepys was a regular visitor at the old inn which survived until towards the end of the last century. A century after Pepys, Dr Johnson and friends within his circle were also regular customers. The Doctor in fact had his own chair in the tavern, now to be seen in 'Johnson's House' (see below). Later visitors included Charles Dickens and Alfred, Lord Tennyson.

In the present Cock Tavern T. S. Eliot (1888-1965) used to hold planning meetings in the early 1920s, over lunch, for the literary journal the *Criterion*. Among regular guests whose advice Eliot, as editor, sought were: Herbert Read, Harold Monro, Bonamy Dobrée, Richard Church and Frank Morley.

Mrs Salmon's Waxworks, 17 Fleet Street. In 1711 Mrs Salmon had installed her waxwork figures in a house near Chancery Lane on the opposite side of Fleet Street. Moved to No 17 by the new owner, a figure on crutches greeted the visitor, whilst Old Mother Shipton, the witch, kicked at the visitor on the way out.

A few doors beyond the public-house, on the first floor of the building at No 17, may be seen the half-timber work of Prince Henry's Room at the entrance to Inner Temple Lane. Built in the years 1610-11, it was one of the few dwellings to survive the Great Fire of 1666. It now houses a small display of Pepysiana (including an original letter of Pepys's for the year 1669) – though the diarist himself has no connection with the house.

From 1795 until well into Victorian times this building housed Mrs Salmon's Waxworks, her collection having been taken over by a surgeon following the original owner's death in 1760. During her own long life, Mrs Salmon had displayed her waxworks at St Martin's-le-Grand, and at Southwark and Bartholomew Fairs. The works, comic, grotesque, some arranged in tableaux, and some operated by clockwork, were seen on several occasions by both Hogarth and by Boswell.

When their housing was moved to Fleet Street the displays were seen by Charles Dickens, and were visited by David in *David Copperfield* (ch.xxxiii).

* * *

At this point the visitor may proceed directly to the remainder of this tour by continuing further along Fleet Street (as below); or, alternatively, incorporate here a visit to the grounds and buildings of The Temple. For those who may wish to do the latter, directions – as from Prince Henry's Room – are gathered in The Temple section.

* * *

A short distance beyond Prince Henry's Room the Gateway entrance leading into The Temple grounds will be found at Middle Temple Lane. A few yards past that entrance, and on the same side of the street, will be seen a plaque, at what is now No 1 Fleet Street, marking the former site of the Devil Tavern. One of Doctor Johnson's favourite meeting-places, the Devil Tavern in fact had its origins in the Apollo Club initiated in the middle of the sixteenth century by the poet and playwright Ben Jonson. In later times the tavern was frequented by Samuel Pepys; and after him Addison, Steele and Swift. It was demolished in 1787.

The bank now occupying this site is the Child's Branch of William and Glyn's. In the building which preceded the present building (of 1879), and was in fact Child's Bank, Charles Dickens located the Tellson's Bank which features in *A Tale of Two Cities*:

Tellson's Bank by Temple Bar was an old fashioned place . . . It was very small, very dark, very ugly, very incommodious . . . the triumphant perfection of inconvenience. After bursting open a door of idiotic obstinancy with a weak rattle in its throat, you fell into Tellson's down two steps, and came to your senses in a miserable little shop with two little counters, where the oldest of men made your cheque shake as if the wind rustled it, while they examined the signature by the dingiest of windows. (II,i)

***

A little back from this location Chancery Lane joins Fleet Street on the opposite, or north side of the street. Within a hundred yards of the junction, on the right-hand side, will be found the Public Record Office – and the public museum which it houses. The Record Office itself contains the national archive of state papers, legal records and a vast range of other documents (occupying a total of 90 miles of shelving). Among its possessions are many of literary interest, including letters by Philip Sidney, Francis Bacon, Ben Jonson, John Milton, Samuel Pepys, Daniel Defoe, James Boswell,

Next to Wren's Temple Bar (of 1670-2), which separated Fleet Street from the Strand, stood Child's Bank – on the left as viewed in this print. In 1678 John Dryden deposited here £50 as a reward for anyone who would discover the thugs employed by Lord Rochester to beat him up in Rose Alley (see Covent Garden). Alongside Child's stands the gable-ended building of the Devil Tavern.

Charles Dickens and Matthew Arnold, together with a document signature by John Bunyan.

Since 1962 Shakespeare's Last Will and Testament, of 25 March 1616, has been stored in the Public Record Office. By this date Shakespeare was a dying man who would survive for another month only. Each of the three pages of the document is signed by Shakespeare; of these, little remains of the first – the lower left-hand corner of the paper having decayed. The other two signatures clearly show an invalid hand. The third and final signature to the Will is prefixed with the affirmative 'By me'; this and the 'William' of the signature are firm enough to show that Shakespeare mustered his strength for the task, then (in the words of

Shakespeare's signature on the third sheet of his Last Will and Testament, showing the failing hand of the dramatist. A transcription of the entire will can be found in E. K. Chambers, William Shakespeare: A Study of Facts and Problems, *ii, 170-4.*   Public Record Office

Schoenbaum) 'collapsed into the wavering scrawl of the surname'.

The Will has incited endless debate and controversy; most particularly over the bequest to his wife, Anne: 'Item I gyve unto my wief my second best bed with the furniture' (that is, together with the bed linen, the hangings, and so on). Since the entry is an interlineation, and the Will had not until then referred to Anne, some commentators have seen this afterthought as, at the least, a lack of Shakespeare's regard for his wife. In fact, the common law of the time entitled Anne to one third of her husband's estate in any case, as well as residence in the family home – so that in these respects the wife was provided for without special clause having to be made.

As to 'the second best bed' other explanations are possible for, as a man of some substance, Shakespeare would have provided for guests to the family home in Stratford. To them, as honoured guests, would have been available the 'best' bed. Thus the 'second best' bed might indeed have been the marital bed, and Shakespeare's recalling of it and its particular mention in bequest to his wife, can be seen indeed as a mark of affection and love. In the end, there is only speculation.

The museum display, necessarily small in relation to the wealth of materials stored within the Public Record Office, is nonetheless certainly worth visiting (Monday to Friday, 1.00pm to 4.00pm). The exhibits are changed periodically and those presented at any one time may not be of exclusively literary interest. The Record Office has, however, produced two publications, with facsimiles, which will be of especial interest to readers of this book and will supplement their visit. They are: *Men of Letters* (1974) and *Shakespeare in the Public Records* (1985), available at the museum bookshop, together with a range of other facsimile materials.

***

Returning to Fleet Street and heading back towards Ludgate Circus, on the left-hand side within a short distance will be found the church of St Dunstan's in the West. The church as it stands today dates from 1833, though a church has occupied the site since the thirteenth century. In the previous church were buried Thomas Campion (1567-1620) and Thomas Carew (1595?-1639?). The poet John Donne (1572-1631) had been its rector for the seven years from 1624; and Izaak Walton (1593-1683), author of the still-popular *Compleat Angler, or the Contemplative Man's Recreation*, one of its vestrymen.

The 'afterthought', penned in as interlineation, which has given rise to endless controversy: 'Item I gyve unto my wief my second best bed with the furniture.'   Public Record Office

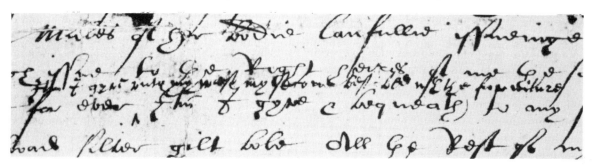

Walton, who had his own ironmongery business in Fleet Street, and lived in nearby Chancery Lane, became one of Donne's firmest friends; and many years after Donne's death he edited a collection of the poet-preacher's sermons, to which he prefixed his *Life of Dr John Donne* (1640). Later he added other biographical accounts of four more Anglican divines (Wotton, Hooker, Herbert and Sanderson), which collectively constitute *Izaak Walton's Lives*.

To the right-hand side of the entrance to the present-day church there is a plaque to Izaak Walton, and inside the church there is a stained glass window 'erected by some Anglers and other admirers of Walton in the month of April 1895'.

* * *

A short distance on from St Dunstan's, on the same side of the street, is Johnson's Court (not named after the Doctor) where, at No 7 – long demolished – Johnson lived from 1765 to 1776. The site of the former house is located with a plaque.

Also in the Court used to be the offices of the *Monthly Magazine*, the periodical which was the first to publish any piece of Charles Dickens's writing. Dickens's friend, John Forster, recorded in his *Life* of the author that the young man dropped the manuscript into the letter-box 'stealthily one evening at twilight with fear and trembling'.

A little beyond here is the opening to Bolt Court where the Doctor died in 1784, though that house too no longer survives, having burnt down in 1819. This was the house at which Johnson suffered the squabbles of various of his dependants and other 'pensioners' to whom he gave welfare.

* * *

Further along Fleet Street, just yards beyond the entrance to that court, a narrow opening leads into Wine Office Court. Here, on the right-hand side, will be found a printed sign recalling an observation made by Johnson to Boswell. The correct, and full, version would read:

> Sir, if you wish to have a just notion of the magnitude of this city, you must not be satisfied with its great streets and squares, but must survey the innumerable little lanes and courts. It is not in the showy evolution of buildings, but in the multiplicity of human habitations which are crowded together, that the wonderful immensity of London consists.
>
> (5 July 1763: Boswell's *Life*)

The London which Johnson loved was the crowded huddle of shops, taverns, houses and

Johnson's house in Bolt Court, to which he moved from Johnson's Court in 1776. In this house he died, and on his death-bed quoted to his physician, Brocklesby, the passage of Shakespeare:

> *Canst then not minister to a mind diseased;*
> *Pluck from the memory a rooted sorrow;*
> *Raze out the written troubles of the brain;*
> *And with some sweet oblivious antidote*
> *Cleanse the stuffed bosom of that perilous stuff*
> *Which weighs upon the heart?*

eating-houses which had quickly restored London after the Great Fire of 1666. Then, most of its wooden buildings had been destroyed, and from the year following the Fire all building had to be of brick or stone. Yet the buildings were still densely packed, and in that respect the sentiment of Johnson's remarks holds good today. For despite all the rebuilding of the last two centuries there remain many little lanes and courts to investigate, in this part of the capital as elsewhere.

The notice recalling these words of the Doctor is set against the wall of Ye Olde Cheshire Cheese. A public house rebuilt in 1667 it is a good example of the rebuilding which took place immediately following the Great Fire.

The Cheshire claims to have been frequented by Johnson and some of his circle – among them Reynolds, Gibbon, Garrick, Dr Burney and Boswell. Though Boswell himself nowhere actually confirms the claim, given its proximity to at least three of his residences – and given the Doctor's predilection for company, conversation and drinking-houses – there is a very likely probability that Johnson would indeed have visited there. What is certain is that in the 1890s the Rhymers' Club did hold regular meetings there, in a room on the second floor. Its members included Arthur Symons, Ernest Dowson, Lionel Johnson, Richard le Gallienne and W. B. Yeats.

Of these only Yeats went on to achieve an unarguable greatness in his poetry. In his *Autobiographies* Yeats refers to 'The Tragic Generation' of his fellow Rhymers – and offers pen portraits of his contemporaries (though in the version published in his lifetime sometimes differing in both detail and expression from his first draft, which did not appear until 1972). Lionel Johnson (1867-1902), for example, became a chronic alcoholic – a habit begun at University on the recommendation of a doctor as a palliative for insomnia. Johnson's austere intellect embraced the orthodoxies of Catholicism, and its dogmas 'stirred his passion like the beauty of a mistress'. Johnson's erudition, and his mastering of languages was impressive, and 'He became', wrote Yeats, 'for a few years my closest friend.' He was, however, 'content that books should be his world' – a renunciation conveyed through the refined aestheticism of his poetry. Johnson in fact died as a result of a fractured skull after falling off a chair in a public house.

Ernest Dowson (1867-1900), on the other hand, produced poetry of expressive but unfulfilled eroticism – of which the best-known remains *Non sum qualis . . .* containing the following verse (whose last line is refrained throughout the poem):

> All night upon my heart I felt her warm heart beat,
> Night-long within my arms in love and sleep she lay;
> Surely the kisses of her bought red mouth were sweet;
> But I was desolate and sick of an old passion,
>   When I awoke and found the dawn was grey:
> I have been faithful to thee, Cynara! in my fashion.

The Cynara of the poem was the young daughter of the keeper of an Italian eating-house in Soho, for whom Dowson conceived an inordinate passion – which she did not return. When he was sober she remained for him an image of ideal love and, in Yeats's words, 'he would not look at [another] woman'; but when drunk, 'any woman, dirty or clean, served his purpose'. Dowson's Cynara 'married the waiter and Dowson's life went to wreck'. Drink (and a fondness for absinthe particularly) and dissipation combined in his early death.

The poetry of Arthur Symons (1865-1945) has something of the same qualities of sexual longing – though its subjects this time are the chance encounters with the 'Juliets' of the night. Symons, it seemed to Yeats, had 'chosen deliberately a life of music-halls and amorous adventure' in order that 'he might have vivid impressions for his verse'. Symons's critical book on the *Symbolist Movement in Literature* (1899), though, did achieve influence. In December 1908 T. S. Eliot (1888-1965) came across a copy of Symons's book at Harvard University. It changed dramatically the conception of poetry which he designed for his own poetry – principally because in Symons's work he there encountered the poetry of Jules Laforgue and the mannered, ironic pessimism of his adopted pose. It provided Eliot with the careful contrivance he required for some of his early work.

A number of other literary visitors are claimed for the Cheshire – among them Conan Doyle, Carlyle, Dickens, Tennyson, Mark Twain and Paul Verlaine. Oscar Wilde is claimed also as a visitor – though the evidence of Yeats's words would refute this: 'It had been useless to invite him [Oscar Wilde] to the Cheshire Cheese, for he hated Bohemia.'

* * *

Beyond the Cheshire the passageway widens and a few steps ahead, connecting with a period house alongside, now stands a modern redbrick building. Formerly at No 6 in the court there stood the house where Oliver Goldsmith (1730-74) had lodgings in the years 1760 to 1762.

Goldsmith was generally well-liked by the Johnson circle, and by Johnson particularly, though Goldsmith was loquacious rather than a genuine conversationalist; he was also gay, vain, unfailingly good-hearted, sometimes naive, and always extravagant when he was in funds. More often than not, however, he was short of money; two years before taking up these lodgings, for example, Goldsmith had accepted work as a proof reader and corrector in Samuel Richardson's office.

Of Goldsmith, Dr Johnson said that 'No man was more foolish when he had not a pen in his hand, or more wise when he had.'

Whilst lodging in the court Goldsmith had written most or all of his novel *The Vicar of Wakefield*, and

The opening section of one of Johnson's essays in The Rambler, *displaying well the learning and characteristic rhetorical style of his didactic prose.*

---

134   THE RAMBLER.   Nº 22.

NUMB. 22. SATURDAY, *June* 2, 1750.

——*Ego nec studium sine divite venâ,*
Nec rude quid prosit video ingenium, alterius sic
Altera poscit opem res, & conjurat amice.   HOR.

Without a genius learning soars in vain;
And without learning genius sinks again;
Their force united crowns the sprightly reign.
        ELPHINSTON.

WIT and LEARNING were the children of Apollo, by different mothers; WIT was the offspring of EUPHROSYNE, and resembled her in cheerfulness and vivacity; LEARNING was born of SOPHIA, and retained her seriousness and caution. As their mothers were rivals, they were bred up by them from their birth in habitual opposition, and all means were so incessantly employed to impress upon them a hatred and contempt of each other, that though Apollo, who foresaw the ill effects of their discord, endeavoured to soften them, by dividing his regard equally between them, yet his impartiality and kindness were without effect; the maternal animosity was deeply rooted, having been intermingled with their first ideas, and was confirmed every hour, as fresh opportunities occurred of exerting it. No sooner were they of age to be received into the apartments of the other celestials, than WIT began to entertain Venus at her toilet, by aping the solemnity of LEARNING, and LEARNING to divert Minerva at her loom, by exposing the blunders and ignorance of wit.

Thus they grew up, with malice perpetually increasing, by the encouragement which each received from those whom their mothers had persuaded to patronise and support them; and longed to be admitted to the table of Jupiter, not so much for the hope of gaining honour, as of excluding a rival from all pretensions to regard, and of putting an everlasting stop to the progress of that influence which either believed the other to have obtained by mean arts and false appearances.

At last the day came, when they were both, with the usual solemnities, received into the class of superior deities, and allowed to take nectar from the hand of Hebe. But from that hour CONCORD lost her authority at the table of Jupiter. The rivals, animated by their new dignity, and incited by the alternate applauses of the associate powers, harassed each other by incessant contests, with such a regular vicissitude of victory, that neither was depressed.

It was observable, that, at the beginning of every debate, the advantage was on the side of WIT; and that, at the first sallies, the whole assembly sparkled, according to Homer's expression, with unextinguishable merriment. But LEARNING would

---

was substantially in debt. To his landlady he owed £36 in rent. To prevent his escaping from the sheriffs whom she had called to arrest him for this debt, she had taken away his clothes. Goldsmith sent to Johnson for help. Johnson thereupon sold Goldsmith's novel for him for the sum of 40 guineas – with an additional 20 guineas for the Doctor's personal assurance as to its merit. Goldsmith's novel appeared in 1766, four years after the sale of its copyright by Johnson.

***

Wine Office Court connects with Gough Square where, at No 17 (continue past to the left of the Goldsmith reference), will be found 'Dr Johnson's House' – the only one of the Doctor's London homes to survive to the present. It is now a museum, administered by a Trust, and has been restored as closely as possible to its condition at the Doctor's time of residence here. It houses a substantial collection of memorabilia and paintings connected with Johnson and his contemporaries. Among the exhibits are the Doctor's Will; his chair from the Old Cock Tavern – a 'gout chair' designed to take the weight off the legs; and, in Miss Williams's Room, the Doctor's letter formally proposing Boswell's election to 'The Club', which met in Gerrard Street. (See Soho section.)

Johnson lived at Gough Square from 1749 to 1759. Here he began publication of the *Rambler* (1750), followed by the *Idler* (1758). And it was during residence here that his beloved 'Tetty' died. He had married Elizabeth Porter, a widow and twenty years his senior, in 1735. There is no doubt that he was devoted to her, and that after their seventeen years of marriage, her death remained keenly felt by him.

21

Samuel Johnson – the engraving (after the painting of Reynolds) which was used as frontispiece to eighteenth century collected editions of The Rambler.

At Gough Square Johnson also laboured at his Dictionary – a project which at its beginning he had thought to complete in just three years. He had first advertised his Plan for the Dictionary in 1747 (addressed to Lord Chesterfield, whose patronage for the project he hoped to obtain), and had been commissioned in 1749 by a syndicate of booksellers to produce the work.

From Lord Chesterfield, in Boswell's words, Johnson received 'continued neglect'. Upon the eve of its eventual publication (in 1755) Lord Chesterfield who,

> . . . it is said, had flattered himself with expectations that Johnson would dedicate the work to him, attempted, in a courtly manner, to soothe and insinuate himself with the Sage conscious, as it should seem, of the cold indifference with which he had treated its learned author . . .

Lord Chesterfield had, in fact, published two papers in which he commended the forthcoming work with fulsome praise. Johnson's reply to his Lordship was devastating; and is surely a classic of the epistolary art. It reads, in part:

> Seven years, my Lord, have now past since I waited in your outward rooms, or was repulsed from your door; during which time I have been pushing on my work through difficulties, of which it is useless to complain, and have brought it, at last, to the verge of completion, without one act of assistance, one word of encouragement, or one smile of favour. Such treatment I did not expect, for I never had a Patron before . . .
>
> Is not a Patron, my Lord, one who looks with unconcern on a man struggling for life in the water and, when he has reached ground, encumbers him with help? The notice which you have been pleased to take of my labours, had it been early, had been kind; but it has been delayed till I am indifferent, and cannot enjoy it; till I am solitary, and cannot impart it; till I am known, and do not want it. I hope it is no very cynical asperity, not to confess obligations where no benefit has been received, or to be unwilling that the Publick should consider me as owing that to a Patron, which Providence has enabled me to do for myself . . .

The garret in the Gough Square house, where most of the work for the Dictionary was done, was 'fitted up like a counting-house', with a long work-surface, at which Johnson's six amenuenses copied out the entries. All the research for the work, however, was conducted by Johnson himself. Though not the first English Dictionary, Johnson's was the first to include definitions, etymologies and exemplar usages drawn from an extensive range of authors. A first edition of the Dictionary is on display in the Dining-Room of the house.

Johnson (1709-1784) straddles the eighteenth century, exemplifying the Age of Reason with his learning, wit, and formidable powers of debate; and as moralist and critic he remains its most influential arbiter of taste and judgement. He imposed himself upon the age as much by the force and extensiveness of his presence and his influence as by the power of his own writings. And by the painstaking labours of his biographer Boswell the largeness of that personality infuses our sense of what 'right thinking' and a tempered sensibility meant to those Augustan times.

* * *

From Dr Johnson's house, you may return to Blackfriars underground station by continuing along Fleet Street as far as Ludgate Circus, then turning right along New Bridge Street. Alternatively, you may wish to continue beyond Ludgate Circus, either to visit St Paul's cathedral or to follow, from Ludgate Circus, the entries gathered in the section Ludgate, St Paul's and Aldersgate.

CITY OF LONDON

THE TEMPLE

CITY OF LONDON

To start this tour begin either at the Aldwych or the Temple underground stations. From Aldwych turn to the right along the Strand, passing by the church of St Clement Danes (sited on its own island in the Strand), and passing through Temple Bar into Fleet Street. Within a short distance of this point the entrance to Inner Temple Lane will be arrived at, on the right – the distinctive half-timber work of Prince Henry's Room (for details see Fleet Street section) which straddles the Lane clearly marking out the entrance. From the Temple underground station, proceed up Arundel Street, directly facing, to the Strand, here turning to the right and locating Inner Temple Lane, as above. Visitors incorporating their tour of The Temple within the Fleet Street visit will be at this point of arrival.

The narrow Gateway entrance to Inner Temple Lane leads to a complex of courts and buildings known collectively as 'The Temple'. In fact the area covered by the Temple comprises two of the present four Inns of Court – the Inner Temple and the Middle Temple – though their division, east and west, is only notionally marked by the line of Middle Temple Lane.

The Temple derives its name from the Knights Templar who were established in London by the early twelfth century and who, through the accumulated gifts of rich benefactors, themselves became wealthy bankers and property-owners. Their growing power, and the threat which that power implied, lead to the suppression of the Order in 1312. The land alongside the river, on which they had built The Temple and their great house, was passed on to the Knights Hospitallers who, in turn, leased a part of the land to a group of lawyers for the purpose of using it as a hostel or lodging-house (an original sense of the term 'inn'). By the middle of the fifteenth century the lawyers had formed themselves into two societies, of the Inner Temple and Middle Temple.

Following the suppression of the Knights Hospitallers in 1539, the ownership of the land passed to the Crown. On making a gift of the land to the two law societies in 1609, James I imposed the condition that the societies must maintain both the Temple and the Master's House.

As the Inns of Court evolved so they began to model themselves on the Oxford colleges – the Benchers representing the roles of college Masters and Fellows – with the function of training their students for the practice of law as barristers.

Among literary people associated with the Inner Temple were Francis Beaumont (1584?-1616), dramatist and poet; Leslie Stephen (1832-1904), essayist and editor of the massive *Dictionary of National Biography* and father of Virginia Woolf; Thomas Hughes (1822-1906), author of *Tom Brown's Schooldays*; and Arthur Henry Hallam (1811-33). The early death of his undergraduate friend Hallam was a traumatic bereavement for Tennyson, occasioning a number of bleak, elegiac poems of private grief ('dull narcotics', as Tennyson himself described them) – before his extended sense of loss issued in the public mourning of *In Memoriam* (1850).

Residents or students of the Middle Temple included the dramatists Thomas Shadwell (1642?-92), William Congreve (1670-1729), William D'Avenant (1606-68), John Ford (1586-1639), John Webster (1580?-1625?), William Wycherley (1640?-1716), Nicholas Rowe (1674-1718) and Richard Brinsley

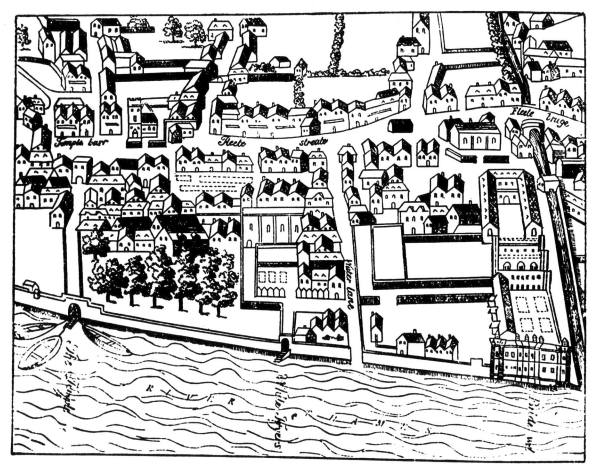

Fleet Street and The Temple, from a plan published by Ralph Aggas in 1563.

Sheridan (1751-1816). Other literary men not specifically referred to (below), who would also have frequented the courts and buildings of the Temple include: the diarist John Evelyn (1620-1706); Thomas de Quincey (1785-1859), remembered for the dream-records and addiction-debate of *Confessions of an English Opium-Eater* (1821); Thomas Moore (1779-1852), the Irish poet; and Sir Walter Ralegh (1552-1618), Elizabethan adventurer and poet.

* * *

On the right-hand side of Inner Temple Lane are Doctor Johnson's Buildings, built in 1857, and named in honour of Doctor Samuel Johnson (1709-84). In the former buildings which occupied the site Johnson resided at No 1 for the five years from 1760.

William Cowper (1731-1800) lodged briefly in the former building in the year 1752; and for nine years from 1808 Charles Lamb (1775-1834) and his sister Mary (1764-1847) resided at No 4.

At the end of Dr Johnson's Buildings, Hare Court issues on the right. In this Court James Boswell (1740-95) took lodgings in the early 1760s, in a building to the right, some time after Doctor Johnson had moved to Inner Temple Lane. At No 1 Hare Court, to the left of the entrance, William Makepeace Thackeray (1811-63) had rooms whilst studying law. As an incidental note, Hare Court also hosted the famous, or infamous, Hanging Judge – Lord Chief Justice Jeffreys – who, as a barrister, had rooms on the west, or far, side of the Court.

* * *

The entrance to Hare Court faces the rounded end of the Temple Church, but before entering the church itself, retrace a few steps back up Inner Temple Lane to where, on the right, stands Goldsmith Building. Follow this walkway alongside the church until, on the left, just before the Master's

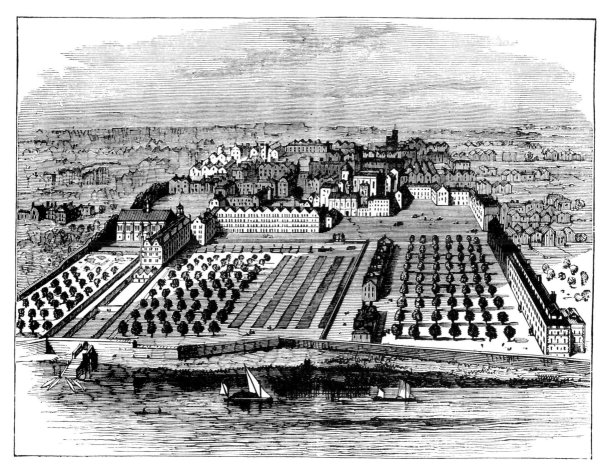

Bird's-eye view of the Temple precincts in 1671.

In 1842 the Benchers of the Temple decided that no more burials would take place in the churchyard, which was to be paved over. The tomb to Goldsmith was erected in 1860, by which time the exact location of the poet's grave was no longer known. The engraving (right) shows the tomb in the autumn of that year, soon after which the old houses pictured beyond the stone were pulled down.

House, you will see a raised stone slab. It carries the inscription: 'Here lies Oliver Goldsmith. Born 10th November 1728. Died 4th April 1774'. The slab, however, does not mark the exact location of Goldsmith's burial-place, which is unknown, but is believed to be very close to this spot. It is inaccurate in a further regard also: there can be very little doubting that the actual year of Goldsmith's birth was 1730.

* * *

Returning to Inner Temple Lane, and circling the rounded end of the church, will lead to Tanfield

Court. At No 2 in the Court lived George Greene (1853-1921), poet and critic, and editor of the two *Rhymers' Club* anthologies of the 1890s (see Fleet Street section).

To the right, facing the entrance to the Temple Church, is Inner Temple Hall, dating from as recently as 1955. The present building replaces the Victorian-Gothic structure of 1868-70 which was destroyed by German bombs in May 1941. That in turn had replaced the medieval hall of the Knights Templar. The ancient hall, in Elizabethan times, hosted much revelry – dancing, mock-trials and masques were all conducted there. The entertainment could be boisterous, especially at Candlemass during the festivities of the Lord of Misrule when, on one such occasion, a fox was hunted by hounds around the hall of the Inner Temple.

Other spectacles could be more decorous and edifying. The earliest English tragedy, *Gorboduc*, written by two Temple members, Thomas Sackville (1536-1608) and Thomas Norton (1532-84) was first performed in the ancient hall. Throughout the sixteenth and seventeenth centuries numerous other plays were also performed here; among them works by Beaumont and Fletcher, William D'Avenant, William Wycherley and John Dryden.

The entrance to Temple Church is on the left-hand side of Tanfield Court. Modelled on the circular design of the Dome of the Rock, the church was built by 1185, the rectangular choir added in 1204. Battlements and buttresses were added, to Wren's design, in 1682, and considerable refurbishment was undertaken in the nineteenth century. Bomb damage during the Second World War Blitz necessitated extensive repair work to the fabric.

On the floor of the Round of the church will be found a number of ancient effigies of recumbent Crusader knights. Somewhere in the church, though the location is unrecorded (the gravestone having disappeared), was buried the dramatist John Marston (1575-1634). Charles Lamb was baptised in the church in 1775.

* * *

On leaving the church, turn left across Tanfield Court, heading for an archway which will lead out into King's Bench Walk. To the left, upon exiting from the archway, are the Mitre Court Buildings, dating from 1830. In the previous buildings occupying the site, Charles and Mary Lamb (see above) lived between the years 1800 and 1808, before they moved to Inner Temple Lane. It was during their residence at Mitre Court Buildings that they jointly composed their famous *Tales from Shakespeare* (1807).

On the far side of King's Bench Walk, facing the archway exit, will be found a row of buildings dating, for the most part, from 1667-8, and built to Wren's design. At No 3 Goldsmith lodged before moving to Brick Court. Victoria Sackville-West (1892-1962), novelist, and her husband, the historian Sir Harold Nicolson (1886-1968), kept No 4 as their London residence during the years 1930-45. George Moore (1852-1933), Irish poet and novelist, lived at No 8 from 1888 to 1896. During his years here he composed what is still probably his most-read work, the novel *Esther Walters* (1894); a story of the trials and tribulations of a young servant girl, written in the tradition of the social realism of Zola. H. Rider Haggard (1856-1925), author of *King Solomon's Mines* and *She* lived for some time at No 13.

Dating from 1838, replacing the lath and timber constructions of the early seventeenth century, on

The medieval Hall of Inner Temple.

King's Bench Walk.

the opposite side of the Walk are the Paper Buildings: 'A row of goodly tenements, shaded in front by ancient trees and looking at the back upon Temple Gardens', as Dickens appositely described the new buildings in *Barnaby Rudge*, published just two years after they had gone up. Sir John Chester, in the same novel, had his chambers located in the Buildings. John Galsworthy (1867-1933) had offices here, at No 3, in the 1890s. Galsworthy had been called to the Bar as a member of Lincoln's Inn in April 1890, and occupied as a young barrister what would seem to have been a position offering a good deal of promise – since his father, one of the senior partners in a firm of solicitors, was ideally placed both to put work his way and to recommend his services to other solicitors. Yet the future novelist and dramatist showed little interest in the promotion of his prospects at the Bar. On one occasion only was he actually called upon to make an appearance in the Law Courts to make a short speech in support of his client. On the day itself Galsworthy was so engaged in discussion with his father, *outside* the Law Courts, that when he did enter the application had already been made by a fellow barrister. Galsworthy thus never did address a judge in his life – though in his novels and plays there are several barristers who do just that, most fluently.

During the years 1800-3, the largely-forgotten Victorian poet Samuel Rogers (1763-1855) lived in the former building on this site. A man of independent wealth, who refused the offer of the Poet Laureateship, he is remembered certainly for one exchange with Tennyson. The younger poet had remarked that he did not know whether his poetry would survive, whether it had the enduring qualities of great verse; to which Rogers replied that he had no doubt whatsoever that his own (Rogers's) most certainly would!

* * *

Returning up the hill, beyond Paper Buildings, Crown Office Row is on the left. The building in the Row, to the right as you enter, faces gardens (to which the public is not admitted). About halfway along the building, opposite the entrance-gate to the gardens, will be found a plaque stating that Charles Lamb was born (10 February 1775) in the Chambers which formerly stood here. The plaque bears the following of Lamb's own words: 'Cheerful Crown Office Row (place of my kindly engendure) . . . a man would give something to have been born in such places.' Lamb's father was a clerk to one of the Benchers of the Inn. Also born here was Charles's sister, Mary (see above), to whom Charles would offer his tender care and affection in their later lives, devoting himself to her protection from his middle twenties until his death – Mary surviving him by thirteen years. The present Row dates only from 1953-5, but in the original building – itself replaced in the 1860s – Thackeray (see above) lived between the years 1848 and 1850. At the time of taking up residence here *Vanity Fair* had just been published (1847-8), and the latter sections of *Pendennis* (1848-9) were still in-the-making.

A little way ahead, on the right, will be found a narrow entrance with some steps up to Elm Court. Fig Tree Court, destroyed by enemy action in 1940, used to adjoin Elm Court at its furthest end (to the right on entering the court). William Cowper (1732-1800) lived for some time in Fig Tree court – and here perpetrated one of a series of attempts at suicide, some of them rather casually contrived. On this occasion he attempted to hang himself with his

The Fountain and Court, looking back to Middle Temple Hall, much as it would have appeared in the days of Charles Lamb.

garter. The garter, to his proclaimed surprise at least, broke 'before eternal death' claimed him.

* * *

From the left-hand corner of Elm Court a small passageway leads out into Middle Temple Lane. Directly opposite is the open yard of Fountain Court where, immediately to the left, a flight of stone steps leads to Middle Temple Hall. The Hall dates from 1573 – a replacement for the original ancient hall which itself lasted for 250 years. Beneath the oak hammerbeam roof, on the low raised dais, stands the Bench Table, 29 feet long and made from a single oak tree. In front of the Bench Table is 'the cupboard', as it is known, a small table said to be made from the hatch of Sir Francis Drake's ship *The Golden Hind*.

The Hall has been the setting for many plays, pageants, and spectacles through the ages. Among them was the first production of Shakespeare's *Twelfth Night*, acted here on 2 February 1601 before an audience which included Queen Elizabeth I.

The Hall may be visited by members of the public between 10.00am and noon on those weekdays when it has not been reserved for a function. Application must be made to the porter's office, just inside the main entrance, to the left.

Fountain Court itself provided the setting for 'a little plot' between Ruth Pinch and her brother Tom, enabling Ruth to meet John Westlock (*Martin Chuzzlewit*).

* * *

Beyond the Hall, on the left, are some steps leading down to Garden Court. Just at the foot of the stairs is No 1 where Thomas Jefferson Hogg (1792-1862), Shelley's friend with whom he was expelled from Oxford, lived in 1816. (See Soho section). At No 2, alongside, lived Oliver Goldsmith for some time.

* * *

The gardens facing these buildings are those traditionally associated with the plucking of the red and white roses, by which action the Lancastrians and Yorkists signalled their respective allegiances. Here, in Shakespeare's *King Henry VI* (Part One, II, iv), the Earl of Warwick proclaims:

> And here I prophesy: this brawl today,
> Grown to this faction in the Temple Garden,
> Shall send between the Red Rose and the White
> A thousand souls to death and deadly night.

In fact the struggle for the crown which ensued, the Wars of the Roses, lasted for thirty years (1455-85) and cost the lives, it has been estimated, of something more like 100,000 men.

* * *

Returning to Middle Temple Lane, and turning left, will be found within a very little distance an entrance to Pump Court (on the right) through a small archway. To the immediate right-hand side of the archway will be seen No 4 Pump Court, a building in which Henry Fielding (1707-54), novelist and playwright, rented rooms for life.

Pump Court's entrance is almost directly opposite Brick Court on the other side of Middle Temple Lane. Only Nos 1 and 4 of Brick Court now remain – Nos 2 and 3 have gone as a result of war damage, and Brick Court now forms a single area with Essex Court. At the former No 2 lived Oliver Goldsmith from 1765 until his death in 1774. Whilst in chamber here this roistering and gregarious Irishman penned *The Deserted Village* (1770), the poem which inhabits a country of the mind where everything is in its idealised order, an order which can exist only in the mind – since the village itself has been destroyed by a rapacious landlord. Here too Goldsmith made his first play, *The Good Natured Man* (1768), notable for its mixing of characters of 'low' social status with those of 'polite' and refined society. At its first production one such scene was hissed down, and had to be dropped. Goldsmith was unrepentant, as his finest comedy, *She Stoops to Conquer* (1773), will show – where the theme of genteel society encountering the low is not allowed to drop.

The rooms below Goldsmith's were occupied briefly by William Makepeace Thackeray (see above) in 1855.

* * *

From Brick Court, return to Middle Temple Lane, turning left where, within a short distance, the Gate House (of 1684) leads out to Fleet Street. To end this tour turn to the left, continuing along Fleet Street, leading into the Strand where, a little distance on, will be seen the Aldwych underground station. Alternatively, if The Temple has been incorporated into the Fleet Street tour and that is to be continued, then turn to the left along Fleet Street. Within just a few yards you will be at No 1 Fleet Street, where you will be able to pick up the reference to the Devil Tavern (Fleet Street section: p16).

Middle Temple Hall.

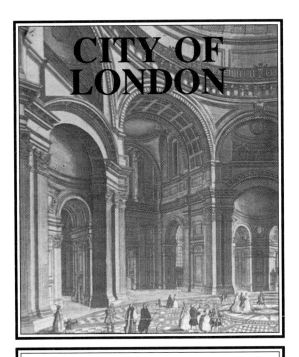

CITY OF LONDON

LUDGATE, ST PAUL'S AND ALDERSGATE

CITY OF LONDON

The following tour describes a large L shape: from Ludgate Circus east as far as St Paul's Cathedral, then north as far as the Barbican Underground station (where begins the next tour, Charterhouse and Smithfield, for those who would like to extend their explorations).

The tour which follows may itself be directly undertaken, for those completing the Fleet Street tour, simply by turning to the left at Ludgate Circus, into Farringdon Street, instead of returning to Blackfriars underground station. At this point they will then be able to pick up the directions (below) to take them to the site of the Fleet Prison.

The tour, however, may also be begun at Blackfriars underground station – from which starting-point there is an additional area to investigate before moving on to Farringdon Street.

From the exit of Blackfriars underground station locate Queen Victoria Street running off to the east. Just into Queen Victoria Street, on the left-hand side, there is the opening into Blackfriars Lane. A few steps ahead is the turning, to the right, into Playhouse Yard.

The whole of the area you have entered was once part of the estate of the Blackfriars Monastery – the order having first established its community in 1221 in Chancery Lane. Under the patronage of Edward I the order grew rich, and its land more extensive.

In 1538, however, following the dissolution of the monasteries by Henry VIII, the monastic land and buildings were divided into separate holdings. The holding which occupied this immediate site was granted to Sir Thomas Cawarden, then Master of Revels to the king. Much of the monastery was demolished, and other parts were let out to shopkeepers and residents.

The upper frater (refectory) of the old monastery stood just into the yard, running north to south. During its occupation by Richard Farrant, Master of the Children at Windsor, the upper floor was used as a theatre, the ground floor the living-quarters for Farrant's family. Though public playhouses, under the Court of Common Council ruling, were not permitted in the area, Farrant got around the prohibition by calling it a private theatre, whose performances by the boy-actors of St Paul's were intended 'for better trayning them to do her Majestie service.' These amateur performances, staged in what is now referred to as the first Blackfriars playhouse, lasted from 1576 until 1584.

In 1596 James Burbage, whose Theatre in Shoreditch was the first purpose-built playhouse (1576), bought the upper frater with the intention of fitting it out as an indoor theatre for use by the Lord Chamberlain's Men during the winter – when the outdoor playhouse of the Theatre (and from 1599, the Globe) would be closed. The re-fitting was designed with three tiers of galleries holding an audience of between 500 and 600. When Burbage died the following year, however, his son Richard did not use the venue; instead he leased it to Henry Evans, one of Farrant's successors as Master of the Children at Windsor, and Nathaniel Gyles, Master of the Children of the Royal Chapel.

Their boy-actors performed regularly here and became very popular – so much so that they rivalled adult companies of players. Within a couple of years the competition they posed was severe enough for Shakespeare himself to write into *Hamlet* (II, ii) a somewhat gratuitous sideswipe at their success. In Rosencrantz's words:

Richard Burbage.

... there is, sir, an eyrie of children, little eyases [nestling hawks], that cry out on the top of question and are most tyranically clapped for't. These are now the fashion, and so berattle the common stages (so they call them) that many wearing rapiers are afraid of goosequills and dare scarce come thither.

In 1608 the lease of the theatre was surrendered to Burbage. He then formed a company of housekeepers [owners], together with his brother Cuthbert, Shakespeare, Condell, Heminge and Sly, to manage the first indoor theatre to operate with an adult company. The King's Men performed here many of the plays previously staged at the Globe – including almost certainly *The Winter's Tale* and *The Tempest* – and possibly even gave alternate performances at the two playhouses on successive days. Clearly the second Blackfriars theatre attracted a far higher proportion of wealthier patrons who, for the added convenience of an indoors performance, would pay the far higher entrance charges; between 6d and 2s 6d.

The performances given in an indoor setting – though again with the same bare thrust stage as at the outdoor playhouses – would have been probably a little more elaborate in their manner of presentation; providing for an entertainment that may have lasted altogether up to four hours. Including music both before and following the play itself, such entertainments moved closer to the character of the court masque.

The second Blackfriars theatre was closed by the Puritans in 1642; in 1655 the building was demolished. A model of the theatre may be seen at the Shakespeare Globe Museum (see The Borough and Bankside).

Somewhere within the old monastic precincts Ben Jonson had a house around the year 1607; and it is certain that Shakespeare bought a house in the immediate loction in 1613. The house was sited a very short distance away from the Theatre, in Ireland Yard, a continuation of Playhouse Yard – and probably at its corner with St Andrew's Hill. In Ireland Yard itself there remains a small section of wall from the original monastic building.

* * *

From Playhouse Yard return to the junction with Blackfriars Lane and turn to the right. Almost immediately there is an opening to the left, Apothecary Street, which in a few yards enters New Bridge Street. Here, turn to the right and continue ahead to Ludgate Circus, crossing over Ludgate Hill (to the right) to enter Farringdon Street. Some fifty or sixty yards up Farringdon Street, on the right-hand side,

A conjectural reconstruction of the Second Blackfriars Theatre.

Street front of the Fleet Prison. Burned down by the Gordon rioters in 1780, the prison was immediately rebuilt to the old plan.

may be traced the site of the old Fleet Prison. Where Caroone House (a modern office block) now stands, replacing the Congregational Memorial Hall – for which there is a commemorative plaque at the main entrance – once stood the Fleet.

A prison existed on that site since Norman times. Twice burned down, in the Great Fire of 1666 and in the Gordon Riots of 1780, the Fleet was finally pulled down in 1846.

From the reign of Henry VIII until that of Charles I many of the prisoners confined in the Fleet had been committed there by the Star Chamber – the court at Westminster which until 1641 punished those 'offences' for which the law had not actually made provision. Many prisoners of the Fleet were therefore, in effect, prisoners of state, and sometimes important people in the public and political world. Subsequently, however, the Fleet became a prison for debtors, bankrupts, and those charged with contempt of court, as well as a range of minor offences. The conditions in the prison were notoriously dismal, and the gaolers corrupt.

Henry Howard, Earl of Surrey (1517?-1547) spent two periods of imprisonment at the Fleet. Howard, always proud and often rash in action, quarrelled with John à Leigh, and was committed to the prison by the privy council. In a petition for his release he attributed his conduct to 'the fury of reckless youth' and promised to control his 'heady will'. Having been released, the following year (1543) he was again sent to the Fleet for a few months; on this occasion for a rampage in the company of others during which he smashed the windows of churches and of citizens' homes. (See also the sections: Moorgate to the Bank, and Eastcheap and the Tower.)

John Donne (1572-1631) was imprisoned in the Fleet for having married without consent (see later entry in this section).

Henry Wriothesley, 3rd Earl of Southampton (1573-1624), Shakespeare's patron – and argued by some to be the 'W.H.' to whom the *Sonnets* (1609) are dedicated – was imprisoned at the Fleet briefly in 1598. Whilst in Paris he learned that his mistress, Elizabeth Vernon, one of Queen Elizabeth's waiting-maids, was pregnant. Hurriedly and secretly he returned from the continent to marry her. The Queen angrily sent Southampton and his wife to the Fleet, though they were soon released.

Two dramatists imprisoned at the Fleet were: Thomas Dekker (1572?-1632), and William Wycherley (1640?-1716). In a sense Dekker took London itself for a theme – its crowded life and especially the lower orders of its citizenry. He contributed to many plays, including *The Honest Whore* (1604), as well as writing seventeen solely – of which *The Shoemaker's Holiday* (1599) remains his best-known. Dekker was almost always poor, at times penniless, and had to rely upon his writings for his income. From 1613 to 1619 Dekker was imprisoned in the Fleet for debt.

Wycherley spent seven years in the Fleet. He had secretly contracted a marriage to Lady Drogheda, whom he believed to be richer than she in fact was. Upon her death in 1681 he inherited her debts. He was released from the gaol upon the intervention of James II who agreed to pay the dramatist a modest annual pension, having been much impressed with Wycherley's comedy *The Plain Dealer*. Upon this play, and *The Country Wife*, rests most of Wycherley's modern reputation.

Other literary men confined to the Fleet included: Sir Thomas Wyatt (1503-43); Thomas Nashe (1567-1601), for his part in the writing, with Ben Jonson, of the lost satire *The Isle of Dogs*; and Richard Savage (see below). And the most famous of all fictional inmates of the Fleet was surely Mr Pickwick – sent here for his refusal to pay the costs and damages awarded to Mrs Bardell when the breach of promise trial found in her favour (*Pickwick Papers*, chs xl, xliii).

* * *

Returning to Ludgate Hill, and just beyond the turning for the Old Bailey, will be found No 42 Ludgate Hill, now Ye Old London public house. Formerly the London Coffee House (1731-1868), this was the regular meeting-place of a club to which James Boswell belonged, and is the same place referred to by Charles Dickens in *Little Dorrit* (I, iii). In the coffee-shop Arthur Clennam sat on the Sunday after his arrival in London, watching

Old St Paul's – detail of an engraving by Hollar, 1647.

people sheltering from the rain 'in the public passage opposite, and listening to the bells ringing "Come to church, come to church . . . they won't come, they won't come"'.

* * *

Approaching St Paul's with the statue of Queen Victoria immediately facing, the area known as St Paul's Churchyard leads off to both sides of the cathedral. In this space surrounding both the Old St Paul's and Wren's replacement, innumerable publishers (or booksellers as then known) conducted their trade. First editions of Shakespeare's works published here include: *The Merry Wives of Windsor, The Merchant of Venice, Richard II* and *III, Troilus and Cressida, Titus Andronicus* and *King Lear* – though issuing from different booksellers. It was to a bookseller in St Paul's Churchyard that Dr Johnson sold the manuscript of Goldsmith's *Vicar of Wakefield.* And it was a consortium of booksellers here who commissioned Dr Johnson himself to write what many readers consider his greatest work, the *Lives of the English Poets.*

Old St Paul's was the fourth church known to have occupied this site; a site which even earlier was once occupied by a Roman Temple dedicated to Diana. The Norman cathedral of Old St Paul's was begun towards the end of the eleventh century, added to subsequently with a cluster of buildings within its precincts, and was one of the largest buildings in England (larger than the present St Paul's). The cathedral became a favoured location for many and diverse ceremonies, thanksgivings, and processions. Following Henry VIII's divorce of Catherine, and the English Reformation of the church which ensued, Old St Paul's lost its high clerical status. The nave became little more than a thoroughfare, Paul's Walk as it soon became known, for tradespeople of all kinds, their market stalls, and their animals. Lawyers and prostitutes both took up their positions in the nave, and there conducted their respective businesses. Though restored, both by Elizabeth I and James I, the cathedral was completely burned down in the Great Fire of 1666.

Wren's Warrant Design of 1675, the third which he submitted, for St Paul's. Though this was the plan finally approved, in the building of the cathedral Wren made a number of changes, including the shortening of the nave and dispensing with the planned steeple.

In his *Diary* for 4 September, John Evelyn reported the event: '. . . the stones of Paules [flying] like granados, the Lead melting down the streets in a streame, and the very pavements of them glowing with fiery rednesse . . .'

* * *

Within the replacement church, Wren's greatest monument, the cathedral of St Paul's, will be found many literary associations. In the north aisle of the nave (to the left upon entrance) will be found a memorial statue to Sir Joshua Reynolds (1723-92), Dr Johnson's friend across many years, and a founder-member of their famous Literary Club. Further along the nave, immediately before the Choir, will be found a memorial statue to the Doctor himself – '*grammatico et critico*'. It displays him in Roman toga and holding a manuscript. Despite the obvious classical association the statue itself can claim little aesthetic appeal.

In the Choir (for which there is an entrance charge), against the south wall, stands a marble statue of John Donne (see above). Poet and preacher John Donne was, in the words of T. S. Eliot, 'much obsessed by death'. Towards the end of his life Donne caused to have made a full-length painting of himself, dressed in a shroud, so that he might see how he would appear in death. This portrait he kept in his bedroom; and it is upon this portrait that the statue is modelled.

It has a further curious history. In the Great Fire of London of 1666 which consumed Old St Paul's, most of the monuments within it were destroyed. Donne's was one of the few to survive. It fell through a hole in the floor into the crypt, and was not recovered for many years. Today it still displays scorch marks of the fire at its base.

As a young man Donne soon acquired a reputation for his genius and accomplishments. These included his scholarship and a command of French, Italian and Spanish gained on his travels, together with those verses of his which freely circulated in manuscript (though were not printed). The secular love poems display an uninhibited delight in sensual pleasure; sometimes allusively or elliptically, but often with unabashed directness they celebrate what he called 'the sport'. With their evident compression and Wit – the latter a most highly-prized quality with his sophisticated readers – they were markers of a highly-individual and athletic mind which could leap from image to image, and their associations, whilst still seeming to hold to the logical development of an argument.

At Christmas 1600, when he was 27, Donne secretly married the sixteen-year-old niece of his employer Sir Thomas Egerton, in whose care Ann More had been placed. For this illicit marriage he was pursued and briefly imprisoned (see an earlier entry in this section). But from about 1615 he was once more in favour, attending the court of King James I, and indeed reading to him at table.

Travelling in France with Sir Robert and Lady Drury in 1612 Donne experienced his celebrated vision, at Paris, in which he saw his wife with a dead infant in her arms. Izaak Walton, in his *Life of Dr John Donne* (1640) records as follows Donne's words to Sir Robert:

> I have seen a dreadful vision since I saw you: I have seen my dear wife pass twice by me through this room with her hair hanging about her shoulders, and a dead child in her arms . . . and am as sure that at her second appearing she stopped and looked me in the face, and vanished.

His wife had indeed had a miscarriage, and at about the same time and day as the vision experienced by Donne. Five years later his wife died at the birth of their twelfth child; seven of their children surviving. Upon the death of his wife Donne resolved never to re-marry.

Having for many years been urged to take holy orders Donne finally did so in 1615, and was almost immediately appointed by James I as his own chaplain. For the last ten years of his life Donne, following other livings and benefices, was Dean of St Paul's. He was the most eloquent of preachers, his sermons displaying an ingenuity which made them events to which crowds would flock.

His last sermon was preached on Ash Wednesday (23 February) before King Charles I at Westminster. He was obviously emaciated, having been very ill for some time. The King remarked that Donne was preaching his own funeral sermon – and indeed there is justice in the remark. Donne, despite his sickness, worked with a passion at the sermon, for which he had chosen this text from Psalm 68: 'Unto God the Lord belong the issues of Death.' Donne himself called the sermon 'Death's Duel'. On 31 March Donne died.

In a letter to Lord Ancrum Donne himself made the distinction between 'Jack Donne . . . and Dr Donne' – from which distinction some readers have

St Paul's cathedral crossing.

been tempted to see his works as separate and independent: the profane love poems as quite distinct from the divine. An alternative view is both more powerful and more complex: that the passion for those 'profane mistresses', as he calls his lovers, somehow became sublimated into a passionate longing for union with his God. This is to recall, too, that Donne had been born into a highly-religious family, one tortured for its Catholic adherence, so that Donne agonized over acceptance of the Anglican creed. Not until probably his thirtieth year did he finally declare for the Anglican religion. And in both the secular and divine love poems will be found the same movement, style and images by which that love is expressed. Consider, for example, the similarity of thought between the following lines:

> To enter in these bonds is to be free . . .
> (Elegie XIX: 'To his mistris going to bed')

> Take mee to you, imprison mee, for I
> Except you enthrall mee, never shall be free . . .
> (Holy Sonnet XIV)

In the crypt of St Paul's (entry to which is charged) will be found memorials to more than 350 people from all walks of life, many of whom have literary associations of one kind or another. Clearly there is not space here to mention them all. But among them will be found, in the south-east section, a memorial to William Blake (1757-1827) inscribed with these lines from his 'Auguries of Innocence':

> To see a World in a grain of Sand
> And Heaven in a Wild Flower
> Hold infinity in the palm of your Hand
> And Eternity in an Hour.

Close by, set into the floor, is the gravestone of Sir Joshua Reynolds – almost alongside the tomb of Sir Christopher Wren. Set into a nearby pillar will be found the memorial to Max Beerbohm (1872-1956), humourist and novelist whose best-known work, *Zuleika Dobson*, is still much-read and admired. Beerbohm's grave is marked by a small stone set into the floor.

On another flank of the same pillar will be found a memorial to Walter de la Mare (1873-1956), his ashes set beneath a marked flagstone in the floor. De la Mare had been a chorister at St Paul's and his subsequent literary career attracted him both adult and child readers. Indeed, the first volume of his poetry which achieved recognition, *The Listeners* (1912), contains the poem of the same title which is still a favourite of many children, and still widely-anthologised. De la Mare achieved distinction too as an anthologist in his own right; his anthology *Love* (1943) remains a classic. The quality of his verse projects typically a numinous, questing atmosphere – a sense of the mysterious invested often in the ordinary and the commonplace.

There is a memorial also to Sir Walter Besant (1836-1900), historian of London, founder of the Society of Authors and (with James Rice) co-author of a number of best-selling novels of their day.

Charles Reade (1814-84), novelist, has a memorial in the crypt. Reade began his writing career as a dramatist, meeting more than modest success – though it is for the classic novel *The Cloister and the Hearth* (1861) that he is known to most readers.

R. H. Barham (1788-1845), who was educated at St Paul's School, subsequently took orders and became a minor dean at the cathedral, is remembered for his *Ingoldsby Legends*; and T. E. Lawrence (1888-1935) is commemorated too. As 'Lawrence of Arabia' he achieved something of a mythic status, the subject of plays, books and a memorable film directed by David Lean. His own account of his war experiences, *The Seven Pillars of Wisdom*, has been hailed by some readers as a fine and distinguished piece of writing; it has been criticised, too, for its fictive versions of history, of the author's own part within it, and for biographical evasions and distortions.

* * *

Circling St Paul's to the south, along St Paul's Churchyard, you will come to New Change. On the

St Paul's and neighbourhood, from Ralph Aggas's plan of 1563.

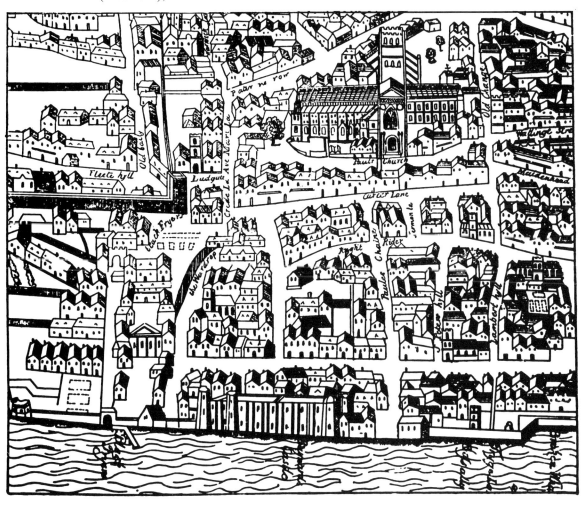

left will be found a plaque which reads: 'Near this spot from 1512 until 1884 stood St Paul's School founded by Dean Colet.' John Milton (1608-1674) and Samuel Pepys (1633-1703) were both students at the school.

New Change leads to the intersection of Cheapside and St Martin's Le Grand with Newgate Street. About 200 yards up St Martin's le Grand (which becomes Aldersgate Street), and on the left-hand side, will be found the church of St Botolph Without Aldersgate. Here, in 1825, the poet Thomas Hood (1799-1845) was married.

Somewhere in Little Britain, the street at the corner of the church, Samuel Johnson (1709-84) lodged as a boy with his mother. Johnson had been a sickly child, and among his ailments was a condition known then as 'the king's evil', an infection of the skin otherwise known as scrofula. A form of tuberculosis which attacks the lymphatic glands, it impaired Johnson's sight and hearing. In the (common) belief that the touch of a royal hand might cure the illness, Johnson's mother brought him to London hoping to intercept the queen and obtain the royal favour of a cure.

A few yards into Little Britain, on the right-hand side, will be found a plaque commemorating 'the scene of Charles Wesley's evangelical conversion, May 21st 1738, in the house of John Bray', which stood on the site adjoining the plaque. The younger brother of John Wesley (1703-91), the founder of Methodism, Charles became a prolific writer of hymns. Among them are many which are much-loved; and as diverse as 'Gentle Jesus, meek and mild . . .', 'Love divine, all loves excelling . . .', together with the carol 'Hark! the herald angels sing . . .'

* * *

Beyond Little Britain and continuing northwards along Aldersgate Street, a flight of steps on the left (clearly marked) leads to an overhead walkway and the entrance to the London Museum – a visit to which is highly recommended. The complex of buildings within which the Museum is located, known as the Barbican, houses an art gallery, concert hall, and theatre (for the Royal Shakespeare Company), in addition to several hundred private apartments. Though there is much to explore within this complex, visitors should be warned that one can get lost within its confusing geography with very great ease.

Charles Wesley.

The Museum's exhibits will take the visitor on a guided tour through the history of London, from prehistoric times through to the present day – and included is a sound and light representation of the Great Fire which consumed the heart of the City. (Admission free. Opening times: Tuesday-Saturday, 10.00am to 6.00pm; Sunday, 2.00pm to 6.00pm.)

* * *

From the Museum return to Aldersgate Street via the overhead walkway. One may then return towards St Paul's and the underground station of the same name, or continue northwards along Aldersgate Street with the complex of the Barbican buildings filling the right-hand view. Some way ahead, on the left-hand side of Aldersgate, is located the Barbican underground station. Here one may end the tour; or one may proceed on to the next tour (Charterhouse and Smithfield) simply by going a few yards beyond the Barbican underground station and turning left into Carthusian Street.

CITY OF LONDON

CHARTERHOUSE AND SMITHFIELD
CITY OF LONDON

The following tour encompasses a fairly small area – the first location within which technically lies just outside the boundary of the City limits proper. One may begin the tour at the Barbican underground station, whose exit issues into Aldersgate Street. Here turn to the left, and within a few yards Carthusian Street will be seen opening up to the left. For those undertaking this tour as a follow-on to the previous section (Ludgate, St Paul's and Aldersgate) they will be at this point of entry to Carthusian Street.

A short distance into this street Charterhouse Square emerges on the right. The land occupied by the Square was bought and donated to the City in the middle of the fourteenth century as a burial place for victims of the Black Death. Some twenty years later, however, the same knight who had donated the land, Sir Walter de Manny, founded upon it a Carthusian monastery. The first monks' cells were completed by the year following, 1371, and most were finished before the end of the century. Each cell was a small two-storey house standing in its own garden. At this monastery, for four years from 1499, Sir Thomas More (1478-1535) was a noviciate and here did penance, wearing a hair shirt, before deciding to return to the public world.

The monastery came into the possession of Henry VIII in 1537, many of the monks there having been executed at Tyburn for failing to acknowledge the King as Supreme Head of the Church. A few years later the monastery passed into private ownership, then through a series of aristocratic owners.

In 1611 Thomas Sutton, a rich commoner, bought the Charterhouse and endowed it as a school, for 'forty poor boys of London', and a hospital for eighty poor gentlemen.

At the north (or top) side of the Square, to the right on entering, will be found the gateway entrance to the buildings which once comprised the Charterhouse School – which transferred to Surrey in 1872. Many of the buildings of Charterhouse were destroyed or damaged in air raids, but have since been restored.

Among the scholars of Charterhouse who later achieved literary distinction were the following: Richard Crashaw (1612-49), one of the most-admired of the 'metaphysical' poets; Joseph Addison (1672-1719), most-remembered as essayist and for his contributions to *The Spectator*; Nathaniel Lee (1653?-92), dramatist; Richard Lovelace (1618-57), Cavalier poet whose eventful life ended in abject poverty; Sir Richard Steele (1672-1729), the contemporary and friend of Addison and like him, most noted as essayist; William Makepeace Thackeray (1811-63), novelist; and Max Beerbohm (1872-1956), essayist, humourist, novelist. Also a pupil at Charterhouse was John Wesley (1703-91), the founder of Methodism, and a writer of some of the favourite hymns in the English language.

Thackeray clearly remembered his schooldays with a vividness; in his novel *The Newcomes* Charterhouse emerges under the title of Greyfriars; whilst in the earlier *Vanity Fair* it appears under the uncompromising title of the Slaughterhouse. Max Beerbohm's recall of his schooldays was expressed in more compact irony: 'My delight in having been at Charterhouse was far greater than my delight in being there'.

Conducted tours of the buildings take place every Wednesday during April to July inclusive, at 2.45pm.

The Charterhouse, from the Square, as it appeared in 1804.

Circling Charterhouse Square, at its lower, furthest end, will be found the entrance to Hayne Street which leads within a very short distance to Long Lane. Turning to the right here, flanking the street ahead will be seen the Smithfield Markets – their present covered, ironwork structures dating from 1868, with the exception of the whole of the poultry section, a replacement of 1963 following the fire which had burned it out a few years previously.

Since 1868 known officially as the London Central Meat Market, only in 1855 did the sale and slaughter of live cattle and horses cease at Smithfield, ending a continuity stretching back to at least the twelfth century when pigs, sheep and cattle were certainly being traded. For most of its history the Smithfield traders operated with few, if any, formal controls. Drovers, either drunk or for the sport of it, were known to stampede their animals – and the origin of the phrase 'a bull in a china shop' may come from just such a history, the fightened animal

taking refuge in one of the numerous small traders' shops surrounding the area from the seventeenth century on.

When regulations were imposed they were ignored for, despite the inadequate conditions, cattle were still being slaughtered in the market through to the middle of the nineteenth century. Charles Dickens's *Oliver Twist* (1837-8) contains a graphic description of the appalling state of affairs to be encountered there:

> ... and so into Smithfield; from which place arose a tumult of discordant sounds that filled Oliver Twist with amazement ... It was market morning. The ground was covered, nearly ankle-deep with filth and mire; a thick stream perpetually arising from the reeking bodies of the cattle, and mingling with the fog ... the hideous and discordant din that resounded from every corner of the market; and the unwashed, squalid and dirty figures constantly running to and fro, and bursting in and out of the throng rendered it a stunning and bewildering scene, which quite confounded the senses. (ch xxi)

***

Long Lane very quickly emerges into the open space of Smithfield itself, facing the markets, with Little Britain turning off to the left.

In 1173 William FitzStephen, a clerk to Thomas Becket, described the whole of this area then just outside the City Walls as: 'a smooth field where every Friday there is a celebrated rendezvous of fine horses to be sold, and in another quarter are placed vendibles of the peasant, swine with their deep flanks, and cows and oxen of immense bulk.' Falstaff, in Shakespeare's *Henry IV, Part Two*, sends his servant Bardolph to Smithfield to purchase horses. And in the same play Falstaff is himself called a 'Bartholomew boar-pig' by Doll Tearsheet.

From 'smooth field' derives Smithfield. As well as a market-place, the open field was used also for tournaments, jousting and sporting events, including wrestling. Criminals were hanged here, for more than four hundred years, until the gallows were moved to Tyburn in Henry IV's reign. Witches were burned, as were heretics – or they were boiled alive. In 1849 excavations just outside the doorway of the church of St Bartholomew the Great (see below) revealed burnt stones and charred human bones.

This is the space which was the venue, too, for the Bartholomew Fair. The history of the Fair is bound up with the origins of St Bartholomew's Hospital, occupying the left-hand flank of open space, as viewed from the corner of Little Britain; and of the church of St Bartholomew the Great, whose entrance is a few yards away to the left along Little Britain. For early in the twelfth century Rahere (d 1144), to whom legend attributes the title of court jester to Henry I before his conversion to a clerical life, undertook a pilgrimage to Rome. During that journey he contracted malarial fever, and experienced too a vision of a winged monster attacking him; from this he was saved by St Bartholomew, the patron saint of healing. In gratitude for his safe delivery, and recovery from the illness, Rahere vowed that upon his return to London he would found there a priory and hospice.

This he did. On land granted to him by the king, Rahere founded in 1123 his Augustinian priory (of which the church of St Bartholomew the Great is the sole remaining part) and the hospital of St Bartholomew – known popularly to many simply as Bart's. Ten years later Henry I granted to the priory the right to hold on the land a fair and to charge tolls as a means of generating income. Thus came about St Bartholomew's Fair, which began on 24 August each year and which quickly established itself as a major venue for trading and for entertainments. The annual Fair, lasting three days, soon became the greatest cloth fair in the country – the narrow Cloth Fair remains, a turning off Little Britain, just yards away from the corner where one has entered.

Through the centuries, though, the Fair as a trading centre began to diminish in significance as it became increasingly given over to popular entertainments of all kinds: human and animal exhibits were on display, strolling players performed, fire-eating and juggling acts played to the crowds, and wrestlers staged their matches. A good deal of licentious and rowdy behaviour accompanied the Fair, and everyone in the crowd was fair game to the cut-purses.

Ben Jonson's comedy *Bartholomew Fair*, first performed at the Hope Theatre on Bankside (see The Borough and Bankside), presents an impression of the event, the play following the fortunes and misfortunes of various of the types attending the

A staircase in the Charterhouse. 'Many old halls, old passages, old chambers decorated with old portraits, walking in the midst of which we walk, as it were, in the early seventeenth century.' Thackeray, *The Newcomes*

Fair. There is, too, a mocking and ridiculing of the Puritans in the figure of Zeal-of-the-land Busy. Yet in fact the Puritans failed to put an end to the Fair, and it continued uninterruptedly until the City authorities, who saw it as a threat to public order, suppressed the event in 1855.

In their days both Pepys and Evelyn visited the Fair, and in 1802 Charles Lamb took his friends Dorothy and William Wordsworth to see the entertainments. Wordsworth, clearly, did not take to the event. In Book Seventh of *The Prelude* (published 1850) Wordsworth recalls that the noise of the musicians and the shouting of the stall-holders produced 'anarchy and din'. The crowds pressed in tightly around the sideshows where 'all moveables of wonder, from all parts' were on display.

> . . . Albinos, painted Indians, Dwarfs,
> The Horse of knowledge, and the learned Pig,
> The Stone-eater, the man that swallows fire,
> Giants, Ventriloquists, the Invisible Girl,
> The Bust that speaks and moves its goggling eyes,
> The Wax-work, Clock-work, all the marvellous craft
> Of modern Merlins, Wild Beasts, Puppet-shows,
> All out o'-th'-way, far-fetch'd, perverted things,
> All freaks of Nature, all Promethean thoughts
> Of man; his dulness, madness, and their feats,
> All jumbled up together to make up
> This Parliament of Monsters . . .

***

By turning to one's left at the open space of Smithfield, a little way into Little Britain, will be seen the narrow entrance way leading into the Priory Church of St Bartholomew the Great. Much altered and restored in successive ages, this church founded by Rahere is the oldest church in London, and should certainly be visited. Inside there is a fine sixteenth-century tomb to the founder.

To this church Wat Tyler, the leader of the Peasants' revolt of 1381, sought refuge having received a knife-wound. In the open field beyond the church the peasants had assembled to make known their grievances to the boy king, Richard II. Fearing for the life of his King, the then Lord Mayor of London, William Walworth, had pulled Wat Tyler from his horse and had stabbed him.

Whilst Tyler was in the church the peasants were persuaded to disperse, to the fields of Clerkenwell further to the north, on the strength of promises made them by Richard II. Tyler was later dragged out of the church and beheaded in the open field, not far beyond the church's entrance.

Baptized in the church in a much later age was William Hogarth (1697-1764), artist and satirist, whose engravings provide a sometimes savage commentary on the manners, morals and conditions of his times.

***

At the church entrance way Little Britain runs off south – to the left on coming out of the church. Somewhere along Little Britain the first copies of the *Spectator*, edited by Steele and Addison (see above), were printed in 1703.

About fifty yards straight ahead on leaving St Bartholomew the Great Church, however, will be found the main entrance to St Bartholomew's Hospital, on the left – the King Henry VIII gate. Just inside the gate, again on the left, is the Church of St Bartholomew the Less, whose parish is the hospital itself. This delightful, fifteenth-century church has a very distinctive, octagonal-shaped nave; a design of 1789 made by George Dance the Younger. Though there are neither gravestones nor memorials to them, here were buried Thomas Watson (1557?-92), poet; and John Lyly (1554?-1606), poet and dramatist.

When, between 1730 and 1759, the hospital was re-built in four blocks around a courtyard, William Hogarth early in that period was made a governor. To the hospital Hogarth donated two large canvases; *The Good Samaritan* and *The Pool of Bethesda*. They now hang on the main staircase (and permission to view them will amost certainly be granted).

**

From the Hospital, Giltspur Street runs away to the south and passes, on the right, the entrance to Cock Lane. On this street, in medieval times, prostitutes were permitted to reside legally and to ply their trade. At the corner of the Lane, at first floor level, there is a gilt statue of a fat cherub – marking the location of Pie Corner, where the Great Fire is reputed to have stopped.

The street itself has a later claim to attention. For in the early months of 1762, crowds flocked to No 33 in the hope of witnessing the Cock Lane Ghost.

At No 33 lived an eleven-year-old girl whose father was a clerk of the church of St Sepulchre (see later entry). The girl claimed to have heard knockings and scratchings whilst she lay in bed. Her father claimed that the 'ghost' was that of his sister-in-law. Reports spread widely, and thousands of people

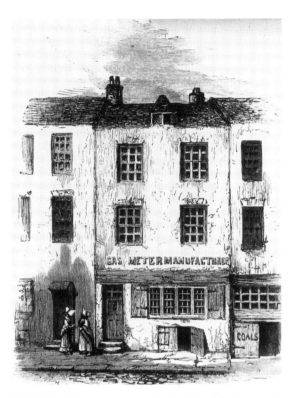

No 33 Cock Lane, a century after its 'ghost' had attracted thousands to the premises. Among the visitors was Horace Walpole: 'The house . . . is wretchedly small and miserable. When we opened the chamber, in which were fifty people, with no light, but one tallow candle at the end, we tumbled over the bed of the child to whom the ghost comes, and whom they are murdering by inches in such insufferable heat and stench.'

visited the house in the hope of witnessing the strange phenomenon. When, in the company of others, Dr Johnson was invited to investigate the affair, he concluded that the girl had been making the noises herself. Johnson's *Account of the Detection of the Imposture in Cock Lane* (published first in the Gentleman's Magazine) clearly rationalises – as have many investigators of such occurrences since – the so-called *Poltergeist* phenomenon.

* * *

Beyond Cock Lane, Giltspur Street then joins Holborn Viaduct, which runs away to the right towards Holborn Circus. But just a little to the left and on the opposite side of the road (on the corner of the junction between Old Bailey and Newgate Street) used to stand Newgate Prison. The Central Criminal Court which now occupies the site was built there between the years 1902-7.

A prison had been in existence on this site from at least the twelfth century – originally the cells being just a few rooms above the gate. The first purpose-built prison was erected there by the early fifteenth century, for there is a 1419 reference to 'the heynouse gaol of Newgate'. By the end of the sixteenth century, however, it had deteriorated badly, and burned down completely in the Great Fire. The replacement building was completed in 1672; the magnificence of its exterior contrasting sharply with the squalid conditions inside its walls. Subsequently, in the years 1770-8, a new prison was built here – to the designs of George Dance the Younger. In the Gordon Riots of 1780 the prison was completely destroyed, reduced to a smouldering heap, several hundreds of prisoners having made their escape. The last prison to occupy the site was built in 1780-3; and was demolished in 1902, to be replaced by the Central Criminal Court (the 'Old Bailey' as popularly referred to) which now stands at this corner. Writing just a few years before its demolition, but in the knowledge that this prison building was to be pulled down, W. J. Loftie assessed its visual impression thus: 'Most antiquaries will be sorry when Newgate Prison is pulled down. It is an admirable example of the architecture of a century ago. Although the height is only 50 feet, the proportions are so good that the mere mass and outline remind one of a Norman keep. It is gloomy, strong, impressive, and evidently intended to look what it is – a prison.'

It was of this last prison that Dickens wrote in *Barnaby Rudge*; in *Great Expectations*; and in *Oliver Twist*, where Fagin awaits his end in the condemned cell.

Though there remain unresolved questions about his identity, it is very probable that the Sir Thomas Malory (c 1410-1471) whom we know as the author of *Morte d'Arthur*, was imprisoned here for many years, in the very first of the prisons to occupy this site. During this time he wrote the great Arthurian legend, translating from French romances, incorporating some English materials, and arranging the whole. This work, founded on chivalric virtues, stands in curious opposition to the few known facts ascribed to the Sir Thomas Malory presumed to be the author. For having been knighted in 1445, and having become a Member of Parliament for Warwickshire, the rest of Malory's life was one of lawless recklessness: his crimes included cattle-raiding, extortion, the stealing of property, rape and various acts of violence.

Also imprisoned in the first Newgate was Ben Jonson (1572-1637), poet and playwright, not long after the staging of his play *Every Man in His Humour* (1598) – for having killed a fellow actor following a challenge.

Christopher Marlowe (1564-93) was confined to the prison on suspicion of his involvement in the murder of a man who died in a fatal sword fight. Marlowe's short, turbulent life – which included duties in Sir Francis Walsingham's English secret service, repeated charges of atheism and homosexuality – itself was ended in a tavern brawl by the Thames, at Deptford Strand. Stabbed to death, there remains the suspicion that he was murdered on the orders of Walsingham, one of the witnesses to the slaying himself having been a member of the secret service, and Marlowe's death having followed several hours of dining, strolling in the gardens, and lengthy conferences with the company there assembled.

Edmund Waller (1606-87), who had entered parliament at the age of just sixteen, suffered a brief period of imprisonment in Newgate; a disgrace from which he recovered to enter parliament once more. Though noted for the wit of his speeches in the House, that quality in his poems can seem somewhat laboured – as, for example, in 'On a Girdle' which lacks the deftness and elaboration to be found in Donne's treatment of the same theme. Others of his poems can, however, show a lyric ease (admired by Dr Johnson) as in some of the conventional love poems.

George Wither (1588-1667) had spent two brief periods confined to the Marshalsea prison (in Southwark) for publications which had offended the authorities. During the Civil War he joined the Parliamentarians, first as a captain of horse, later rising to the rank of major commanding the garrison of Farnham Castle in Surrey. There he was captured by the Royalists led by Sir John Denham

Newgate Prison, the last of the prisons to occupy the site.

George Wither.

Sir John Denham.

(1615-69). Denham, a fellow poet, allowed Wither to escape hanging with the jest that while Wither lived he, Denham, could not be the worst poet in English.

After the restoration Wither lost his fortune and in August 1660 was imprisoned at Newgate before being transferred to the Tower in March of the following year.

Among Wither's work are the broad diamond-shaped poems of the sequence in *Faire-Virtue* (1622), an experiment with the geometry of poetic form (pre-dating George Herbert's innovation for the design of 'Easter Wings') which Dylan Thomas was to employ in the twentieth century.

Robert Southwell (1561-95), whose best-known poem is certainly 'The Burning Babe', had broken the law excluding Jesuits from England and from his confinement at Newgate was taken to Tyburn and there hanged. Southwell had served his noviciate-ship with the Society of Jesus in Rome. In 1586 he travelled back to England to continue his mission which, despite all perils, he succeeded in doing for a period of six years, before being informed upon and arrested. Following thirteen applications of torture Southwell was sent to Newgate for two-and-a-half years before achieving the martyrdom which moti-vated him (an ambition made clear in his letters and journals). Whilst in prison he composed most of the poems which make up his work.

Daniel Defoe (1660-1731), the 'father of the English novel' was sent to the second of the purpose-built prisons at Newgate for seven months for a seditious libel. In his satire *The Shortest Way With Dissenters* he had advocated the persecution of dissenting sects – but in the assumed guise of a High Anglican Tory. For this deception he was three times put in the pillory and condemned to serve the prison sentence. During his confinement at Newgate, Defoe composed his defiant *Hymn to the Pillory*, a mock-Pindaric ode, which was sold in broadsheet in the streets and which helped to bring public sympathy to him.

Among the thieves who achieved notoriety and who spent time imprisoned at Newgate was Jack Sheppard (1702-24), about whose life Defoe wrote an account which appeared shortly after Sheppard's hanging at Tyburn.

Sheppard was known for his remarkable series of escapes from captivity; the most impressive of them being from the third floor of the high tower at Newgate. In his cell there he had been handcuffed, and manacled and chained to the floor. Nonetheless,

The Old Bailey Sessions House, as it appeared in 1750.

somehow he made his escape from the cell and clambered to freedom across the roofs of the buildings, having had to unlock various doors to apartments in the buildings in order to get onto the roofs in the first place.

In the nineteenth century Sheppard became the hero of the novel, *Jack Sheppard* (1839), by Harrison Ainsworth (1805-82) – the author of dozens of bestselling novels, all of which were based on fastidious researching of fact.

Another famous criminal, also held at Newgate, and also the progenitor of fiction was Jonathan Wild (1682-1725). Known as the Thief-Taker General, his name was taken by Henry Fielding (1707-54) for the satirical hero who pursues his life of crime with the intention of achieving greatness at 'the tree of glory', the gallows. (*Jonathan Wild the Great*, 1743.)

The eighteenth-century poet and friend of Dr Samuel Johnson, Richard Savage (1697?-1743), was another imprisoned in Newgate. In November 1727 he had killed a gentleman by the name of James Sinclair in a tavern brawl. In fact he was condemned to death for this affair, but was pardoned in the March of the following year.

Charles Dickens confessed to a 'horrible fascination' with Newgate, visiting it on several occasions. And for a vivid and graphic account of Newgate and its conditions in the early part of the nineteenth century readers might like to refer to Charles Dickens's 'A Visit to Newgate' (in *Sketches by Boz*, 1836).

Biographical accounts of the more notorious criminals confined at Newgate began to be collected from 1773. *The Newgate Calendar*, first published in 1824-28 in four volumes, collected together many of these accounts; and *The Chronicles of Time, or the New Newgate Calendar* (in two volumes) followed in 1886.

Before the building of the present Central Criminal Courts an Old Bailey sessions house stood alongside the prison. It was in this courtroom that the fictional trial of Darnay proceeded in Dickens's *A Tale of Two Cities*. Here, too, was enacted the celebrated trial of 1895 in which Oscar Wilde (1854-1900) sued the Marquis of Queensberry for libel; the consequence of which was his own criminal

Oscar Wilde, photographed about 1882.

prosecution and imprisonment.

Queensberry, a man of great resentment and sudden flares of unpredictable behaviour, had objected to Wilde's friendship with his son, Lord Alfred Douglas. The immediate cause of Wilde's prosecution of the Marquis was the latter's note which he had left for Wilde at the Albemarle Club. The note read: 'To Oscar Wilde posing as a somdomite' (the Marquis's spelling was as erratic as his conduct).

In the train of events which followed, when Wilde was himself challenged to justify his behaviour, he made that extempore and justly-famous speech on the 'Love that dare not speak its name' – a line from one of Douglas's poems. The rhetoric of that response reads in part:

> The 'Love that dare not speak its name' in this century is such a great affection of an elder for a younger man as there was between David and Jonathan, such as Plato made the very basis of his philosophy, and such as you find in the sonnets of Michelangelo and Shakespeare. It is that deep, spiritual affection that is as pure as it is perfect. It dictates and pervades great works of art like those of Shakespeare and Michelangelo, and those two letters of mine, such as they are. It is in this century misunderstood, so much misunderstood that it may be described as the 'Love that dare not speak its name', and on account of it I am placed where I am now. It is beautiful, it is fine, it is the noblest form of affection . . .

Wilde was prosecuted on indecency charges. In the present Old Bailey a book, in effect, came up for trial in 1960 when Penguin Books were prosecuted for making an obscene publication. The publishers were in the event found not guilty of publishing an obscene article: the paperback edition of the unexpurgated version of D. H. Lawrence's *Lady Chatterley's Lover*. A number of leading literary persons were called upon, or volunteered, to give their evidence in favour of the book's literary merits and the moral purport of the work. Helen Gardner and E. M. Forster, among many others, gave their judgements; T. S. Eliot, who spent several days waiting to be called, was not required to give testimony.

* * *

Just on the right of the junction of Giltspur Street (via which one has issued to the point across the way from the Old Bailey) with Holborn Viaduct is the Church of St Sepulchre. Much of the church was rebuilt by Wren following the Great Fire, and has been restored several times since then. The original Crusaders' Church on this site was founded in the twelfth century.

Buried in the church is Roger Ascham (1515-1568). Though the location is not marked, it seems very probable that he would have been buried in the Easter Sepulchre, now the Musicians' Chapel.

Ascham was tutor to Princess Elizabeth, later Queen Elizabeth I, for a period of at least two years. Ascham had distinguished himself in classical studies, was an accomplished musician, and had a developed enthusiasm for archery – which he had practised since his youth. In 1545 he published *Taxophilus*, a treatise on archery in two parts, a work with which he hoped to gain the favour of Henry VIII. Part I presents the argument in favour of archery both as recreation and as an instrument of war; Part II consists largely of practical hints as to how to develop proficiency in the art.

Between 1563 and his death Ascham composed the second text for which he is still remembered: *The*

> The
>
> Ballad of Reading Gaol
>
> By
>
> C. 3. 3.
>
>
> Leonard Smithers
> Royal Arcade London W
> Mdcccxcviii

Title page facsimile of the first edition of Wilde's Ballad of Reading gaol, *of which only 400 of the projected 800 copies were actually printed, though further impressions followed quickly upon the immediate success of the poem. Found guilty as charged at his trial, Wilde had been sentenced to the maximum term of 2 years' imprisonment which, from November 1895, he was transferred to serve at Reading Gaol, Berkshire. Discharged on 18 May 1897, Wilde began the writing of the* Ballad *in July, exactly one year and one day after the hanging on 7 July 1896 in Reading Gaol of Charles Thomas Wooldridge (the C.T.W. of the dedication) for the murder of his wife, Laura Ellen, out of jealousy. C.3.3. refers to the cell in which Wilde was held at Reading Gaol.*

Scholemaster, a plaine and perfite way of teachyng children to understand, write, and speak in Latin tong. Published by his widow two years after the death of Ascham (whose last words are reported to have been, 'I desire to depart and be with Christ'), *The Scholemaster* is notable for two principal recommendations. The first, representing Ascham's humanist stance, is the condemnation of corporal punishment of the student; Ascham asserts that gentleness, not force, is a more certain means of inducing learning in the child. The second, an invention of Ascham's which has found favour with many linguists and teachers of languages, is the device of 'double translation'. In this procedure a passage in Latin is presented by the teacher with a general explanation, and the pupil is to construe and parse the words, making a translation of the text. Later, this translation is turned back to Latin by the pupil when it may then be compared with the original from which the whole exercise began.

Within the last few years a society of archers has dedicated to the memory of Ascham a bell in the tower of the church.

* * *

Turning right on leaving the church, Snow Hill will be seen leading off to the right. It was in the house of a grocer friend, Mr Strudwick, somewhere in Snow Hill that John Bunyan (1628-88) died (see section: City Road).

A few hundred yards along Holborn Viaduct and on the opposite side of the road there stands the Guild Church of St Andrew. The present church was designed by Sir Christopher Wren and built in the years 1684-90, replacing a church on the same site.

When Agnes Wickfield was staying at the house of her father's agent in Ely Place, just off Holborn Circus (see below), David Copperfield's meeting with her at 'the appointed time was exceeded by a full quarter of an hour, according to the clock of St Andrew's' before Copperfield could 'muster up sufficient desperation' to pull the bell at the house. (*David Copperfield*, ch xxv).

There are a number of other literary associations which belong to St Andrew's. Baptized in this church was Richard Savage (see above), who claimed to be the illegitimate son of the Earl of Macclesfield. The balance of evidence suggests that the claim was false, though the first account of this claim appeared as early as 1726. In the year following Savage's death Dr Johnson published his version of the *Life of Savage* based on contemporary accounts, and on his own knowledge of the man whom he had met in 1737. They had parted in July 1739 when Savage left for Bristol. In January 1743 Savage died of a fever in the Bristol Newgate where he had been confined for debt.

Ann Radcliffe (1764-1823) was baptized in St Andrew's. Inspired by Horace Walpole's *Castle of Otranto*, the first of the English 'Gothic' novels, Radcliffe's own *Mysteries of Udolpho* (1794) proved to be a hugely successful novel.

Benjamin Disraeli (1804-81), who became both Prime Minister and a prolific novelist, was born of Jewish-Italian stock. But at the age of thirteen he was baptized into the Christian faith at St Andrew's.

In this church William Hazlitt (1778-1830) married his first wife, Sarah Stoddart, with Charles and Mary Lamb attending; Charles as best man and Mary as bridesmaid. The parents of Charles and Mary Lamb were buried here too.

And Richard le Gallienne (1866-1947), poet and a member of the Rhymers' Club (see Fleet Street) was married here.

***

From St Andrew's one may continue along Holborn (to Chancery Lane underground); or turn sharp left into Andrew Street (becoming Shoe Lane then St Bride Street) to Ludgate Circus, thence to Blackfriars. Alternatively, one may locate Ely Place, just off Charterhouse Street which leads away from the north, or farthest, side of Holborn Circus.

Ely Place, a private street guarded by beadles, as Crown property is outside of the jurisdiction of the City of London. Midway down the Place is the church of St Ethelreda, whose crypt dates from the middle of the thirteenth century, incorporating walls of an even older date.

The site of Ely Place was formerly occupied by the House of the Bishops of Ely. John of Gaunt retired here in 1381, following the sacking of his own Savoy Palace in the Peasants' Revolt (see The Strand). It is at Ely Palace that, in Shakespeare's *Richard II*, Gaunt makes his 'sceptr'd isle' speech ('. . . this blessed spot, this earth, this realm, this England.')

Ely House and most of the other buildings were demolished in the last quarter of the eighteenth century, replaced by the present brick terraced houses. In one of these, Charles Dickens set the residence of Mr Waterbrook, in *David Copperfield*, and it is at Ely Place also that David renews his friendship with Tommy Traddles.

***

From Ely Place one may turn to the left, along Charterhouse Street; and left again into Farringdon Road and on to the underground station of the same name.

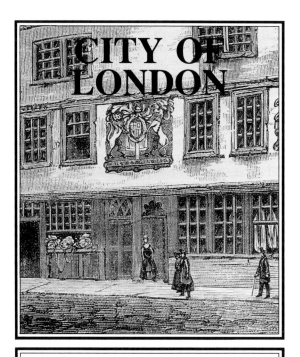

CITY ROAD

ISLINGTON

The area contained within this section actually lies within Islington, beyond the City itself. It is included at this point because it may be used to provide a preface to a series of linked tours which follow, and which will take the visitor into the heart of the City.

Islington itself being outside the City it provided a place of refuge from outbreaks of the plague, and proved to be also a gathering-place for dissenting sects – who in turn instituted in the area a number of academies and meeting-houses.

Indeed, most of the following references have their place within the context of non-conformism. And since the first two of these – Wesley's Chapel and House, and Bunhill Fields Cemetery opposite – are within a minute or so of Old Street underground station these visits may be self-contained. Following those references, however, an optional follow-on route will take the visitor to the starting-point of the section Moorgate to the Bank.

* * *

At Old Street take the subway exit No 4, which issues in City Road. A short distance ahead, on the left, will be seen the Chapel, founded in 1777 and opened the year following, by John Wesley (1703-91). Leader of the Methodist movement, Wesley travelled thousands of miles in his ministry, whilst still finding time for a prolific output of writings – pamphlets, treatises, and collections of hymns. His *Journal* has been praised by readers for its humour, and for its detailed observations of mankind and the spiritual life.

In the crypt of the Chapel there is a Museum of Methodism, tracing its history from beginnings in the eighteenth century through to the present day.

Wesley's tomb is located at the rear of the Chapel, in the small graveyard there.

Alongside the Chapel is Wesley's House (open: weekdays, 10.00am to 4.00pm; Sunday, following morning service which is at 11.00am). The House, in which Wesley died, contains numerous exhibits – including Wesley's furniture and clothes, letters, and other personal memorabilia.

* * *

On the opposite side of City Road lies Bunhill Fields Cemetery. The fields of Bunhill (derived almost certainly from 'Bone Hill') were first enclosed with a

John Wesley.

The tomb of John Bunyan.

brick wall in 1665-6, originally intended by the Corporation of London as a burial ground for victims of the Great Plague – though they were in fact used as an ordinary cemetery. Within two or three decades of opening the cemetery had become associated with the burial of nonconformists.

Among the many buried here are: John Bunyan, Daniel Defoe, Isaac Watts, and William Blake. Directions to the locations of these burial-places may be read from the plan of the cemetery posted on the wall of the hut beside the central pathway.

John Bunyan (1628-88) was born at Elston, Bedfordshire. In *The Grace Abounding to the Chief of Sinners* (1666), a confessional autobiography, he describes '[his] father's house' as 'being of that rank that is meanest and most despised of all the families in the land' – for his father was a tinsmith. Despite their poverty his parents, recognising the gift of an exceptional child, managed to find the money for his schooling. By his own account Bunyan experienced dreams and visions and troubled thoughts at an early age – though it must be recalled that his account of childhood is shaded by the adult author's deep conviction of sinfulness and a keenly-developed puritan sensibility. Bunyan's sense of Providence, God's working agency on earth, is acknowledged in his own account of four youthful escapes from death: twice from drowning, once from the bite of an adder which had crossed the path he and a companion were walking, and a fourth escape as a young soldier. At the age of seventeen, during the civil wars between Charles I and his parliament, Bunyan served in the parliamentary ranks, and was present at the siege of Lichfield in 1645:

> When I was a soldier I, with others, was drawn out to go to such a place to besiege it. But when I was just ready to go, one of the company desired to go in my room; to which, when I had consented, he took my place; and coming to the siege, as he stood sentinel, he was shot in the head with a musket bullet and died.

At nineteen he married a devout but poor Church woman whose dowry of two books (*The*

Plain Man's Pathway to Heaven and *The Practice of Piety*) became their regular reading-matter. In 1653 Bunyan joined a nonconformist church in Bedford, and shortly afterwards – chosen by the congregation, as was the custom among dissenters – began preaching there. In 1656 his wife died, leaving him with four young children. Bunyan re-married three years later, and the year following was arrested for preaching without a licence. There followed twelve years of imprisonment at Bedford Gaol. It was during this long confinement that he wrote, among other works, *Grace Abounding*.

Upon his release from the 'den' (Bunyan's word for his cell) of Bedford Gaol, he returned to preach at his former church, but was again imprisoned a few years later. During this confinement he completed the first part of *The Pilgrim's Progress from this world to that which is to come*. This 'similitude of

Bedford Gaol, the damp 'den' where Bunyan was imprisoned. During his second term of imprisonment, for 6 months in 1675, he wrote the first part of Pilgrim's Progress, *'mine own self to gratifie'.*

a dream', or allegory, was not published until 1678. Though Bunyan himself had no doubts about the merit of the work he was, of course, intimately aware of the puritan aversion to the fictional treatment of spiritual matters.

Bunyan's concern for others shows through the tribulations of his own history and is, indeed, illustrated in the final 'errand of mercy' of his life. Bunyan had stopped at the London house of a friend, Mr Shadwick, a grocer – whose house was in Snow Hill, Holborn. From there he had travelled to Reading, in Berkshire, where he had used his good influence to reconcile a father with his son. On the return to London he was caught in a heavy shower of rain. Feeling ill upon arrival at Snow Hill, and his own spirits depressed, Bunyan developed a fever. The fever lasted ten days, Bunyan dying on 31 August 1688.

Daniel Defoe (1660?-1731) was born in London, the son of James Foe, a butcher. At some point in his late thirties he changed his name, by which time he had travelled widely on the continent, married, and served in the protestant William III's army. In that cause he produced also *The True-born Englishman* (1701), a satirical poem which attacked the popular prejudice against a foreign-born king.

In the year following, Defoe's pamphlet *The Shortest Way with Dissenters* appeared, and quickly became notorious. In this Defoe, himself a Dissenter but in the assumed role of an ecclesiastic, demanded the suppression of *all* dissent as a means of satirising the church authorities' intolerance of Dissenting movements – a protest for which he was fined, actually served rather less than six months imprisoned at Newgate, and was three times put in the pillory at Temple Bar. From the hooting and pelting he suffered there on his first appearance, by the time of his third appearance at the end of July the mood of the populace had changed and he was accounted a hero. Crowds of people applauded him and brought flowers to bedeck the pillory.

Defoe's career and, it has been argued, his character, never recovered fully from this episode of his life – and perhaps the humiliation of the pillory more than the imprisonment. He had already recovered from one major personal crisis. More than ten years previously he had been declared bankrupt following some kind of speculative venture, but he had largely redeemed those debts. For several years before his trial and imprisonment he had been the manager of a tile factory at Tilbury. Thus Defoe had worked himself back into fairly prosperous circumstances. Following his release from Newgate, however, Defoe's situation was frequently impecunious; without secure income, but with the need to support a large family, he became much shiftier in his dealings with people and affairs, practising deceit and subterfuge. Character and career found their coincidence in his profession of government spy.

He became an agent for Edward Harley, the

Daniel Defoe.
By courtesy of the Rector of St Giles, Cripplegate

Whig prime minister – who almost certainly had been instrumental in securing Defoe's release from Newgate. When Harley fell, Defoe's services were retained by the Tory government – Defoe transferring allegiance again upon the return of Harley. In the exercise of his duties Defoe made extensive and extended journeys through Scotland, reporting privately on the Jacobite movement. Defoe's journalism was at the service of his masters too, and it is possible (though only one speculative possibility among several) that a duplicity practised in this role for his masters might have contributed to the mystery of his final months. For between the years 1716 and 1726 he posed as a tory political journalist, and in the early part of that period he found employment with a Jacobite publisher, Nathaniel Mist, becoming Mist's editor for the *Journal* which he published. In accordance with the deal he had struck with Lord Townshend, the principal secretary of state, Defoe's role was to soften or suppress treasonable articles and to inform the government administration of what was going on in Jacobite circles. Mist himself served a term of imprisonment for his activities and, discovering Defoe's treachery – so it is believed – swore his revenge and pursued Defoe.

What is certain is that in 1729, following the marriage in the spring of his daughter Sophia to Henry Baker, Defoe left the family home at Newington and disappeared – taking refuge first in London and then in Kent, returning then to lodgings in Ropemaker Street (see below). Defoe may have been hiding from Mist. His reasons may have been financial, the escape from creditors following a failed speculation, or have had some connection with the transfer of property to one of his sons, made on the condition that the son continued to provide for his mother and unmarried sisters – obligations which the son did not fully discharge. For in the autumn of that year the Newington home was broken up, and Defoe might have believed that he must separate from the family. Whatever the true cause of Defoe's seclusion he continued to write pamphlets, as vigorous in tone as ever, thus countering another suggestion – that Defoe was suffering from some kind of mental illness, including the hallucinatory conviction that he was being pursued.

On 26 April 1726 Defoe died of a stroke in the Ropemaker Street lodgings – a short distance away from the place of his birth in Fore Street – his wife and seven children all surviving him.

As journalist, editor, pamphleteer, and from the age almost of sixty, a novelist also, Defoe assembled a prodigious output of writings – though there exists scholarly questioning as to whether the canon of work attributed to him issued in fact from his own pen. The novels for which he is most widely-known (including: *Robinson Crusoe, Moll Flanders, A Journal of the Plague Year*, and *Roxana*) combine an energetic prose with a journalistic eye for the selection of detail. In the last two or three decades a good deal of critical work has shown that these fictions, written as continuous narratives, are indeed constructed to a design and carefully crafted. And certainly, in these moral fables, Defoe set down many of the major lines of development for the subsequent history of the English novel.

Isaac Watts (1674-1748) is probably best-known as a writer of hymns. Among those which he penned and which have achieved lasting popularity are: 'There is a land of pure delight . . .', 'When I survey the wondrous cross . . .', 'Jesus shall reign where'er the sun . . .', and 'O God, our help in ages past . . .' He is remembered too by some generations of readers for his children's verse (from *Divine Songs for Children*, 1715), mostly in a vein which combines piety with sentimentality. 'A Cradle Hymn', for example, opens with the following stanza:

> Hush! my dear, lie still and slumber,
> Holy angels guard thy bed!
> Heav'nly blessing without number
> Gently falling on thy head.

There are lines from others of his poems which have achieved a detached life of their own or have amended lives as proverbs: lines such as 'How doth the busy little bee', 'Satan finds some mischief still for idle hands to do', and:

> Let dogs delight to bark and bite,
> For God hath made them so . . .

His other poetry, little-read today, displays a technical experimentation with the metrics of verse – in an age when the heroic couplet became more or less the automatic form – employing, for example, blank verse form, Sapphics, and 'the poulter's measure' (alternate lines of 12 and 14 syllables).

Watts was born in Southampton, the son of a clothier, and the eldest of nine children. After an education at a nonconformist academy at Stoke Newington he became a private tutor, at the same time preaching at an independent chapel in London. Because of failing health he had to relinquish some of his pastoral duties.

From 1712 Watts lived with his friends and patrons, Sir Thomas and Lady Abney. Following the death of Sir Thomas, Lady Abney transferred to Stoke Newington, Watts remaining in her household until his death. He never married.

William Blake (1757-1827) was apprenticed as an engraver, a skill which he was later to employ both to illustrate his own books of verse and also, for some of his 'inspired' works, as a medium for direct composition.

Throughout all of his works there is a sense of a mystical cast of mind and a revolutionary sensibility. Certainly his own self-education finds an embodiment in the wholly-original modes of expression which he developed – including his invented systems of mythology, often of a complex symbolism and personification; as deployed in, for example, *The Four Zoas*.

Tomb of Isaac Watts.

Whether in this epic and extended form or in the briefer lyrical mode of *Songs of Innocence of Experience*, Blake's poetry offers a consistent and powerful critique and condemnation of society, its false values, and the wickedness of man's treatment of man. It is, as Blake himself announced repeatedly, prophetic poetry; his inspirations being the King James Bible and the poetry of Milton.

Blake, perhaps above all, was the apostle of the Imagination – believing that only through the exercise of that power could one achieve essential being. Indeed, again and again in Blake's work imagination equates with the real nature of man – and the lack or impoverishment of imagination accounting for man's unredeemed nature, and restorable only through the imagination.

Blake's own revolutionary spirit confined itself to his creative works; he was not, in the common sense of the word, an activist. In 1782 he had married Catherine Boucher. Though the marriage was childless their relationship, after some difficulties, was close and dependent. Blake died, it is reported, a fulfilled and contented man. A few months before he died at Fountain Court (see section: The Strand), he wrote to George Cumberland, one of his patrons:

> I have been very near the Gates of Death & have returned very weak & an Old Man feeble & tottering, but not in Spirit & Life, not in The Real Man The

Imagination which Liveth for Ever. In that I am stronger & stronger as this Foolish Body decays . . .

Here, explicitly, is stated the equation between the Imagination and the Spirit – 'Man The Imagination'. In his unyielding insistence that it is this equation which proclaims and makes man human, Blake can be regarded as a precurser of the English Romantic movement of writers – whilst at the same time his work remains distinctively apart from any concensus or group effort, his poetry being always and wholly individualistic.

* * *

Having visited Bunhill Fields Cemetery, there are several options. One may return to Old Street underground station, either to end the tour or to go on to Moorgate underground station to commence the next tour. Or, one may walk directly down the City Road until one reaches Moorgate.

Alternatively, there is a short diversion one may take – which may be of particular appeal to those interested in the history of the English theatre.

At the far side of Bunhill Fields Cemetery, there

Tombstone of William Blake.

is an exit into Bunhill Row. Almost opposite will be seen the opening into Dufferin Street. At the far end of Dufferin Street, at the junction with Whitecross Street, Fortune Street leads away. Immediately into Fortune Street, and on the right-hand side, will be seen a commemorative plaque marking the site of the Fortune theatre.

The first Fortune theatre, modelled on the round, wooden structure of the Globe theatre at Bankside (see: The Borough and Bankside) was built here in 1600 for the theatre impresario and manager Philip Henslowe and his partner in this venture Edward Alleyn, one of the most notable actors of his day. Alleyn made his reputation at another Bankside theatre, the Rose, also managed by Henslowe. From the substantial wealth Alleyn accumulated, not all of it income directly from his acting, Alleyn endowed Dulwich College, an educational establishment for poor boys. From the diary and notes which Henslowe left derives a good deal of knowledge of some of the minor Elizabethan playwrights (such as Drayton, Rowley, Chettle, and Day), together with specifications for the Fortune theatre itself.

The first Fortune was burned down in 1621. It was re-built, this time as a brick structure – a square facade with windows let in at each storey level. Officially closed by the Puritans in 1642, illegal performances continued there until it was pulled apart by soldiers in 1649, to be demolished completely in 1661.

* * *

From the Fortune theatre site return to Bunhill Row, turning to the right. Some way along, on the right-hand side of the Row, all trace gone, used to stand the house where died John Milton (1608-1674), whose home it had been for the previous eleven years.

He took up residence here with his third wife, Elizabeth Minshull, following their marriage in 1663. With them were Milton's three daughters from his first marriage. Totally blind since 1652 – the year, coincidentally, of his first wife's death – it was at Bunhill Row that Milton composed his epics *Paradise Lost* and *Paradise Regained*, together with his poetic drama *Samson Agonistes*.

* * *

At the end of Bunhill Row there is a junction with Chiswell Street. A little to the left of this corner Moor Lane leads off ahead. A few yards into Moor Lane, Ropemaker Street opens on the left. Some-

The second Fortune Theatre.

where along this street, then probably almost as narrow as an alleyway, Daniel Defoe (see above) took refuge in lodgings for the last months of his life.

* * *

Ropemaker Street soon empties into Moorgate where, on the right and a little way ahead, will be found the entrance to Moorgate underground station, where one may choose to end this brief tour. Alternatively, one may proceed directly to the next tour by continuing a little further down Moorgate, locating the site for the entry which begins that section (Moorgate to the Bank).

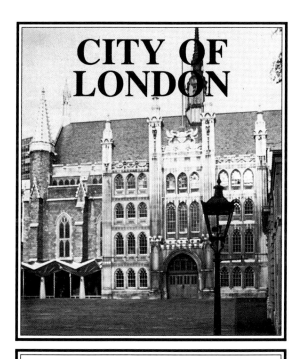

CITY OF LONDON

MOORGATE TO THE BANK
CITY OF LONDON

The area of the City included in this section will take the visitor to the heart of its financial and banking empires. The route mapped out here includes a number of locations with notable historic associations, where the visitor with time to spare may well wish to linger. The tour has been designed, however, to end at the Bank underground station – so that those who so choose may immediately go on from this section to explore the references gathered in the following section, The Bank to London Bridge.

* * *

The tour begins at Moorgate tube station. On leaving the station turn to the right where, further along Moorgate itself, and just before the junction with London Wall, will be found the location where John Keats (1795-1821) was born. On the righthand side of the street, at what is now the Moorgate public-house (No 85), between the first and second floors of that building will be seen a commemorative plaque. The site was formerly occupied by the Swan and Hoop Inn, and John Keats was born above the livery-stable run by his father. Having come up from the West Country to work as an ostler, John Keats's father had married his employer's daughter, Frances Jennings. The father, Thomas, died as a consequence of a fall from a horse when John was nine; and when he was fifteen his mother died of tuberculosis – from which disease John would himself die.

* * *

Immediately beyond this site London Wall crosses Moorgate. To the right, some fifty or sixty yards beyond the junction, and bearing to the right will be seen Fore Street. Somewhere along this street, though the location is not known, Daniel Defoe (1660-1731), who has a number of associations with this part of the City, was born.

The street which formerly ran north from Fore Street, on the right, to connect with Chiswell Street was in the eighteenth century the famous Grub Street to which Dr Johnson referred in his *Dictionary* as one where a number of hack writers congregated: 'whence any mean production is called grubstreet.' From 1830 the name of the street was changed to Milton Street (not named after the poet); and in the 1960s the street disappeared with re-development.

* * *

Where Fore Street joins with Wood Street a little distance further on there is an entrance to the Parish and Ward Church of St Giles Without Cripplegate. The entrance way leads into an open space which faces the modern complex of the Barbican buildings, with the entrance to the church to one's left.

A church has stood on this site since Saxon times. The present church dates from 1030, was extended in 1340, restored in 1545 and 1897 – and extensively restored after bombing in 1940.

Among those who worshipped at St Giles were Sir Thomas More (1478-1535), whose parents married here in 1474; Daniel Defoe (see above), who attended as a young man; and John Bunyan (1628-1688), who worshipped here as a child. Edward Alleyn (1566-1626), actor and theatre-proprietor, also attended St Giles. Alleyn's playhouses included the Rose at Bankside, and the Fortune a little north of the City limits (see section: City Road) – both owned jointly with Philip Henslowe, whose step-daughter he married. Upon her death in 1623 he then married John Donne's daughter, Constance.

John Foxe (1516-1587), author of the *Protestant*

Milton's Bible: the entries, in his own hand, on the blank page opposite the opening of the Book of Genesis.

Book of Martyrs, was buried here, as was John Milton (1608-1674). Milton, who was born in nearby Bread Street, just off Cheapside to the south of St Giles, lived at various times in close proximity to the church. His burial place, the same grave as that of his father, is marked by a tablet in the floor just beside the pulpit and to the left of the centre aisle. There is a record that in 1793 Milton's grave was opened and his corpse interfered with. The coffin having been prised open, the corpse 'which was clothed in a shroud, and looked as if it had only just been buried' was then exposed:

> . . . one of the overseers, then endeavoured to pull out the teeth but, being unsuccessful, a bystander took up a stone and loosened them with a blow. There were only five in the upper jaw, but they were quite white and good. They together with some of the lower ones [the men] divided between them. A rib bone was also taken and the hair from the head which was long and smooth was torn out by the handful. After this the caretaker Elizabeth Grant took the coffin under her care charging sixpence to anyone who wished to view it. Later she reduced her fee to threepence and finally to twopence.

To the right of the centre aisle there is a Victorian eagle lectern which commemorates Bishop Lancelot Andrewes (1555-1626) who for seventeen years, from 1588, was vicar of this church. In addition to his sermons and devotional prayers he is remembered as one of the translators of the Authorised (King James's) Version of the Bible. Against the right-hand, or south wall of the church will be found four marble busts. Dating only from the turn of the present century they represent: Daniel Defoe, John Milton, John Bunyan and Oliver Cromwell (who also worshipped here, and was indeed married in the church).

A little further along the south aisle there is a statue of John Milton which, however, invites fuller attention. Though made in 1904 it is based on the likeness of a bust sculpted originally in 1654 – by which time Milton's first wife had died, leaving behind three daughters, and he had lost his sight completely. At that period Milton held governmental office – as Secretary for Foreign Tongues to the Council of State, in the Commonwealth – and had published many of those pamphlets in which, over a period of some twenty years, he espoused and championed various religious, political and moral freedoms. These works included *Of Education* and *Areopagitica* (both 1644), and the two *Defences of the English People* (1651 and 1654). Not until the early 1660s would Milton compose, by dictation, the long-deferred epic *Paradise Lost* (completed 1665, first published 1667).

A memorial tablet to Helen Lucy (d 1634) in the south aisle recalls the legends of Shakespeare's sudden departure from Warwickshire to escape prosecution for supposedly stealing deer from Sir Thomas Lucy – to which family Helen belonged. Research has shown, however, that there was no deer-park on the Lucy estate of Charlecote at the time, and that the Lucy family did not establish one there until the eighteenth century. The opening passage from *The Merry Wives of Windsor* – with its puns on luces (freshwater pike, and featured on the Lucy coat of arms) and louses – often cited in support of the story is, as Peter Alexander (editor of the Tudor Shakespeare) expresses it, 'more probably the origin of the story itself.' Alternative explanations of the legend and its variants may be traced in Schoenbaum in his documentary life of Shakespeare (see Bibliography). That Shakespeare once lived close to St Giles has been established, however – in Silver Street (now gone) off Wood Street.

A Shakespeare connection with St Giles that does now appear to hold good refers to William's youngest brother Edmund. For in the Parish register for 12 August 1607 appears the following burial entry: 'Edward sonne of Edward Shackspeere Player base borne'. The lack of scrupulous distinction between like-sounding names is a feature of such records commonly encountered, and that fact has led to the identification of Edmund as the father of the illegitimate child, Edward. Edmund survived the death of his son by a few months only (for details, see The Borough and Bankside section).

* * *

Leaving St Giles and turning to the right into Wood Street and continuing beyond its junction with London Wall, Love Lane enters on the left. At the corner of Love Lane where it bears left into Aldermanbury there are some small gardens, the remains of the churchyard of St Mary Aldermanbury Church. In these gardens there is a bust of William Shakespeare; it is mounted on top of a pedestal memorial to John Heminge and Henry Condell, both of whom were buried in the churchyard.

Seven years after Shakespeare's death Heminge and Condell, his friends and fellow-actors, issued the first collected edition of his plays: the First Folio of 1623. Shakespeare's last few years had been spent in Stratford, where he had retired with, it seems, no intention himself of collecting together his works into a definitive edition. Though some of Shakespeare's plays had been published in his lifetime, with or without his authority, there was good reason why playwrights of his time would be loath to publish stage works; there was no copyright to protect them from booksellers producing pirated copies, and in any case publication could well result in a loss of takings at the playhouse itself – and therefore was a procedure not favoured by either actors or managers where a play was drawing good houses.

Heminge and Condell, members and managers of the group with which Shakespeare had acted for some twenty years (the Lord Chamberlain's Men, later the King's Men) were ideally suited to discharge the self-appointed task of editing the plays, for they could compare printed copies of single works with manuscripts which they held in their own possession. As their address 'To the Great Variety

The title page of the First Folio of 1623, compiled by Heminge and Condell. The 'stuffed dummy' figure of Martin Droeshout's inexpert engraving has been variously described, and dismissed – as in Gainsborough's 'Damn the original picture of him . . .' Ben Jonson's verse inscription, on the flyleaf facing the title page, perhaps points an ironic comment: '. . . Reader, looke/ Not on his picture, but his Booke.'

of Readers' makes plain, they were well aware of the financial risk to themselves: hence their exhortation to the public to buy a copy of the work – '. . . read and censure. Do so, but buy it first. That doth best commend a Booke, the Stationer saies'. But their admiration for the plays can not be doubted, nor their intention 'to perfect of their limbes' the 'diverse stolne, and surreptitious copies, maimed, and deformed by the frauds and stealths of injurious imposters.'

The memorial acknowledges the immense debt which posterity owes to them for their labours.

* * *

From the gardens, heading in the opposite direction along Aldermanbury and within a few yards, there is a passageway off to the left which leads into a large open space. Here, on the left, stands the Guildhall, the seat of government of the City of London; to the right stands the Church of St Lawrence Jewry.

The Guildhall dates from the fifteenth century. The porch, of 1430, still provides the main entrance; whilst the main structure of the Hall – though both altered and repaired – was completed a decade after. Beneath the Hall is a large medieval crypt, the most extensive in London.

Straight ahead beyond the entrance to Guildhall, steps to the right lead into the Great Hall – where will be seen the large monuments to several distinguished men of the nation.

The Hall has also been the location for several famous historical trials. Of these perhaps the best-known was the trial of Lady Jane Grey, tried here with her husband, Lord Guildford Dudley, in 1553 – the same year as Archbishop Thomas Cranmer, principal author of the English liturgy, was also tried at the Hall.

On 13 January 1547, Henry Howard, Earl of Surrey (1517-47), and his father the 3rd Duke of Norfolk, were tried together here before the Privy Council on charges of high treason and found guilty.

Two years of Howard's youth had been spent at Windsor as the companion of Henry VIII's natural son, Henry Fitzroy, Duke of Richmond. Surrey's subsequent history as soldier and courtier was marked by many checks to his career – to which his own impetuosity contributed significantly.

When it was known that Henry VIII was dying, towards the close of 1546, there was competition between Lord Hertford and Surrey's father, Norfolk, as to which of them should be appointed regent or protector during the minority of Henry's son, the Prince Edward. Surrey pressed hard his father's claims.

Earlier in that same year Surrey had sought, and been refused by the College of Arms, permission to quarter the family arms and include heraldic emblems of Edward the Confessor. Despite the refusal Surrey had nonetheless gone ahead with the change.

Hertford and his supporters construed this action as a treasonable design. They therefore pressed that a charge be laid before the Privy Council – together

The Guildhall.

with other charges added by Surrey's enemies. These included most notably the accusation that Surrey had sought to persuade his own sister to offer herself as the king's mistress in order to secure royal influence. Certain of his enemies also accused Surrey of affecting foreign dress and manners and of keeping an Italian jester.

Father and son were arrested and sent to the Tower in December 1546. Henry VIII personally assisted in drawing up the paper which set forth the allegations against them, on his presumption that Surrey's ultimate aim was to set aside Prince Edward from the throne in order to assume it for himself. Though nothing constituting evidence was presented at the trial, Surrey and his father were found guilty and were sentenced to death. (See also section: Eastcheap and the Tower.)

The Guildhall Court, since rebuilt, was chosen as the location for a fictional trial: that of Mr Pickwick's trial for breach of promise to Mrs Bardell in Dickens's *Pickwick Papers* (see ch xxxiv). It is as a result of this case that Pickwick, refusing to pay damages after the case has been found in Mrs Bardell's favour, is sent to gaol.

Housed within the Guildhall there is a very fine Library entered via flights of stairs leading off from the main lobby of the building. The Library houses the finest collection of books, prints, maps and drawings of London across the ages. Windows in the Old Library celebrate the printers William Caxton, Wynken de Worde (shown as Caxton's apprentice, as indeed he was for some years); Bishop Coverdale, translator of the Bible into English; John Milton; and John Stow, historian of London. More recent stained-glass windows in the Guildhall crypt (not open at all times) display as their subjects: Geoffrey Chaucer, Sir Thomas More, William Caxton, and Samuel Pepys.

***

The church of St Lawrence Jewry faces the Guildhall across the open space between. The former church was designed by Sir Christopher Wren and built in 1677 to replace the older church which burned down in the Great Fire. All but the walls and tower of the Wren church were destroyed in a firebomb raid on the City in December 1940. The present church was built in the years 1954-57, restored to the design of Wren.

Henry Howard.

In the right-hand aisle, one of the stained glass windows celebrates Sir Thomas More (see above) who preached in the older church. In the same older church was baptized Thomas Middleton (1570?-1627).

***

From St Lawrence Jewry, turning right along Gresham Street, within a few yards will be seen Milk Street leading off to the left. Somewhere along this street Sir Thomas More was born.

Just yards beyond Milk Street the next turning off to the left is Wood Street, which very soon emerges at a junction with Cheapside. Somewhere along this section of Wood Street was located the shop where Robert Herrick (1591-1674), Cavalier poet, was apprenticed as a goldsmith to an uncle. It is possible, though not certain, that Herrick had been born in Wood Street.

In the section of Wood Street beyond Goldsmith Street (which enters on the right) formerly stood the Cross Keys Inn (then No 128), the coaching inn where Charles Dickens (1812-70) first arrived in London, from Chatham, as a young lad of ten years of age. Dickens recalled the journey many years later:

> Through all the years that have since passed, have I lost the smell of damp straw in which I was packed – like game – and forwarded, carriage paid, to the Cross Keys, Wood Street, Cheapside, London? There was no other inside passengers, and I consumed my sandwiches in solitude and dreariness . . .

The Cross Keys had also been recalled by Dickens as the location at which Pip, in *Great Expectations*, arrives in London. Later (ch xxxiii) Pip entertains Estella in 'a private sitting room' at the Cross Keys, there ordering tea for them.

At the corner of Wood Street with Cheapside, on the right-hand side, there is the remaining churchyard of St Peter's, destroyed in the Great Fire. There may still be seen the plane tree where sang the thrush in Wordsworth's 'The Reverie of Poor Susan':

> At the corner of Wood Street, when daylight appears,
> Hangs a Thrush that sings loud, it has sung for three
>   years:
> Poor Susan has passed by the spot, and has heard
> In the silence of morning the song of the Bird.
>
> 'Tis a note of enchantment; what ails her? She sees
> A mountain ascending, a vision of trees;

The tree at the corner of Wood Street, as it appeared in the last quarter of the nineteenth century.

> Bright volumes of vapour through Lothbury glide,
> And a river flows on through the vale of Cheapside . . .

* * *

Just a little to the left of the junction of Wood Street with Cheapside, leading away from its far side, will be seen Bread Street. Born in Bread Street were John Donne (1572-1631), and John Milton (see above) – though the location of neither house is known with certainty. Milton's house was at the sign of the Spread Eagle; and it is known that the house became a tourist attraction during the latter stage of Milton's life, so great was his fame.

Just beyond the junction with Cheapside, on the right-hand side of Bread Street and probably just a few yards into the street, stood the famous Mermaid Tavern (from certainly early in the fifteenth century until destroyed in the Great Fire), the meeting-place for many of the wits and literary men of the early seventeenth century. Among those who attended the tavern, and formed the Friday Street Club, were: Ben Jonson, John Donne, Sir Walter

Ralegh, Francis Beaumont and John Fletcher. Their meetings were said to have been instigated by Ralegh (who was later to select Jonson as travelling tutor to his son). Tradition also insists that Shakespeare was present at these meetings. The tradition in all likelihood is accurate, but as a matter of historical record it has been pointed out that such gatherings at the Mermaid took place following Shakespeare's retirement from London to Stratford. Shakespeare's presence, therefore, could have occurred only on return visits to London. For two return visits there exists documentary evidence, and a third may be reasonably inferred. Given the years of Shakespeare's residence in London, his involvement with the stage, the friendships with fellow-writers and -actors, it seems reasonable to claim that other unregistered visits would have been made also.

Beaumont's 'Lines to Ben Jonson' point to the character of the conversation which animated the company gathered at the Mermaid:

> What things have we seen
> Done at the Mermaid! Heard words that have been
> So nimble, and so full of subtile flame,
> As if that everyone from whence they came
> Had meant to put his whole wit in a jest,
> And had resolv'd to live a fool, the rest
> Of his dull life.

John Keats's poem, 'Lines on the Mermaid Tavern', later re-animated the legend of the place:

> Souls of poets dead and gone,
> What Elysium have ye known,
> Happy field or mossy cavern
> Choicer than the Mermaid Tavern?

* * *

At his point there is a small detour which most visitors will wish to take: some thirty or forty yards into Bread Street there is a narrow entrance on the left leading through to Bow Lane and the Church of St Mary le Bow. A church has stood on this site since Norman times. The immediately preceding church here was burned down in the Great Fire, the present church being to a design of Wren – largely re-built following bombing in the Second World War. It was the sound of the bells from the earlier church here which, in the legend, recalled Dick Whittington to London to make his fortune and to be four times Lord Mayor of London.

The term Cockney now applies to anyone born within the sound of Bow bells, as well as denoting a characteristic speech-form. Originally, the Middle English *cokeney* meant 'a cock's egg', that is, a small egg containing no yolk, as occasionally laid by the hen. By extension the term was applied by country-dwellers to townsfolk, the latter presumed by them to know nothing of country matters and therefore to be ignorant.

In 1817 the reviewer Lockhart, writing in *Blackwood's Magazine*, coined the phrase the 'Cockney School' to refer to a group of writers which included Shelley, Keats, Leigh Hunt, Hazlitt and Lamb. Either by their subject or their style their writings, as Lockhart conceived things, had departed from the high classical ideal.

* * *

Both Bread Street and Bow Lane (for those who have visited the church) within a very short distance join with Watling Street to the south. Heading left along Watling Street, and just yards away at its junction with Queen Victoria Street, is the Church of St Mary Aldermary.

Its title of 'alder' [older] is taken to mean that its beginnings are older than those of the church of St Mary le Bow. Of the earlier medieval church which stood here, some parts of its walls have been incorporated into the present building. After the Great Fire destroyed the original, Sir Christopher Wren re-built the church to its Gothic style – that being a condition of the benefactress who financed the re-building. The benefactor of the medieval church was Richard Chaucer, vintner, the poet's step-grandfather.

In the former church Samuel Pepys (1633-1703) was married to his fifteen-year-old bride, Elizabeth St Michel (see also: Eastcheap and the Tower).

In 1663 John Milton (see above) married in St Mary Aldermary church his third wife Elizabeth Minshull, with whom he appears to have enjoyed a contented harmony.

* * *

About a hundred yards further east along Queen Victoria Street, and on the opposite side of the road beside a subway entrance to the Bank underground station, will be found Walbrook. And a little way into Walbrook is sited St Stephen Walbrook Church. Yet another of Wren's churches, it has recently been restored after nine years' work, and should certainly be visited. At the centre of the spacious, light interior is a huge, round altar stone by Henry Moore.

The interior of St Stephen Walbrook (1672-9), one of the finest of Wren's churches.

Sir John Vanbrugh (1664-1726), himself an architect, and a Restoration playwright of prose comedies, notably *The Provok'd Wife* and *The Relapse*, is buried in the church. Written to 'amuse the gentlemen of the town', Vanbrugh's plays contain some marvellously comic invention; and none more so than the vain, complacent and affected dandy Lord Foppington in *The Relapse* (a character he adapted and developed from Colley Cibber's *Love's Last Shift*).

Vanbrugh's burial place in the church is not known; neither is there any memorial to him within the church.

The tour may be ended here by returning to Queen Victoria Street and the subway entrance to the Bank underground station. Or one may proceed directly to the next tour, The Bank to London Bridge, simply by continuing further along Queen Victoria Street, where it merges into a confluence of seven roads. Leading off to the right is Cornhill, the corner of which marks the starting-point for that tour.

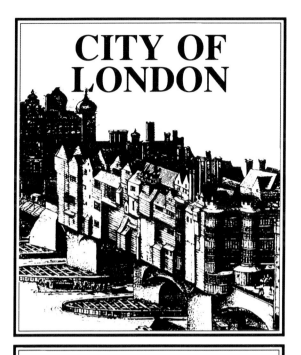

CITY OF LONDON

THE BANK TO LONDON BRIDGE
CITY OF LONDON

This tour will take the visitor around a small area of the City, largely its financial and banking section, before leading on to London Bridge At that point, for those who wish to continue touring, there are the options of continuing east, towards the Tower of London, or heading south, across the river, into Southwark.

Immediately at the Bank underground station stands the unmistakable building of the Bank of England. Dating originally from 1734, largely reconstructed in the late 1780's, the Bank was dubbed the 'Old Lady of Threadneedle Street' by Richard Brinsley Sheridan in a debate in the Commons during the Napoleonic Wars. That title it has retained.

Kenneth Grahame (1859-1932) joined the Bank of England after coming down from Oxford, and served there for many years, becoming secretary to the institution. Grahame's depiction of childhood set in the English countryside proved a contemporary success (*The Golden Age*, 1895), but it is, of course, for the later *The Wind in the Willows* (1908) that he is chiefly remembered.

* * *

Opposite the Bank will be seen the junction of Threadneedle with Cornhill.

Somewhere off Cornhill, and probably some way into it, Daniel Defoe (1660-1731) was once in business, as some kind of 'middleman' merchant. But just into Cornhill, on the right-hand side at No 17, is the bank where T. S. Eliot (1888-1965) first started to work for Lloyds Bank for what would be a total of eight years. In March 1917, through a friend of his wife's family, Eliot joined the staff of the Colonial and Foreign Department after a period of schoolteaching. In July of that year his collection *Prufrock and Other Poems* was published; and in the month preceding that event he had been offered an assistant editorship on the *Egoist* magazine – the start of what was to be, in effect, a life-time of editing.

Here he worked in the basement, beneath the thick glass inserts set into the pavement – the click of heels overhead clearly audible.

Fellow employees who worked with Eliot at this period of his life remembered him as somewhat aloof, sometimes 'living in a dreamland', and often breaking off suddenly 'in the middle of dictating a letter . . . [to] grasp a sheet of paper and start writing quickly when an idea came to him . . .'. He dressed formally, indeed with an over-nice precision: 'Immaculate black jacket and sponge-bag trousers, and his large tortoise-rimmed glasses which, at the time, were a new thing and not generally worn, even at managerial level'. After no more than three years here Eliot was transferred to Lloyd's Head Office in Lombard Street (see below). But he was to return to the Colonial and Foreign Office at Cornhill in 1923, at first as joint head, but later as sole head of the Foreign Office Information Bureau.

Eliot left the employ of the bank in 1925 to join the Directors of the publishing house of Faber and Gwyer (later Faber and Faber), in which position he would remain for the rest of his life. (See Bloomsbury I section.)

* * *

Immediately beyond the bank, Change Alley opens. A little way into the Alley, there is a turning to the left. A few yards along, at another intersection of the Alley, on the right-hand side, will be found a

plaque which reads: 'The site of Garraway's coffee-house. Rebuilt 1874'.

Founded in the sixteenth century by Thomas Garway, a tobacconist and coffee merchant, Garraway's lasted for more than two hundred years. It is cited by Defoe as a meeting-place frequented by people of quality. The place was referred to in Henry Fielding's *Amelia* (1751), and is mentioned in several of Charles Dickens's novels – including *Martin Chuzzlewit*, *Little Dorrit*, and *The Uncommercial Traveller*. The best-known of Dickens's references to Garraway's, however, remains that of the *Pickwick Papers* (ch xxxiv) where it is the location at which Mr Pickwick drew up his 'chops and tomato sauce' letter to Mrs Bardell.

* * *

Returning to Cornhill, still on the right-hand side and a few yards beyond Change Alley, is sited No 32, the present building now occupied by the Cornhill Insurance Group. At the entrance to the

Garraway's Coffee House, many of whose patrons were engaged in trade and exchange, viewed shortly before it closed down in 1872. Change Alley, its location, was described by Jonathan Swift as a 'narrow sound though deep as hell', in his ballad on the South Sea Bubble.

building is a double wooden, carved door. Designed by B. P. Arnold, the eight carved panels of the doors were carved by Walter Gilbert – the doors being placed there is 1939.

The eight panels of the doors, four per door, depict some of the historical associations of Cornhill. The bottom panel of the left-hand door presents a scene from Garraway's, whilst the bottom panel of the other door shows the meeting which took place between two of the Brontë sisters and William Makepeace Thackeray in the building which formerly stood on this site. Then No 65 Cornhill, it was occupied by the Brontës' publishers, Smith, Elder and Co.

Title page facsimile of the first edition of Jane Eyre.

A panel of the carved wooden door at 32 Cornhill depicting the meeting between Thackeray and Charlotte and Anne Brontë at the publishing house of Smith, Elder and Co.   Courtesy Cornhill Insurance Group

The Brontë sisters, Charlotte (1816-55), Emily (1818-48) and Anne (1820-49), together with their brother Branwell, were brought up at Haworth, Yorkshire, a middling-size but remote moorland village of about 5,000 inhabitants where their father was perpetual curate from 1820. They spent a good deal of their childhood inventing and writing of fantasy-worlds which in some way clearly compensated for the lack of immediate adventure in their closed community.

In 1846 the sisters had published pseudonymously their *Poems* under the names of 'Currer, Ellis and Acton Bell', the costs of publication paid for by themselves. Financially the venture was a failure – only two copies of the volume were sold – but its appearance was undoubtedly a spur to the sisters to continue and complete other writings which they had worked on. After something like eighteen months of submitting their first novels to various publishers, Thomas Newby accepted Ann's *Agnes Grey* and Emily's *Wuthering Heights*. Charlotte's *The Professor* was turned down, and would be published only after its author's death.

Charlotte began work on *Jane Eyre*. Her final submission of *The Professor*, though it did not bring her an acceptance from Smith, Elder, at least gave her a good deal of encouragement. So when completed, it was to that publisher which she sent the work, where it was accepted immediately. Thus in October 1847 there appeared Charlotte's work in print, followed in the December by Anne's and Emily's.

Of the three it was *Jane Eyre* which created an immediate sensation, being both highly proclaimed and, by a few, vituperatively condemned. A first-person narrative, it stimulated other novelists to experiment with the fictional autobiographical form. The title pages of the first editions of *Jane Eyre* in fact advertised the novel as 'An Autobiography, Edited by Currer Bell'. Through the words of the heroine the novel also spoke out against the restraints and constraints imposed upon women, and the suffering which they consequently endure (see especially ch xii).

For the second edition of the novel, issued in December, Charlotte inserted a dedication of the work to Thackeray. At that time Thackeray's *Vanity Fair* was being issued in monthly numbers. Unknowingly, Charlotte had drawn a parallel between her fictional Rochester and Thackeray himself. Thackeray's wife had developed melancholia after the birth of her third child, and had attempted suicide in 1840; her mental powers collapsed and she was declared insane. The coincidence of the fictional with the actual circumstances of insanity further encouraged rumour and speculation as to the identities of the Bells, those authors whose names were carefully contrived to make their sex undetermined.

Conjecture was heightened deliberately by Newby, the publisher of Emily's and Anne's novels, who had also accepted for publication Anne's *The Tenant of Wildfell Hall*. This he brought out in June 1848, promoting it in such a way as to imply it was by the same, singular, author of *Jane Eyre* and *Wuthering Heights*. Since Newby had also offered *The Tenant*, under the same presumption, to an American publishing-house with whom Smith, Elder had contracted for Currer Bell's next novel, Charlotte's publishers were naturally offended. In response to their letter to Haworth, Charlotte and Anne travelled to London on 27 July to make themselves known to Smith, Elder at Cornhill, and thus to confirm their separate identities. During this short stay in London they were introduced to Thackeray, who had admired *Jane Eyre* intensely.

* * *

Further along Cornhill, on the same side of the road and just beyond the opening to Ball Court, will be found a plaque on the modern building, at No 39, marking the birthplace of Thomas Gray (1716-71) who was born in a house on this site. Gray, who became a friend of Dr Johnson and his circle, produced one of the best-known, and best-loved of all poems in the English language: the 'Elegy written in a Country Church-Yard'. The son of a scrivener, he was educated at Eton where he became a friend of Horace Walpole, undertaking with him a tour of France and Germany in the years 1739-41.

On the tour, however, they quarrelled and returned separately; though four years later they

Charlotte Brontë.

had repaired their friendship. Walpole subsequently published Gray's two other major works – *The Progress of Poesy* and *The Bard* – on his press at Strawberry Hill, as well as issuing a very fine edition of the *Elegy*.

From 1742 Gray lived at Cambridge, from which he made many travels and visits, including numerous trips to London where he took lodgings at various times, including an extended stay close to the British Museum where he pursued his researches. For Gray's contemporary reputation rested not only on his poetry but also on his scholarship, and some of his later poems reflect his inquiries into Norse and Celtic verse.

Immediately alongside the site of Gray's birthplace is St Michael's Church, where the father of the poet was buried.

* * *

Cornhill joins with Gracechurch Street which leads away to the right. A short distance down Gracechurch Street, Lombard Street emerges on the right.

The first small opening to the left on Lombard Street is Plough Court. At the entrance to the Court there is a plaque noting that Alexander Pope (1688-1744) was born in a house that once stood in the Court. The house was, in fact, at the bottom of the Court, facing Lombard Street.

Further along the street, on the right-hand side, is the Church of St Edmund the King. In this church Joseph Addison (1672-1719) married the Dowager Countess of Warwick in 1716. By this time Addison had achieved wealth and fame both in his political life – he held posts of Secretary to the Lords Justices, Secretary for Ireland and Secretary of State – and in his literary. Together with Richard Steele he had founded the *Spectator* in 1711, a daily paper which had established his reputation as an essayist; Addison had contributed 274 of the essays which the *Spectator* carried throughout its existence of less than two years. Some of the most enduring, and endearing, of these essays are the ones which feature Addison's invention of 'Sir Roger de Coverley', an old-fashioned squire, a comic character whose good-natured though sometimes absurd behaviour and manners enliven the events at the Club of which he is a member.

Addison's brief marriage to the Dowager Countess was made uneasy by her jealous and possessive temperament; and the liaison may be partly to blame for the break-up of Addison's friendship with Steele (especially since Steele's life-style was of a more riotous and reckless character), a rift which was never healed.

The house in which Pope was born. Here Pope's father conducted his business as a linen merchant. The house was afterwards taken over by a firm of chemists.

Joseph Addison.

Further along Lombard Street, on the left-hand side at the junction with Abchurch Lane, was sited Pontack's, a fashionable London eating-house which stood there from towards the end of the seventeenth century until the latter part of the following century. Jonathan Swift was a visitor there, as was John Evelyn, who refers to it in his *Diary*. Among other contemporary references it is named in plays by William Congreve and Sir Richard Steele. The site is currently occupied by a National Westminster bank, a modern building.

On the opposite side of the street will be found, at Nos 71 and 72, the Lloyd's bank Head Office to which T. S. Eliot (see above) transferred in 1920 to join the Information Department, where the major

The church of St Mary Woolnoth.

responsibility of his work was involved with the settling of pre-war debts.

In addition to his regular banking work Eliot had undertaken an arduous regime of editing, the writing of philosophical articles and book reviews, together with the giving of Workers' Educational lectures. A combination of long hours of work and poor health, together with domestic strain, induced the breakdown of 1921, to recuperate from which he obtained three months' leave from the bank. Bertrand Russell noted in the second volume of his *Autobiography* that upon first meeting Vivienne, whom Eliot had married in 1915 (and with whom Russell had a brief and, he insisted, unsatisfactory affair) he thought her mentally ill – 'a person who lives on a knife edge.'

Though much of the writing for *The Waste Lane* had been completed before Eliot's three months' of absence from the bank, the final sections remained to be composed, as remained also decisions about its final organisation. First at Margate in Kent and then in a clinic at Lausanne, Eliot completed the writing of the remaining sections. At Lausanne in particular Eliot now seemed able to write with a freedom he had not known for years – almost in a trance, as he described the experience in a letter to Virginia Woolf.

At Paris, both on the outward journey (November 1921) and on the return home (January 1922), Eliot consulted Ezra Pound, with whom he had been in correspondence, on the poem. The surgery which Pound advocated, and which Eliot accepted, substantially altered the presentation of the entire poem, giving to it an episodic and fractured identity. When the uncorrected manuscript of the poem appeared nearly fifty years later it was possible to see just how extensively Pound's intervention had re-shaped the original conception. The original manuscript of one thousand lines had been cut to the 433 of its published version. An edition of the uncut poem, prepared by Mrs Valerie Eliot (Eliot's second wife) appeared in 1971.

At No 2 Lombard Street there was formerly a small bank, at which worked Mr Beadnell, his family living in the house next door. Whilst a young man Charles Dickens (1812-70) fell in love with Beadnell's daughter, Maria, and used often to call upon her at the Lombard Street home. Her father did not approve of the relationship because Dickens at that time appeared to have little prospect of financial security.

In middle-age Dickens did meet Maria again, following letters which she sent to him. He found her a 'grotesque revival' of the young woman he had once known, and avoided thereafter any further meetings between them.

* * *

The corner of Lombard Street joins with King William Street, an acute turn to the left. At that junction stands the Guild Church of St Mary Woolnoth. The present church dates from the eighteenth century, but in the earlier church on this site Thomas Kyd (1558-94) was baptized. Kyd's most famous play, *The Spanish Tragedy*, the most famous also in its own age, was a pioneer of the Elizabethan revenge tragedy; and was to have a significant influence upon the work of Shakespeare.

St Mary Woolnoth features in Eliot's *Waste Land*. The morning crowd which had crossed London Bridge on its way to work

> Flowed up the hill and down King William Street
> To where Saint Mary Woolnoth kept the hours
> With a dead sound on the final stroke of nine.

The quality of the final sound, which Eliot referred to as 'A phenomenon which I have often noticed', signifies not only the hour at which office work began, but also perhaps the hour at which most modern state executions have taken place.

* * *

From the church turn the corner and follow King William Street to its junction with Cannon Street. Just to the left may be seen a subway entrance to the Monument underground station. Approximately here, a little way into the space where the roads merge (in Great Eastcheap as it was known), was once located the Boar's Head Tavern. At this inn Shakespeare assembled Falstaff, Prince Hal and their drinking friends in *Henry IV, Part One*. Here Falstaff recounts to Prince Hal the 'bravery' of his exploits at the Gad's Hill robbery. The tavern, opened early in the sixteenth century, was known to Shakespeare, but would not have been in existence during the actual historical period of the Prince.

The sign of the Boar's Head Tavern, carved in stone, which marked the site of the tavern re-built after the Great Fire. Here, in Goldsmith's daydream, he proposed his toast: 'Let's have t'other bottle. Here's to the memory of Shakespeare, Falstaff, and all the merry men of Eastcheap!'

Destroyed in the Great Fire, the Boar's Head was re-built in brick. In that building Oliver Goldsmith composed his *Reverie*. The Boar's Head was finally demolished in 1831 to make way for the approaches to the second London Bridge.

* * *

A short distance ahead and off to the left of King William Street as it leads to the Bridge will be found Monument Street, where stands the Monument itself at the junction with Fish Street Hill. Here one turns to the right. (Details of the Monument are gathered in the section: Eastcheap and the Tower.) At the foot of Fish Street Hill is Lower Thames Street. A little to the left and on the opposite side of the street stands the Church of St Magnus the Martyr.

The original church to stand on this site, dating from the eleventh century, burned down in the Great Fire. In the years 1563-6 Miles Coverdale (1488-1568) was rector of the church. Ordained a priest in 1514 Coverdale adopted Lutheran views and, during extended employment at Antwerp, he translated, from Latin and German versions, the Bible into English. Published in 1535 it is the first complete Bible in the English language – some of its sonorous phrases later finding their way into the so-called 'Authorised Version' (1611).

The church of St Magnus the Martyr.

The church of St Magnus was re-built in 1671-6 to a design of Wren, with some later alterations, notably the addition of the steeple in 1705. The interior of the church produces a splendid visual effect:

> . . . the walls
> Of Magnus Martyr hold
> Inexplicable splendour of Ionian white and gold.

So T. S. Eliot's lines in *The Waste Lane* (III, 'The Fire Sermon') describe one aspect of its appeal; in the Notes accompanying the poem Eliot refers to the interior of the church, which contains a number of statues and shrines, as 'one of the finest among Wren's interiors'.

In the churchyard Miles Coverdale was re-buried in 1840 upon the demolition of St Bartholomew-by-the-Exchange, in which church he had first been buried.

Here may be seen too some of the stones from the old London Bridge, immediately alongside which the church was sited.

* * *

Lower Thames Street used to house the Billingsgate Fish Market, a little further on – to whose workers Eliot also referred in the same section of *Waste Land* as his mention of the church. The Market, however, closed in 1982, transferring operations to the Isle of Dogs.

Beyond London Bridge the street continues as Upper Thames Street, where Geoffrey Chaucer (1340?-1400) was born and spent his childhood amid the bustle of wharfside commerce.

* * *

From St Magnus the Martyr one may return to the Monument, where one may end this tour at the underground station, or follow the route to the east collected under: Eastcheap and the Tower.

* * *

Alternatively one may cross London Bridge, continuing on into Borough High Street, where one may then follow the Southwark tour or end at London Bridge station (underground or British Rail).

Crossing the bridge will provide the visitor with fine views of the riverside. The London Bridge of the children's rhyme ('London Bridge is falling down . . .') spanned the river some sixty or so yards downstream – to the left on crossing to Southwark. That stone bridge, replacing earlier wooden structures, was begun in 1176, and acquired in the course of time superstructures of houses, three to seven storeys high, a gatehouse, and a chapel. The massive piles on which the nineteen arches of the bridge rested constricted the flow of the river, increasing considerably the run of the current. These conditions promoted the dangerous boatman's sport of 'shooting the bridge'.

It became the custom to display, on spikes above the gatehouse, the heads of traitors and felons – the heads being first parboiled and then dipped in tar to preserve them. The head of Sir Thomas More (1478-1535) was thus displayed before his daughter retrieved it and had the head buried in a vault of St Dunstan's church, Canterbury.

In the eighteenth century the houses were removed from the bridge which was itself taken down following the building of a new bridge in 1823-31. That bridge, replaced by the present structure in 1967-72, was sold to American property-developers, transported to Arizona, and re-erected at Lake Havasu City.

Miles Coverdale.

Detail from Hollar (1647) showing Old London Bridge.

CITY OF LONDON

EASTCHEAP AND THE TOWER
CITY OF LONDON

At the corner of Fish Street Hill and Monument Street, just yards away from the Monument underground exit, stands the Monument itself. Designed by Christopher Wren with the collaboration of Robert Hooke, the Monument was erected in 1671-77 to commemorate the Great Fire of London of 1666. A fluted Doric column of 202 feet, it is supposed to stand exactly that distance west of the fire's starting point.

Surmounting the column is an urn with a golden globe (recently re-gilded) rising from flames. Wren's original intention was to place a large statue of the King, Charles II, at the top of the column. The King objected, claiming reasonably enough, 'After all, I didn't start the fire.' The platform of the column, reached by an internal spiral staircase of 311 steps, is open to the public for a small charge.

When James Boswell climbed the Monument on Saturday 2 April 1763, he recorded the following impression:

After dinner I sauntered in a pleasing humour to London Bridge . . . I then went up to the top of the Monument. This is a most amazing building. It is a pillar two hundred feet high. In the inside, a turnpike stair runs all the way up. When I was about half way up, I grew frightened. I would have come down again, but thought I would despise myself for my timidity. Thus does the spirit of pride get the better of fear. I mounted to the top and got upon the balcony. It was horrid to find myself so monstrous a way up in the air, so far above London and all its spires. I durst not look round me. There is no real danger, as there is a strong rail both on the stair and balcony. But I shuddered, and as every heavy wagon passed down Gracechurch Street, dreaded that the shaking of the earth would make the tremendous pile tumble to the foundation.

* * *

The great catastrophe which the Monument commemorates started in Farriner's bakehouse, just yards away in Pudding Lane. On the night of 2 September, just before 2.00am, a workman alerted the inhabitants to a fire. The flames spread quickly. Nonetheless the Lord Mayor, Sir Thomas Bloodworth, who had been called out of his bed, thought the fire no exceptional event. Before returning to his bed he remarked: 'Pish! A woman might piss it out!' – one of the most memorable of mis-judgements in history.

The fire raged for four days and burned out the medieval heart of the city. Fanned by easterly winds and fed by the mainly timber constructions it encountered, efforts made to halt its progress – including the pulling down of houses in its path to create fire-breaks – proved ineffectual.

John Dryden's 'Annus Mirabilis' (1667) which takes as its twin themes the Great Fire and the Dutch Wars (of 1665-66) recreates a sense of the awesome power of the conflagration. The Fire is pictured as a living, devouring creature; as here, and in other longer sections of description:

> The fire meantime walks in broader gross;
> To either hand his wings he opens wide;
> He wades the streets, and straight he reaches cross
> And plays his lengthy flames on the other side.
>
> At first they warm, then scorch, and then they take;
> Now with long necks from side to side they feed;
> At length, grown long, their mother-fire forsake,
> And a new colony of flames succeeds.

A friend of Dryden was Samuel Pepys (1633-1703). Pepys's *Diary* (for the years 1660-69) presents a remarkable, confessional portrait of his own life and times, his private flirtations and lecheries no less than his involvement with the public world of events and people. In a varied, distinguished history not without its setbacks, he rose in his public career to become Secretary to the Admiralty. In this post he achieved great distinction, making the fleet into an efficient force, and introducing a variety of innovations. At the time of the Great Fire Pepys was living in Seething Lane (about half a mile to the east of the Monument) and was Surveyor-General of the Victualling at the Navy Office. His *Diary* contains eloquent, eye-witness reporting of the fire's beginnings, progress and aftermath.

At first, awakened by one of his maids at about three in the morning, he thought the fire 'far enough off'. By seven the fire seemed 'not so much as it was, and further off'. Not until his maid reported to him that she had heard that 300 houses had already burned down, did Pepys make a thorough observation. First he went to Allhallows Church, at the end of Seething Lane, to view the fire from the top of its tower. Then he took a boat close to London Bridge. From there he saw:

> Everybody endeavouring to remove their goods, and flinging into the river or bringing them into lighters that lay off; poor people staying in their houses as long as till the very fire touched them, and then running into boats, or clambering from one pair of stairs by the water-side to another. And among other things the poor pigeons, I perceive, were loth to leave their houses, but hovered about the windows and balconys till they were, some of them burned, their wings, and fell down.

It was Pepys, in fact, who carried the news of the fire to the King, and to his brother the Duke of York.

Towards evening, from an ale-house on Bankside, the 'horrid malicious bloody flame' appeared 'as only one entire arch of fire from this to the other side of the bridge, and in a bow up the hill for an arch of above a mile long: it made me weep to see it'.

The *Diary* records Pepys's preparations to save his own goods and possessions – including the digging of a pit in the garden, on the evening of 4 September, in which to deposit 'my Parmazan cheese as well as my wine and some other things'. By two o'clock the following morning the fire had reached Allhallows Church, blackening its tower. Yet, to Pepys's great surprise and relief, by seven that evening the fire was beginning to abate. Pepys described the desola-

Samuel Pepys.

tion he found when he walked through the burned-out parts of the city ('our feet ready to burn'). Characteristically, he adds: 'I also did see a poor cat taken out of a hole in the chimney joyning the wall of the [Corn] Exchange, with the hair all burned off the body and yet alive'.

In all, the Great Fire destroyed more than 13,000 dwellings; and 460 streets were laid waste in the devastation which covered 436 acres. Among the many churches destroyed was Old St Paul's.

Today the view from the balcony of the Monument is restricted in some directions by new, tall buildings, though it yields nonetheless a magnificent panorama of the city. In Charles Dickens's day the view was unopposed. John Willett, in Dickens's *Barnaby Rudge* (ch xiii) gives his son Joe 'sixpence . . . to spend in the diversions of London', adding:

> . . . and the diversion I recommend is to go to the top of the Monument, and sitting there. There's no temptation there, sir – no drink – no young women – no bad characters of any sort – nothing but imagination. That's the way I enjoyed myself when I was your age, sir.

* * *

Pudding Lane is just a very short way along Monument Street. At the top of the Lane, Eastcheap (which soon becomes Great Tower Street) runs off to the right. Within a few minutes' walk Mark Lane enters Great Tower Street from the left. A short way into Mark Lane, on the right-hand side, Hart Lane emerges. Just into this turning, on the right, will be seen the Parish Church of St Olave.

Dedicated to St Olaf, the patron saint of Norway, and founded in the eleventh century, much of the church was wrecked by bombing in 1941. The church as it stands today has been restored and was re-opened in 1954. What remains of its earlier constructions are the tower (dating from the fifteenth century and added to in 1732), the 17th-century vestry, and a 12th-century crypt.

In a vault beneath the communion table were buried both Samuel Pepys (see above) and his wife Elizabeth (d 1669). On 1 December 1655 Pepys had married the fifteen-year-old Elizabeth St Michel when Pepys was aged 22. From the October of the following year they began to live together as man and wife. From the July of the year 1660 in which Pepys opened his *Diary*, they lived in Seething Lane and later in Crutched Friars (continuation of Hart Street). The *Diary* presents a remarkably frank portrait of their lives together. There was love for each other, and Pepys was often struck with remorse for his treatment of his wife. That he treated her badly, however, is amply evidenced.

Pepys was a man who, in addition to his undoubted talents and those abilities which procured him high office, energetically pursued the pleasures of life. He took delight in music, people, conversation, had a natural curiosity for all manner of knowledge, enjoyed enormously food and drink – and the pursuit of women. Yet there was a calculating prudence about his liaisons, so far as the *Diary* allows us to judge, since all of the young women with whom he 'had mon plein plaisir of elle' belonged to much inferior social positions. They included barmaids, shopgirls, servants, prostitutes. Yet while he pursued his enjoyments, and spent lavishly on them, he was miserly towards his wife, challenged the household accounts frequently, and kept her personal allowance as low as he could contrive it to be.

For occasional adventure Pepys prowled the streets. Nor was he above using his office and influence to attain his desires; such as in the lengthy affair with a Mrs Bagwell whose husband's career in the navy Pepys personally superintended. Nor was he always discreet. Elizabeth's jealousies and suspicions burst into anger on many occasions, the most fiery of which were provoked over Deb Willet.

Towards the end of September 1667 Elizabeth employed Deb as a maid. Pepys's first sight of her presaged the subsequent history:

> . . . though she seems not altogether so great a beauty as she [Elizabeth] had before told me, yet indeed she is mighty pretty: and so pretty that I find I shall be too much pleased with it . . . I may be found too much minding her, to the discontent of my wife . . .

In the June of the year following Elizabeth asked for a separation so that she might go and live in France by herself. Pepys, as on many occasions, became conciliatory and managed to bring them back on good terms with each other. In the October, however, Elizabeth's repeated suspicions of Deb were confirmed when she saw husband and maid in each other's arms. Deb had to go, dismissed – but despite his promises Pepys still made secret assignations with Deb. Elizabeth's suspicions were not assuaged, and in the January of 1669 erupted into a violent argument, ending with Pepys going to bed on his own, leaving Elizabeth lighting fresh candles and stoking the fire. The diarist records:

> At last, about one o'clock, she came to my side of the bed, and drew my curtains open and with the tongs red hot at the ends, made as if she did design to pinch me with them.

Though severely strained, the marriage survived for, despite all the arguments and deceptions, there was a strong bond of affection. As part of the reconciliation Pepys and his wife together went on a two-month continental tour to Holland, Flanders and France. On the return leg of that trip Elizabeth contracted a fever – from which she died three weeks after returning to England in 1669. Pepys did not re-marry.

In the sanctuary of St Olave's Church, high up on the north wall, will be found the sculpted white marble bust of his wife which Pepys had placed there. It was so located that Pepys might look upon her likeness during services. From the time that Pepys became Secretary to the Admiralty (1673) he was a regular worshipper at the church.

* * *

Gateway to the churchyard of St Olave's.

The gateway to the churchyard of St Olave's is in Seething Lane, immediately to the right on leaving the church. The gate, of 1685, is ornamented with skulls above and at either side of the arch. To Charles Dickens's Uncommercial Traveller (in 'City of the Absent') it was his favourite churchyard:

> It lies at the heart of the City and the Blackwall Railway shrieks at it daily. It is a small small churchyard, with a ferocious strong spiked iron gate, like a jail. This gate is ornamented with skulls and cross bones, larger than life, wrought in stone; but it likewise came into the mind of Saint Ghastly Grim that to stick iron spikes a-top of the stone skulls, as though they were impaled, would be a pleasant device . . . hence there is attraction of repulsion for me in Saint Ghastly Grim, and, having often contemplated it in the daylight and the dark, I once felt drawn to it in a thunderstorm at midnight.

* * *

A short way further into Seething Lane there are small gardens on the left, just beyond Pepys Street. The gardens mark the approximate site of the house where Pepys lived during his time at the Navy Office (which was itself very close by, more or less opposite the church). In the gardens is a bust of the diarist made by Karen Jonzen (1983).

* * *

At the end of Seething Lane, and on the far side of Byward Street which becomes Tower Hill, will be seen the Church of Allhallows by the Tower (to get to which turn right for a pedestrian crossing). A church has stood on that site since the seventh century, though much of the present church was rebuilt following bomb damage in 1940. The tower, however, from which Pepys watched the progress of the Great Fire, still stands.

Buried in the church was Henry Howard (1517-47), though his body was removed from there shortly afterwards by one of his sons, Henry, and re-interred at the church of Framlingham, Surrey.

Just beyond the church Tower Hill leads down to the entrance to the Tower of London.

* * *

An important medieval construction, the Tower has been variously a fortress, palace, prison and military arsenal. Begun as a fortress by William the Conqueror, from which both to protect and control the city, it has been added to substantially in subsequent times. At the centre of the site stands the White Tower, a massive Norman keep completed around 1079, which now houses an extensive collection of arms and armour dating from the Middle Ages to 1914. Two encircling lines of walls and towers were added in the 13th century. The Bloody Tower belongs to the 14th century. Inside the inner wall, beneath the Waterloo Barracks added in 1845, are housed the Crown Jewels of the English monarchy.

The Tower is associated with many events in English history, and particularly the imprisonment of many royal or noble persons, as well as others famous (or infamous) for a variety of reasons. Many of its prisoners were executed here, a continuity which stretches from medieval history through to comparatively recent times – several spies having been shot there during the two World Wars. And murdered here were 'the little princes in the Tower', as Shakespeare describes them in *King Richard III* (1591).

Shortly after the death of Edward IV in April 1483, the twelve-year-old Edward was escorted to the Tower by Gloucester in his role of Protector. In June the Queen consented to allow his younger

The earliest painting of London, showing the Tower with London Bridge and the City beyond. An illuminated manuscript painting, from the frontispiece to a collection of poems made by Charles, Duke of Orleans. The Duke, taken prisoner at Agincourt, was brought to the Tower and held to ransom for 25 years. The Duke is pictured in the White Tower just before his release in 1440. He is shown also, on horseback, leaving through a gateway following his release.   British Museum

brother to join him. For some time the two boys were seen playing in the gardens, but soon they were seen less and less, appearing only occasionally at the windows of the tower's apartments.

Commissioned by one of the gentlemen in the service of Richard, their uncle, the young Edward V and his brother the Duke of York were smothered by two assassins in a second-floor room of the Garden Tower. The tower was later re-named the Bloody Tower in recognition of the deed.

There is a sequel to the story. In 1674, whilst demolishing a staircase on the south side of the White Tower, workmen discovered a chest containing the skeletons of two children. On the orders of Charles II the remains were re-buried in the Innocents' Corner of Westminster Abbey.

Some of the bloodiest associations with the Tower belong to the Tudor Period. Shakespeare's version of the murder of the princes came, in the main, from one of Henry VIII's most famous victims: from Sir Thomas More's *History of Richard III* (first full edition 1557), a work which did not appear in any form until after his death. More (1478?-1535) was a man of brilliant intellect who, having studied law, rose rapidly in the public world, whilst devoting his time to literature also.

After entering Parliament in 1504, he became a Privy Councillor in 1517, and finally Lord Chancellor in 1529. From this post he resigned in 1532 over Henry VIII's claim to be Supreme Head of the Church. He had also consistently refused to accept the legitimacy of Henry's divorce from Catherine of Aragon, whom Henry had married at the Tower in 1509. In 1534 More was arrested and committed to the Tower, confined in fact to the Bell Tower. On 1 July 1535 he was tried and convicted, on perjured evidence, of treason. On 6 July he was beheaded. His head, it is recorded, was displayed at London Bridge, and his body interred in the Chapel Royal of St Peter, within the walls of the Tower. The head was later buried in a vault at St Dunstan's, Canterbury; and it is possible that on the orders of his daughter the body was re-interred at Chelsea Old Church.

More's best-known work remains *Utopia*, written originally in Latin and first published on the continent, at Louvain, in 1516. The imaginary island of Utopia (a coined Greek word meaning 'no place': *ou* – not, *topos* – place) provided the setting in which More could display the ordered, rational, hierarchical harmony of an idealised state contrasted against the European reality of his times; where manipulation, extortion, war and a range of social evils prevailed.

Whilst confined to the Tower and awaiting execution More prepared his *Dialoge of Comfort agaynst Trybulacion*, a work mirroring his own condition, though set in the form of a debate between a Hungarian nobleman and his nephew as to how to conduct themselves in the face of a cruel and conquering Turk.

Also imprisoned by Henry VIII was Sir Thomas Wyatt (1503-42). As a courtier and diplomat Wyatt held various offices in Italy, France, Spain and the Netherlands. He thus had opportunities to experience directly some of the cultural forms of the continental High Renaissance. To Wyatt is credited the introduction of the sonnet form into English, via his translations and versions of the Italian poet Petrarch.

According to contemporary accounts Wyatt had been one of Anne Boleyn's lovers before her marriage to the king in 1533. Perhaps because he freely confessed to the fact he suffered only a period of imprisonment in the Tower, during 1536. Whilst

Sir Thomas Wyatt, an engraving after the portrait by Holbein.

there, however, he was compelled to witness the execution of others of Anne Boleyn's actual or supposed lovers.

In addition to Wyatt's modelling of the sonnet, his poetry extends across a wide variety of verse forms, including songs, rondeaux, ballades and carols. The experimentation sometimes leads to an awkwardness, but there is a sense of integrity to many of Wyatt's poems which can seem lacking from much of the verse of the period. There are 'songs' of a simple, unadorned directness; and there are reflections such as this – on 'Honesty':

> Thoughout the world if it were sought,
>   Fair words enough a man shall find;
> They be good cheap, they cost right nought,
>   Their substance is but only wind.
>   But well to say, and so to mean,
>   That sweet accord is seldom seen.

In the history of English literature, Wyatt's name is commonly linked with Henry Howard, Earl of Surrey (see above). Howard was one of Wyatt's literary followers; though not a close friend, he certainly admired the other man's poetry. Their work in fact appeared together, posthumously, in a collection of 1557 called *Songs and Sonnets* (though usually referred to as *Tottel's Miscellany*, after its compiler). Howard was a soldier and courtier, to whom belongs the credit for two major innovations in English poetry. He introduced blank verse into English with his translation of Books II and IV of Virgil's *Aeneid*; and he invented that form of the sonnet later to be taken up by Shakespeare and sometimes referred to as the 'English' sonnet. In this form, there appear three quatrains, the lines alternatively rhyming, followed by a rhymed couplet.

Surrey was the cousin of Catherine, Henry VIII's fifth wife whom he married in 1540 and two years later had beheaded at the Tower. Surrey himself, who had been in and out of favour throughout his career, was finally arrested, imprisoned in the Tower, and executed on charges of treason. His father, who had been tried with him and similarly sentenced, escaped execution with the death of Henry VIII. (See: Moorgate to the Bank.)

The handsome and accomplished Henry Wriothesley, 3rd Earl of Southampton (1573-1624) spent the last two years of Queen Elizabeth's reign in the Tower. From an early age Southampton had been a patron of writers – in the words of Thomas Nash, 'a dear lover and cherisher as well of the lovers of poets as of the poets themselves'. Among those whom he patronised was William Shakespeare who had dedicated to him the poems *Venus and Adonis* (1593) and *Lucrece* (1594), the latter indicating an even closer relationship.

In 1590 he had been introduced at court and presented to the Queen. There he met the Earl of Essex, with whom he established a lasting friendship. A decade later, in February 1601, Essex and Southampton led an attempt to oust their enemies from court, and failed.

They were arrested, sent to the Tower, tried on charges of treason at Westminster Hall, and found guilty. Essex was executed before the end of the month, but Southampton's sentence was commuted to life imprisonment.

On the accession of James I to the throne, orders were given for the release of Southampton who returned to court, received favour and high honour – and was involved in a succession of court quarrels and brawls.

Sir Walter Ralegh (1552-1618) was first briefly imprisoned at the Tower, in 1592, by Henry VIII's daughter Elizabeth I for seducing and marrying one of her maids of honour, Elizabeth Throckmorton. After this episode he regained the Queen's favour. As adventurer and explorer he is best known for his exploration of Guiana, the founding of the first Virginia colony, and his leading of the attack which sacked the Spanish fleet at Cadiz Harbour in 1596.

One of the first acts of Elizabeth I's successor, James I, was to have Ralegh arrested and imprisoned in the Tower. On largely fabricated charges of high treason, Ralegh was held for thirteen years (1603-1616). Some rooms in the Bloody Tower, where he was confined, may be seen today furnished in the style of his times. During this long imprisonment he was permitted to engage in chemical experiments in a converted hen-house in the grounds, and to walk the ramparts for exercise. He was also allowed to have his wife and son with him, and to have visitors. Some of these helped to supply him with the many books he required for the writing of *The History of the World* (1614). Within this work, dealing with Greek, Egyptian and Biblical history, are also to be found some fine meditative passages reflecting on mortality, death, and God's judgement of man – of which this is one example:

In this time ['the last and seventh' age of man] it is, when . . . we, for the most part, and never before, prepare for our eternal habitation, which we pass on unto with many sighs, groans, and sad thoughts, and in the end, by the workmanship of death, finish the sorrowful business of a wretched life; towards which we always travel both sleeping and waking; neither have those beloved companions of honour and riches any power at all to hold us any one day by the glorious promise of entertainments; but by what crooked path soever we walk, the same leadeth on directly to the house of death, whose doors lie open at all hours, and to all persons. For this tide of man's life, after it once turneth and declineth, ever runneth with a perpetual ebb and falling stream, but never floweth again: our leaf once fallen, springeth no more; neither doth the sun nor the summer adorneth us again, with the garments of new leaves and flowers.

Released from the Tower to seek out the gold mine he claimed to have discovered some twenty years previously in Guiana, and failing to return with the spoils, charges of treason were once more applied to him. He was held again in the Tower before his execution at Westminster in 1618.

Whilst Ralegh was suffering his long period of imprisonment at the Tower, Sir Thomas Overbury (1581-1613) was cast into one of its dungeons.

Sir Thomas Overbury.

Overbury's name now attaches to those 'characters' (only some of which issued from his own pen) which were appended to the posthumous second edition of his poem *A Wife* (1614). These prose descriptions, of types not individuals, were developments of the classical Greek models; those impressions of Theophrastus which were concerned to delineate types of vice. *The Characters or Witty Descriptions of the Properties of Sundry Persons by Sir T.O. and others* began as a private amusement, circulating in manuscript, to which John Webster and Thomas Dekker are known to have contributed as well as Overbury himself.

The picture of 'An Amorist' shows the characteristic qualities of the 'Overburian character'. It reads, in part:

[An Amorist] Is a man blasted or planet-strooken, and is the dog that leads blind Cupid; when he is at the best his fashion exceeds the worth of his weight. He is never without verses and musk confects [sachets of perfume], and sighs to the hazard of his buttons. His eyes are all white, either to wear the livery of his mistress' complexion or to keep Cupid from hitting the black . . . His arms are carelessly used, as if their best use was nothing but embracements. He is untrussed, unbuttoned and ungartered, not out of carelessness, but care; his farthest end being but going to bed . . .

Whilst some details of Overbury's imprisonment and death in the Tower remain a mystery, the outline of events is clear enough to suggest collusion and intrigue at court.

Overbury had a close friendship with Robert Carr, Viscount Rochester. Carr was pursuing a relationship with Frances Howard, Countess of Essex, whom Overbury considered to be a woman of abandoned character. He therefore encouraged Rochester to take the Countess as a mistress, but counselled him passionately not to take her as wife.

The Countess succeeded in divorcing her husband, the Earl of Essex, with the intention of marrying Carr. To be rid of the embarrassment of Overbury's presence, the court was induced to offer him a diplomatic post on the continent; an offer which he refused.

On 26 April 1613, therefore, Overbury was sent to the Tower. Rochester took this to be merely a temporary expedient. But the Countess, now his wife, determined to have Overbury murdered. To that end she contrived the dismissal of the encumbent governor of the Tower, so that in early May Sir

Gervase Helwys was appointed to the post. Essex entered into a conspiracy with Helwys and others.

Compound poisons – which included, among other substances, white arsenic, ground diamond, and mercury – were systematically administered to Overbury. Within the space of three months Overbury's health had become critical.

Then, on 14 September, Overbury was given a final 'clyster of corrosive sublimate', from which he died the next day. His body, disfigured with sores and ulcers, was wrapped in a sheet and hurriedly buried in the chapel.

In the year of Overbury's death Rochester was made Earl of Somerset. And two years after that advancement the plot against Overbury was discovered. Four of the Somersets' accomplices, including the governor, were tried and put to death. The Somersets themselves were also arrested, and sent to the Tower in July 1615. In May of the following year they were put on trial, and found guilty. After six years of imprisonment they were pardoned and released from the Tower.

To Sir William D'Avenant (1606-68), poet and dramatist, attached the tradition – which he himself initiated – that he was the natural son of William Shakespeare. John D'Avenant kept the Taverne (later re-named the Crown), a drinking-house at Oxford. Here, on his journeys between London and Stratford, Shakespeare is supposed to have stayed. The legend that he also shared a bed with the wine-house keeper's wife dates from William D'Avenant's drinking-bouts with Samuel Butler (author of *Hudibras*) and others. Whether he believed what he asserted, was jesting or, more remotely, was claiming that his own writing was descended from Shakespeare's, the legend took root. When, in the middle of the eighteenth century, William Chetwood tried to assess the family resemblance by comparing the frontispiece portrait of D'Avenant's *Works* with the likeness of Shakespeare, he claimed to detect a similarity; but had to conclude that 'the want of a Nose gives an odd Cast to the Face.' For, as a result of a mercury treatment for syphilis, D'Avenant had lost his nose – a fact which made him the object of much cruel humour and satirical comment.

D'Avenant's plays – in particular *The Wits*, his comic masterpiece, and *The Unfortunate Lovers* – were staged frequently following the Restoration when they proved to be popular entertainments, admired, among others, by Samuel Pepys.

Sir William D'Avenant.

At an early stage of the Civil War D'Avenant came under suspicion as a royalist sympathiser. He escaped to France, where he served as a royal messenger. In 1650, starting out on a journey to Virginia, he was intercepted by a parliament ship, taken prisoner, and transported to London. There he served two years as a prisoner in the Tower before his release was secured.

George Villiers, 2nd Duke of Buckingham (1628-87), poet, wit and satirist – and himself satirised by John Dryden (see Soho section) – spent altogether four periods of confinement at the Tower.

Charles I, out of affection for their father, brought up George and his brother Francis with his own children. At the outbreak of the Civil War Buckingham joined the King at Oxford, then going into exile on the continent. He returned in 1657 to marry Mary Fairfax, who had been promised to the Earl of Chesterfield. In October of that year Cromwell's council ordered the arrest of Buckingham, an order which he managed to evade until the August of the following year. Upon capture he was sent to the Tower where he remained for six months; released on his word that he would not aid the enemies of the Commonwealth.

On the return of Charles II to the throne

Buckingham became a gentleman of the royal bedchamber, and was appointed a Privy Councillor. He was reputed also to be the richest man in England. But after an indecent scuffle at court, in which blows were exchanged with the Marquis of Dorchester, he was sent for a brief period to the Tower. He was released soon after making his apology.

Between June and September 1667 Buckingham was again imprisoned in the Tower – because of a rift with Charles II who suspected Buckingham of treasonable devices and of intriguing with republicans.

Upon his return to court Buckingham was restored to his position in the King's bedchamber, and took up once more the title and duties of Privy Councillor. His influence over the King was instantly repaired, and indeed must have been extended rapidly; for in his *Diary* entry for 27 November of the year of Buckingham's release, Samuel Pepys recorded the following observation which had been offered to him: 'The king is now fallen in and become a slave to the Duke of Buckingham.'

Ten years later Buckingham (together with three other lords – Shaftesbury, Wharton and Salisbury), was sent to the Tower for refusing to ask pardon over questions raised about the constitution of the House. After five months Buckingham was set free, initially for one month, though that release was made permanent through the good influence of Nell Gwynn.

Buckingham's career was marked by intrigues, a ceaseless search for power, and an overweaning personal vanity; and, to his credit, a consistent advocacy of religious tolerance.

In the last days of the Commonwealth George Wither (1588-1667), poet, had been sent to Newgate prison for his long poem *Vox Vulgi . . .*, which had offended the Commons. From there, on the orders of the House, he was committed to the Tower. After the Restoration a petition was presented on his behalf to the King; as a result of which his wife was allowed access to him. He was released finally in July 1663, having given a bond as to his future good behaviour. (See also: Charterhouse and Smithfield.)

Samuel Pepys (see above) suffered a brief period of confinement to the Tower in 1669. He was arrested with many others, some thirty of whom were actually executed, for supposed complicity in the 'Popish Plot' invented by Titus Oates. Oates had alleged that the Catholics were planning to murder the Protestants and assassinate the King. Pepys, a good Protestant, who was visited in prison by his fellow-diarist John Evelyn, was soon released and all charges against him were dropped.

John Evelyn described John Wilmot, Lord Rochester (1647-80) as 'a profane wit'. In a period which assiduously cultivated the quality of wit and produced many contending for recognition, Rochester was perhaps the most outstanding of all the wits of the Restoration times. His satires, which he could produce freely, made him feared – and opened him to the charge, among many others, of atheism (which then and earlier meant any deviation from orthodoxy). The opening to *A Satyr Against Mankind* shows something of the characteristic style, together with an ability to compose within the metre using varied speech-units and -rhythms:

> Were I (who to my cost already am
> One of those strange prodigious Creatures Man.)
> A Spirit free, to choose for my own share,
> What Case of flesh, and Blood, I pleas's to weare,
> I'd be a Dog, a Monkey, or a Bear.
> Or any thing but that vain Animal,
> Who is so proud of being rational . . .

In fact the range of Rochester's poetry is much broader than that of satire only, and certainly on sexual themes some of his verse is unrestrainedly explicit – though there are, too, some very fine love lyrics, such as the 'Song' – 'Absent from thee I languish still . . .'

Rochester's life was one of debauchery, drunkenness, brawls and duels, and the engagement in countless 'japes' perpetrated with his gentlemen cronies. The excesses of his living combined with disease to attack his health, and in his last years he became (in the words of Graham Greene), 'an embittered and thoughtful man who would die in 1680 of old age at the age of thirty-three'.

At the age of eighteen Rochester, encouraged it would seem by Charles II, began his courting of Elizabeth Mallet of Enmore, Somerset – whose mother and guardians hoped to attract for her a suitably wealthy and titled suitor. They had in mind for her Lord Hinchingbrooke, the son of Lord and Lady Sandwich. On 26 May 1665 Elizabeth dined with her grandfather at Westminster, leaving after supper with one of her guardians, Lord Hawley. At Charing Cross their carriage was stopped by armed

Stylised portrait (dated 1665-70) of Lord Rochester, showing him offering a crown of laurels to his pet monkey. National Portrait Gallery, London

men acting under the direction of Rochester. Elizabeth was forcibly transferred to another coach in which two women were waiting to receive her.

Rochester was arrested at Uxbridge, but without Elizabeth, who had still not been found two days after the abduction. The King issued a warrant to the governor of the Tower to take Rochester prisoner.

For three weeks Rochester was held in the Tower – whilst, incidentally, the plague was spreading rapidly, reaching its climax in September. On 19 June Rochester petitioned the King for his release, which was granted. And at the end of the following January Rochester married Elizabeth, the King this time a party to their elopement.

From Charles II Rochester continued to receive many favours; even though he lampooned and satirised the King in a number of cruel poems – as in this extempore epitaph which Rochester made for Charles:

Here lies a great and mighty king,
Whose promise none relies on;
He never said a foolish thing,
Nor ever did a wise one.

On this occasion, though, the King had the last word. He replied: 'My words are my own, but my acts are my ministers'.

More than ten years after his short imprisonment Rochester returned to the vicinity of the Tower. Rochester had been banished from court because of an incident at Epsom in which one of his companions had died. To escape the King's punishment Rochester took up lodgings in Tower Street, 'next door to the sign of the Black Swan at a goldsmith's house'. There he set up as 'Alexander Bendo', and each day from 3 in the afternoon until 8 at night the mountebank doctor offered his quack cures for all sorts of ailments, specialising in restoring beauty to women – and offering fortune-telling as well.

George Granville, Lord Lansdowne (1667-1735) established his reputation with plays and verse. The plays now seem slight (*She Gallants, Heroick Love*), and the verse is crafted and workmanlike rather than inspired, or inspiring. Nonetheless, at its best, it can achieve an epigrammatic tautness, as in the following – from what is probably Granville's best extended composition in verse, the 'Meditation on Death':

> One destin'd period men in common have,
> The great, the base, the coward, and the brave,
> All food alike for worms, companions in the grave.

Because such compactness frequently occurs, though unexceptional in thought or feeling, and tedious read at length, Granville's verse has proved a rich mine for compilers of dictionaries of quotations.

Granville became a Member of Parliament in 1702 and a Privy Councillor in 1712. But on the accession of George I he fell out of favour. There is evidence to suggest that Granville was indeed involved in a scheme to re-instate the Pretender (James, son of James II) to the throne, by helping in the planning of a rising to begin in Cornwall. From September 1715 until February 1717, therefore, he was held at the Tower as a suspected person. Upon release, he was restored to his seat in the House.

* * *

On leaving the Tower, at the top of Tower Hill and on the opposite side of the road, will be seen Trinity Gardens (where the Seamen's War memorial is sited). In the gardens will be found the small paved area which marks the site of the ancient scaffold. Among more than 125 who were executed here were Sir Thomas More and Henry Howard, Earl of Surrey.

The executions held here, attended by large crowds, were not always neatly and efficiently conducted – in a number of cases the executioner bungling the job. The execution of Sir Thomas More was accompanied by a certain grimly sardonic humour, however. Informed that the traitor's sentence of being drawn and quartered had been commuted by the King to beheading, More replied: 'God forbid the king shall use any more such mercy on any of my friends'. On the day of execution More asked for assistance to help him mount the scaffold, with the words: 'I pray you, Mr Lieutenant to see me safe up and for my coming down let me make shift for myself.' And at the last moment More removed his beard from the block, saying, 'Pity that should be cut that has not committed treason.'

* * *

The entrance to Tower Hill underground station will be found just beyond and to the right of the gardens.

The Shakespeare Memorial window, Southwark Cathedral.

KEY

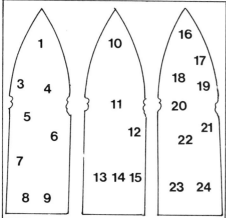

1. Bottom and Puck
2. Titania
3. Malvolio
4. Olivia and Maria
5. Falstaff
6. Jacques and Touchstone
7. Portia
10. Ariel
11. Prospero
12. Caliban
16. Romeo and Juliet
17. Richard II
18. Richard III
19. Othello
20. King Lear
21. Lady Macbeth
22. Hamlet

Nos 8, 9, 13, 14, 15, 23, 24 The Seven Ages of Man (see Jacques's speech, *As You Like It* (II, vii)).

SOUTHWARK

THE BOROUGH AND BANKSIDE
SOUTHWARK

Extending south of the river from London Bridge to beyond Blackfriars Bridge, much of the original area of Southwark is today a busy commercial and industrial centre. The modern administrative borough of Southwark, of course, now extends considerably beyond this first area. Southwark, or 'south work', was the bridgehead at the southern end of the old London Bridge – the *sud werk* of the Viking wars.

By medieval times Southwark had established a reputation for drunkenness, lechery and general immorality. Though there were respectable parts of Southwark, the reputation was not undeserved. Criminals escaping across the river from the City, for example, sought refuge in its crowded huddle of taverns and dwellings. There they were out of reach of the City authorities. Not until 1550, in fact, did 'the borough' (as it is still sometimes referred to) come within that jurisdiction when it became Bridge Ward Without.

The Bankside area of Southwark was the most notorious – for its docks, gaming-houses, innumerable drinking-houses, and 'stewes' (brothels). Its prostitutes were known as 'Winchester geese' since a good part of the land on which Southwark developed was owned by the Bishops of Winchester and, until officially closed down by Henry VIII in 1546, the revenues both from rent and from fines (imposed upon practitioners of the oldest profession for breaking the rules drawn up by the bishops themselves) went into the Winchester coffers. The trade, of course, continued beyond its banning, and in just a few decades the brothels had re-opened. Yet other parts of Southwark were owned by the Archbishop of Canterbury and the Abbot of Bermondsey.

Throughout its time of development, and adding to Southwark's growing population, there came a good many foreign settlers who, unable to set up their businesses in the City, carried on their trades south of the river. They included, for example, weavers, brewers and leather-workers.

Southwark became also a lodging-place for country gentlemen attending parliament, and generally a stopping-point for travellers who rested there before crossing the river to the walled City. Southwark, sited as it was, became additionally a natural place to gather for those about to travel south, towards Canterbury – where companies of pilgrims would make their way to the shrine of St Thomas à Becket.

* * *

The tour as described in this section concentrates only on northern locations, close to the river, within the borough. From London Bridge station (underground or British Rail), London Bridge Street leads away to the left to join with Borough High Steet. At the junction with the High Street, turn to the left. An alternative starting-point is the Monument underground station, from which one crosses over London Bridge, leading directly into the Borough High Street – the route suggested also for those intending to explore Southwark as a follow-on tour to the section The Bank to London Bridge.

Once into the Borough High Street the first location will be found in not much more than a couple of minutes' walk, passing by other locations to which you will shortly return when heading back towards the river.

On the left-hand side of the present Borough High Street, opposite and just below its junction

The Tabard Inn of the seventeenth century, repaired and enlarged in the reign of Queen Elizabeth. The courtyard faced directly onto the street.

with Southwark Street (which enters the High Street to your right) will be found the narrow opening to Talbot Yard, currently used as a service entrance to Guy's Hospital. By 1306 there stood on this site, beyond the entrance and a little way into the open space of the yard, the Tabard Inn. Its sign was the short, sleeveless surcoat as worn by knights and heralds. Here, on 16 April 1387

> Bifel that in that seson on a day
>   [it happened]
> In Southwerk at the Tabard as I lay
> Redy to wenden on my pilgrimage
>   [go]
> To Canterbury with ful devout corage,
>   [ardour, desire]
> At night was come into that hostelrye
>   [inn]
> Wel nine and twenty in a companye,
> Of sondry folk by aventure yfalle
>   [by chance fallen]
> In felawship, and pilgrimes were they alle
>   [companionship]
> That toward Caunterbury wolden ryde.
>   [wished to]

The pilgrims whom Geoffrey Chaucer (1340?-1400) gathered together at the inn at the commencement of his *Canterbury Tales* offer a representative cross-section of his contemporary society – with the exception of the higher nobility. The details of so many of his characters are so individual that commentators are tempted to see them as portraits drawn from life; or at least based on actual persons known to Chaucer. Certainly the Host of the Tabard has been identified; as Harry Bailly, a Southwark publican and a Member of Parliament. And the sly humour of Chaucer furnishes ample reason why the Host should have offered with such alacrity to accompany the pilgrims on their journey when he shows us a view of the inn-keeper's termagent of a wife. When, elsewhere in the *Tales*, the Host says, 'I beat my knaves [servants]' –

> She bringeth me forth the greate clobbed staves,
> And crieth, 'Slay the dogges everyone,
> And break them, bothe back and every bone!'

At sunrise ('whan that day began to sprynge') the day following the gathering of Chaucer's characters at the Tabard – probably, therefore, about 5.00am or a little earlier – Chaucer's band of pilgrims set off on their journey to Canterbury. The original Tabard Inn was pulled down in 1629, its replacement surviving until 1875. Today, sadly, not even a plaque marks the point of departure of the most famous pilgrim-band in the whole of English literature.

* * *

From Talbot Yard retrace your steps, heading back towards London Bridge. Within a few yards will be found the George Inn, set back from the road within a cobbled courtyard. The only galleried inn remaining in London, originally its flanks extended around three sides of the courtyard. The side which remains dates from 1677, its authentic character preserved today. The George was certainly frequented by Dickens, and used by him also as the setting in which Tip Dorrit wrote his begging letter to Arthur Clennam (*Little Dorrit*, I, xxii).

* * *

Heading in the same direction along Borough High Street, and on the same side of the road a short distance on, will be found White Hart Yard. Here formerly stood the White Hart Inn, a hostelry which lasted until 1889 – though it had twice burned down (in 1669 and 1676). At this inn Dickens's Sam Weller, cleaning boots, is first introduced to the reader – and it is here that Mr Pickwick first meets Sam (*Pickwick Papers*, ch x).

The same inn is referred to in Shakespeare's *Henry VI, Part Two*, as the headquarters of Jack Cade's rebels. Cade's popular revolt of 1450 against the misrule of Henry VI had taken him into London itself. But forced to retreat across London Bridge, Shakespeare has Cade address his 'Rabblement' of followers:

> Hath my sword therefore broke through London gates that you should leave me at the White Hart in Southwark? I thought ye would never have given out these arms till you had recovered your ancient freedom . . .

* * *

From this point continue towards the river, crossing to the other side of Borough High Street. Some little distance ahead, close to the bridge, will be found a set of steps leading down to the remaining churchyard of Southwark Cathedral, and to the south door of the church.

The George Inn, the only galleried tavern remaining in London.

Though the nave dates only from the 1890s, and many other parts of the structure have been altered or restored, Southwark Cathedral is nonetheless widely regarded as London's second finest Gothic edifice – after Westminster Abbey. Founded in the 7th century by a community of nuns, a priory of canons erected here in 1106 a large Norman church. Subsequently burned down in 1206 it was replaced by the Gothic design still to be seen in many of the cathedral's features.

The medieval priory church was known as St Mary Overie or Overy – a title usually conjectured to be a corruption of 'over the river'. (An alternative conjecture might be 'over 'ere'.) After the suppression of the priory in 1539, a new parish of St Saviour's was created. The church became a cathedral in 1905 with the enthronement of the first bishop of Southwark. Hence the full title of Southwark's mother church is: the Collegiate and Cathedral Church of St Saviour and St Mary Overie.

Against the north wall of the nave will be found the effigy and canopied tomb – renovated in red, green, black and gold – of John Gower (1330-1408). The head of the effigy rests upon three volumes of Gower's works: for all of which he attained fame, but on one of which only now resides his place in English literature. *Speculum Meditantis* was written in French, *Vox Clamantis* in Latin, and *Confessio Amantis* in English – written for Richard II. Together, within the lifetime of one writer, they show not only Gower's erudition, but the emerging state of the English language. Whereas Latin had been the language of scholars and ecclesiastics, French had been the language of educated society and, until 1362, of lawyers and the law courts – and the language too of many cultural forms, such as romances. Though versions of English were once more generally known by the beginning of the fourteenth century (and had begun to spread among the upper classes around the middle of the thirteenth century), little literature in the language existed. The work of Gower – and even more the work of his friend Geoffrey Chaucer – was therefore important in fashioning a language which could be an assured literary medium. Together they took the language of London – itself a mixture of speech-forms with a pre-dominance of East Midlands, with Kentish and other features – and from that dialect of their times they fashioned the beginnings of modern standard English.

John Gower.

Gower's *Amantis* recounts tales of love, told by a priest of Venus (Genius) to whom the lover Amans is making confession. Collected under the headings of the Seven Deadly Sins the tales illustrate the changing character of love and the behaviour of lovers.

From 1377 until his death Gower lived in the priory of St Mary Overie, devoting himself to his writing. It is thought that he remarried when nearly seventy; and it is certain that he went blind around the year 1400.

Beyond the Gower tomb you will come to the choir of the church. And set into the slabs of the choir, between the stalls, will be found in a row the memorial stones to John Fletcher (1579-1625), Philip Massinger (1583-1640), and Edmund Shakespeare (d 1607).

From the age of seventeen, Fletcher had been left to find his own way in the world upon the death, in poverty, of his father – a minister, first, in Sussex before rising to the office of Bishop of London. Fletcher's education at Cambridge was cut short through the death of his father, and some years after this Fletcher turned up in London. From about the age of twenty-five, if not sooner, Fletcher took to writing plays, producing a prolific list of comedies and tragedies, both solely and in collaboration with others. Within a few years he met Francis Beaumont, who was to become his collaborator in playwriting, as well as a close personal friend. Indeed so close was the friendship, and so Bohemian their style of living, that Aubrey was led to comment that they shared everything in common including a mistress – though that may have been false report. Credited with the sole authorship of at least sixteen plays, among his collaborators – in addition to Beaumont – on numerous other plays were: William Rowley, Ben Jonson, Thomas Middleton, George Chapman, and William Shakespeare. Fletcher died of the plague in the summer of 1625, during which outbreak there were something like 35,000 victims.

Fletcher collaborated also with Philip Massinger on probably a dozen or more plays. Massinger had left Oxford in 1606 without having taken a degree. Arrived in London he too soon entered the friendship of dramatists, and may have begun some anonymous collaborative work quite soon following his introduction to that society of writers. Massinger's collaboration with Fletcher may date from 1613, when Beaumont married, or a little later – from the year of Beaumont's death in 1616.

Massinger died in his sleep at his home, which is known to have been located close by the Globe theatre. He had gone to bed the night before in apparent good health. As in the case of Fletcher's funeral, the actors of Bankside attended the service.

Massinger himself wrote or shared in the writing of some 55 plays – of which the comedy *A New Way to Pay Old Debts* remains the best-known, and certainly the masterpiece among those of which he was sole author. Still given performance today this comedy was extremely popular with theatre audiences throughout the later eighteenth and early nineteenth centuries.

Between these inscribed stones to the two playwrights rests the commemorative slab of Edmund, the younger brother of William Shakespeare. Of the little which is known of him, he was at that time an actor then lodging in Maid Lane (which ran east to west, connecting with the southern end of Rose Alley and Bear Gardens – the line of that part of present-day Park Street); though it is not known with which company he acted. It is probable also that he fathered a child baptized just a few months' previously at the Church of St Giles Without Cripplegate (see Moorgate to the Bank).

The parish record notes: 'December 31. Edmund Shakespeare, a player, buried in the church with a forenoone knell of the great bell'. He was just twenty-eight, and the youngest child of Shakespeare's parents.

Some inferences can be made, however, from the parish register and fee book entries. Edmund's was an expensive funeral. It cost twenty shillings, when the cost of an ordinary churchyard burial was two shillings, and the charge for tolling the lesser bell was one shilling. Clearly someone wished to mark Edmund's death, and it seems very probable that his brother William, who by then was a man of financial substance, met the expenses. And it has been further speculated that Edmund's burial was arranged as a morning service (afternoon burials being the usual convention) in order that Shakespeare's fellow-actors could attend, being required perhaps for afternoon performance at an indoor venue.

In the south aisle of the choir, just in front of the retro-choir (to where it was moved in 1919) will be found the recumbent effigy and canopied tomb of Bishop Lancelot Andrewes (1555-1626). Saint, scholar and the most powerful, intellectually-argumentative preacher of his day, Andrewes's more recent reputation rests upon his affirmation in the work of T. S. Eliot to whom Andrewes was 'a writer of genius'. Eliot's interest in Andrewes dated from at least 1919, since in the November of that year he published in the *Athenaeum* an article on the sermons of Andrewes and of John Donne. This, together with Eliot's subsequent interest, probably from around 1926, in Andrewes's *Preces Privatae* (devotional prayers) issued in the collection of essays *For Lancelot Andrewes: Essays on Style and Order* (1928). Eliot's poem 'Journey of the Magi' borrows from one of Andrewes's sermons preached before King James I at Whitehall in 1622. In the midst of an argument to establish linguistic, latinate distinctions, Andrewes's prose becomes suddenly arrested with the hard detail which considers the 'time of their [the Magi's] coming':

> It was no summer progress. A cold coming they had of it at this time of the year, just the worst time of the year to take a journey, and specially a long journey in. The ways deep, the weather sharp, the days short, the sun

farthest off, *in solstitio brumali* [in the winter solstice], 'the very dead of winter' . . .

    And these difficulties they overcame, of a wearisome, irksome, troublesome, dangerous, unseasonable journey . . .

In the south aisle of the nave there will be found the 1912 memorial to William Shakespeare – an alabaster figure reclining (in an awkward posture) in front of a relief of the Southwark of his times. Above, a stained glass window (unveiled by Dame Sybil Thorndike in 1954) depicts a number of characters from Shakespeare's plays. Across the bottom of the three windows are realisations of the Seven Ages of Man, recalling Jaques's speech from *As You Like It* (II, vii), beginning:

> All the world's a stage,
> And all the men and women merely players;
> They have their exits and their entrances;
> And one man in his time plays many parts,
> His acts being seven ages . . .

Between the three lancet-shaped windows which carry those figures are set two small windows inscribed with the lines from the speech (beginning 'Our revels now are ended . . .') which Prospero delivers following the entertainment he has conjured for his daughter Miranda and her lover Ferdinand (*The Tempest*, IV, i):

> These our actors,
> As I foretold you, were all spirits and
> Are melted into air, into thin air:
> And, like the baseless fabric of this vision,
> The cloud-capped towers, the gorgeous palaces,
> The solemn temples, the great globe itself,
> Yea, all which it inherit, shall dissolve
> And, like this insubstantial pageant faded,
> Leave not a rack behind.

***

Upon leaving the cathedral turn to the right, through the gateway leading from the churchyard. Then turn right again towards the river. Immediately ahead will be seen the schooner Kathleen & May in St Mary Overy's Dock. To the left will be seen the Southwark Heritage Visitor Centre (open 9.00am to 5.00pm Monday-Friday). Alongside the Centre will be seen Pickford's Wharf (Clink Street) leading off to the west.

Just ahead and on the left along here stand the remains of Winchester House, the large palace of the Bishops of Winchester – the last of whom to live there was Lancelot Andrewes. The round window of the Great Hall of the palace was revealed in the 1960s within a modern warehouse.

A few yards further along you will come to a large warehouse, again to your left, which now houses the Clink Exhibition. For close to this location formerly stood the Clink Prison – the original of the expression 'in the clink' – burned down in the Gordon Riots of 1780. The Exhibition attempts to recreate something of the history and the conditions of the Clink and the brothels of Bankside. (Exhibition open 10.00am to 6.00pm seven days a week: admission charge).

Directly ahead of this warehouse the street passes beneath a railway arch. To your right, as you emerge from beneath the arch, may be seen the fading blue (wooden) plaque reminding the visitor of the existence here of the Clink Prison itself.

***

On exiting from the railway arch a little to the left will be found the entrance to Park Street – between which and the riverside itself were to be found the major congregations of theatres, taverns, and dwellings which comprised Bankside.

An area west of St Mary Overie's and stretching alongside the river as far as Blackfriars Bridge, by Elizabethan times Bankside was, according to Thomas Dekker, 'a continual ale-house'. To the puritan City authorities it was a concourse of corruption; a suburb notorious for its prostitutes, rogues and vagabonds. It was a centre, too, for other popular pleasures – notably the spectacles of bull and bear-baiting. And it housed most of the watermen who ferried their rowing-boats across the Thames for hire – with shouts of 'Westward Ho' or 'Eastward Ho' to indicate whether they were plying upstream or down. Their trade increased many-fold when Bankside became the major location for London's theatres, its actors, playwrights and managers.

But Bankside also became the major centre for the theatre, and the remarkable flowering of drama which the playhouses of the times, and an eager playgoing public, engendered in the Elizabethan-Jacobean age. And remarkable, too, is the fact that these developments took place despite official objection and opposition.

For to the City fathers of the Elizabethan age, actors were themselves representatives of immoral, dissolute living. In 1580, for example, the then Lord Mayor declared players to be 'a very superfluous

sort of men'. And the City corporation concluded that the Rose (the first of the Bankside theatres) was no more than a meeting-place for 'thieves, horse stealers, whore-mongers, cozeners, connycatching persons, practicers of treason and such other like'.

Yet the theatre was also genuinely one of the most popular of entertainments, drawing its audiences from all walks of life. And despite the official contempt in which they were held, theatre people clearly took their part in the life of the community. It is known, for instance, that Edward Alleyn, actor, was a vestryman at St Mary Overie's and that Philip Henslowe (who owned the Rose Theatre) was both vestryman and warden.

Until 1575-6 plays were generally performed in the courtyards of City Inns. After several attempts to suppress them the civic authorities of the City of London appointed the Lord Mayor and his aldermen to be censors of both plays and playhouses. Such impossible restrictions prompted the building of purpose-made theatres outside of the City limits. The first of these (the Theatre, 1576, and the Curtain Theatre, 1577) were built in Shoreditch, a

Hollar's view of Bankside (1647) from the tower of St Mary Overie's church. The labels for the Globe and the Beere bayting have been transposed.

northern suburb outside of the City walls, but within walking distance for its inhabitants. These were followed, at Bankside, by the Rose Theatre, 1587, the Swan Theatre, 1595, and then by the most famous of all Elizabethan theatres, the Globe, in 1599. Later still Henslowe had the Hope built (1613), serving the dual purposes of bear-garden as well as theatre.

The Swan (whose location was on the western edge of Bankside, just on the far side of present-day Hopton Street below its junction with Upper Ground Street) is the only one of these theatres for which an internal view exists – though doubts also exist about its verisimilitude. Built by Francis Langley, the Swan was sketched by a Dutch priest, Johannes de Witt, on a visit to London in 1596. A pen and ink copy of his drawing, made by a friend Arend van Buchell, provides the only known contemporary view of the inside layout of an Elizabethan playhouse, though many features of the design and its implications for production remain an unresolved debate.

Puritan objections to theatre were not altogether without foundation. Where so many people gathered together in so small a space there was indeed the risk of the plague being spread rapidly. For to many modern theatre-goers it is perhaps surprising to discover just how small these Elizabethan playhouses in fact were. The external measurements of the Globe are usually reckoned to have been no more than about ninety feet in diameter, a figure arrived at from the known size of the first Fortune theatre (see City Road section). The exact size of the Globe may be established in the future (see below), a matter which may in its turn resolve a continuing scholarly debate as to what number of persons could be contained within such a playhouse. De Witt himself reckoned that the Swan, the largest of the Bankside theatres, could hold about three thousand people – an estimate thought by some to be greatly exaggerated. Yet a paper by D. A. Latter (in the *Shakespeare Survey*, 1975), based on the construction of a model of an Elizabethan playhouse (derived from the known dimensions for the Hope and Fortune contracts and calculating seating-space by taking into account the audience's sight-lines) also arrives at a figure very close to 3,000 as a maximum – an estimate now gaining wider acceptance. An interesting experiment conducted on the now known inner dimensions of the Rose playhouse would appear to put such a figure within realistic bounds (see below). *Average* attendances, it has been suggested, may have been between 1,000 and 2,000.

The 'groundlings', who stood throughout the performance, paid one penny for entrance. These would be, in the main, shopkeepers, craftsmen, apprentices. Two-penny and three-penny seats in the galleries would be taken by professional men, courtiers, and even members of the nobility. For those who wished to make conspicuous their attendance there were available one-shilling 'rooms' or boxes at the side of the stage. Entrance fees would be collected by the 'gatherers' and put into locked boxes – the original of the term 'box-office'.

Plays would be staged generally in the afternoons. If darkness fell, torches or baskets of tarred rope would be lit.

Puritan critics claimed that people attended the theatre for immoral purposes, especially to make

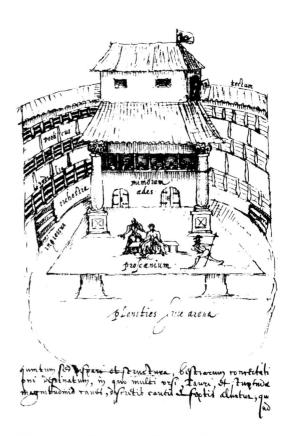

The pen and ink copy of de Witt's drawing of the interior of the Swan theatre.

assignations – 'the winking and glancing of wanton eyes'. Some of this charge was no doubt true. There was sometimes a general rowdiness too, members of the audience shouting their views, even taking part in the action on the stage. Between the acts of a play additional songs, dances, even acrobatics, might be performed; and at the conclusion of a play there might be more entertainment of a similar kind.

Throughout the production pies, pasties, and other food might be sold and eaten; some might play cards, and booksellers would offer their pamphlets for sale. The air would be blue in fact – with the haze of tobacco smoke. The Elizabethan theatre operated therefore under very different conditions to those of modern theatre. Yet theatre unquestionably appealed to all sections of society – and was indeed a favourite pastime. The love of theatre was genuinely enjoyed, and there was therefore a huge demand for new plays. In its three busiest years, for example, the Rose produced fifty-five new plays – including several of Marlowe's.

A model of the Swan theatre.   By courtesy of the Shakespeare Globe Museum

Today a new sense of excitement awaits the visitor to Bankside because of the momentous events of 1989: the discovery, within months of each other, of the foundations first of the Rose playhouse, in February, followed by those of the Globe itself, in early October. There is, too, the development taking place of the International Shakespeare Globe Centre, and the splendid museum which it operates. Certainly something – and in time a good deal more, one trusts – of Bankside's Elizabethan past may be retraced today.

From the eastern end of Park Street (arrived at through the railway arch) and a short distance along, just yards before the bridge carrying Southwark Bridge Road across the street, there will be found a large rectangular plaque commemorating the Globe theatre and the Southwark of those times. The plaque features a relief of Shakespeare's face against a view of Elizabethan Bankside, with the Globe prominently shown.

The exact location of the Globe has now been established, resolving finally the debate caused by the inconsistencies among contemporary maps and panaoramas. The Globe site is a little to the west of the location notionally marked by the plaque.

At the time of writing (December 1989) only a small section of the playhouse's foundations have so far been identified, and these stretch further beneath the Grade II listed buildings of Anchor Terrace (which face onto Southwark Bridge Road) and probably beneath the foundations of Southwark Bridge Road itself. The small area so far exposed by the team from the Museum of London Department of Greater London Archaeology reveals parts of three concentric rings of wall foundations. The smallest section is of a substantial brick foundation. Close by was found a layer of crushed hazelnut shells – which may have provided some kind of flooring (see the Rose, below). Thirteen feet to the east of the smallest brick section there has been revealed a foundation of chalk blocks with timber stakes, representing the outer line of the Globe foundations. About six

95

The commemorative plaque marking the nearby site of the Globe playhouse.

feet beyond that section there is another brick foundation, the outermost of the three. Since this foundation turns at right angles into the line of the outer wall at one end, and at the other there is a similarly-directed foundation trench, it appears likely that this outline shows the base of an outside stair tower. Such a tower is in fact shown quite clearly in Wenceslaus Hollar's engraving of 1647 which features the second Globe.

A few interesting objects have been found on the excavated site. Two Charles I farthings were discovered in the top of the hazelnut layers. These provide dating evidence, the reign of Charles I ending in 1649 and the second Globe known to have been pulled down in 1644. Also found were a number of clay pipes and pieces of pottery, together with lots of brick and tile fragments.

The area of the Globe revealed and briefly put on public display has been back-filled for the winter of 89/90, whilst the future of the Globe site remains unresolved. Should the site be scheduled then no further archaeological excavations could be undertaken without express consent of the Secretary of State for the Environment. Such a move would at least guarantee the integrity of the remains, the fraction so far revealed and the remainder still concealed. And from a strict rescue-archaeology perspective it might be argued that there is no need to excavate the site further in any case, since the remains are not in any danger; they *are* preserved and, left undisturbed, they would remain protected. Of course there are many who would like to see the whole of the Globe site excavated and all the remains exposed, perhaps to be put on public display. To meet both of these requirements, however, would interfere with the Anchor Terrace buildings, of 1835, the façade of which is itself listed. Clearly it would be possible, viewed simply as an engineering task, to shore up the façade, demolish the interiors of the buildings, and so get at the remaining sections of the Globe. Equally clearly, however, preservationists will object to that procedure. Nor is it at all certain that once permanently exposed the remains of the Globe theatre could themselves be preserved – the exposed remains of the Rose playhouse could well provide guidance over the years as how best to proceed with the Globe. Despite the difficulties, and

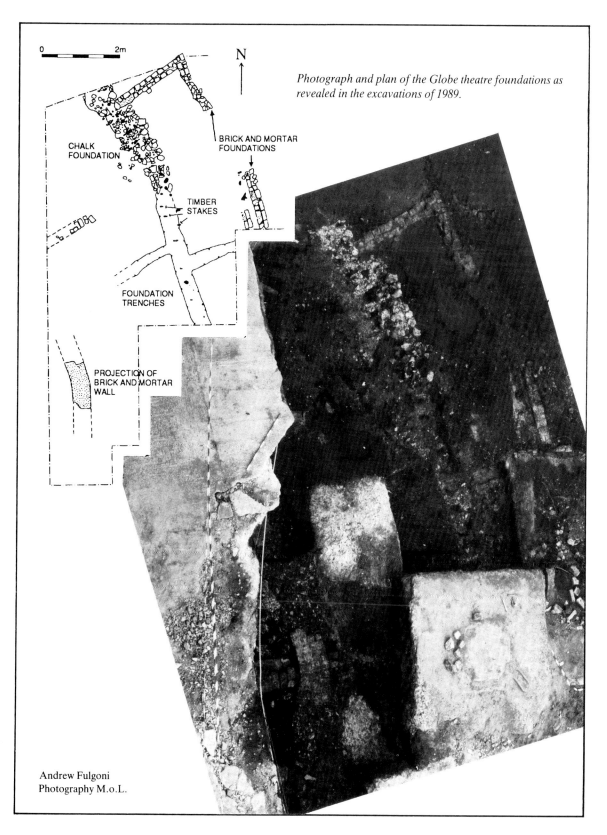

Photograph and plan of the Globe theatre foundations as revealed in the excavations of 1989.

Andrew Fulgoni
Photography M.o.L.

the possible controversies which will be engendered, one may speculate that some further excavation *will* proceed – but under what conditions is less easy to predict.

If the future of the Globe site is uncertain, its origin has been established in some detail. James Burbage had built the first playhouse at Shoreditch. Upon the death of their father his sons Cuthbert and Richard inherited the Theatre. Having failed to re-negotiate for the lease on which the theatre stood, and building materials being very expensive, the Burbages together with ten or twelve workmen had the Theatre taken down. They contrived to do this at Christmastide 1597 (28 December), and at night, when the owner of the land, who claimed also owner-ship of the theatre because it was on his land, was away at his country home in Essex. The Burbages had the dismantled materials ferried across the Thames, and the building re-erected on Bankside as the Globe. Its new name derived from its sign; that of Atlas holding up the world.

The Burbages retained half of the ownership of the new theatre, the other shares being divided among five members of the theatre company known as the Chamberlain's Men, and later, the King's Men. One of that five was Shakespeare, of whom it is known that for some of the early years of the Globe theatre he would have been in lodgings some-where in Bankside. Richard Burbage, it is almost certain, played the lead role in *Hamlet* in early productions at the Globe. And there is a tradition that Shakespeare himself played the part of the Ghost – though no final proof of that exists. Cer-tainly, however, most of Shakespeare's greatest plays were given their first productions at the Globe, including *Othello*, *Macbeth*, and *King Lear*.

The first of Shakespeare's plays to be produced at the Globe – the first at least for which there is any kind of documentary evidence – might well have been *Julius Caesar*. For on the afternoon of 21 Sep-tember 1599 Thomas Platter, a visitor from Ger-many, recorded having seen, with his companions, a play on Julius Caesar acted at the playhouse. In all probability that play was Shakespeare's own.

The very first of Shakespeare's plays to be com-posed with the Globe in mind, however, can fairly clearly be deduced as that of *Henry V*, the Prologue to which refers its listeners to features of the theatre itself: the 'wooden O' of its design, the enclosed 'cockpit', and the 'scaffold' or stage:

> But pardon, gentles all,
> The flat unraised spirits that hath dar'd
> On this unworthy scaffold to bring forth
> So great an object. Can this cockpit hold
> The vasty fields of France? Or may we crown
> Within this wooden O the very casques
> That did affright the air at Agincourt?

In June 1613 the original Globe was burned down when the thatch of the roof caught fire at the dis-charge of a peal of ordnance to announce the entrance of the King in *Henry VIII*, to the writing of which both Shakespeare and Fletcher contributed. The whole construction of the playhouse rapidly burned down; though the time taken to do so varies by report between one and two hours. Thomas Lorkin, in his letter of 30 June, reports that

> ... the whole house burned so furiously, as it con-sumed the whole house, all in less than two hours, the people having enough to do to save themselves.

Three days after the event, Sir Henry Wotton (not himself present on the day) having gathered the details of the event, made the fullest report of the disaster in a letter to his nephew. The letter is inter-esting not least because it confirms the fact that the play was staged with substantial ceremony, that it was a *spectacle*, and its presentation included, for example, finely attiring the actors. One excerpt from Wotton's long letter reads:

> ... I will entertain you at the present with what hath happened this week at the Bankside. The King's Play-ers had a new play, called *All is True*, representing some principal pieces of the reign of *Henry VIII*, which was set forth with many extraordinary circumstances of pomp and majesty, even to the matting of the stages; the Knights of the Order, with their Georges and Garter, the guards with their embroidered coats, and the like ...

Wotton's letter turns then to the matter of the fire itself:

> Now, King *Henry* making a masque at the Cardinal Wolsey's house, and certain canons being shot off at his entry, some of the paper, or other stuff, wherewith one of them was stopped, did light on the thatch, where being thought at first but an idle smoke, and their eyes more attentive to the show, it kindled in-wardly, and ran round like a train, consuming within less than an hour the whole house to the very ground.

Beyond 'a few forsaken cloaks' left behind by fleeing members of the audience, Wotton concludes:

Detail from Hollar showing the second Globe. Note the external structure on the side of the building, possibly a staircase, the foundations of which may be those revealed in the 1989 excavation (see text).

... only one man had his breeches set on fire, that would perhaps have broiled him, if he had not by the benefit of a provident wit put it out with Bottle-Ale.

It has been conjectured by some, however, that there may have been other losses; manuscripts of plays, perhaps some of Shakespeare's, lost in the fire. The suggestion is speculation only, of course, but certainly credible.

An anonymous versifier of the times saw the event of the burning down of the Globe in rather more rumbustious terms:

This fearfull fires beganne above,
   A wonder strange and true,
And to the stage-house did remove,
   As round as taylors clewe;
And burnt downe both beame and snagg,
   And did not spare the silken flagg.
Oh sorrow, pittifull sorrow, and yett al this is true.

Out runne the knightes, out runne the lades,
   And there was great adoe.
Some lost their hattes, and some their Swordes;
   Then out runne Burbidge too;
The reprobates, though drunke on Munday,
   Prayd for the Foole and Henry Condye.
Oh sorrow, pittifull sorrow, and yett all this is true.

No shower his ranne did there downeforce
   In all that Sunne-shine weather,
To save that great renowned howse;
   Nor then, O ale-howse, neither
Had itt begun belowe, sans doubte,
   Their wives for feare had pissed itt out.
Oh sorrow, pittifull sorrow, and yett all this is true.

(From: *A sonnett upon the pittifull burning of the Globe playhouse in London*)

Those Puritans who had continuously opposed the theatre saw the providential hand of God in the destruction of the Globe. The following year, however, the Globe was rebuilt, 'in farre fairer maner than before' – financed by public subscription and a royal grant to the King's Men. Though no new plays of Shakespeare were produced in the second Globe, the repertoire of the company's plays included works by Beaumont and Fletcher, Middleton, Webster, and D'Avenant, among others. Which plays in the repertoire were performed at the second Globe is not certain, since they may have been produced during winter seasons at the Blackfriars indoor theatre on the other side of the river (for details see: Ludgate, St Paul's, and Aldersgate) – or indeed some titles may have featured in both theatres.

The second Globe, like all theatres, was closed down by the Puritans in 1642 during the Commonwealth. Two years later the ground landlord had the structure demolished in order to develop the site.

* * *

Beyond the Globe site, a little further along Park Street past the bridge on the right-hand side, will be seen the site of the first of the two most important and exciting archaeological finds – in the context of English literary culture – discovered in Bankside. For here, in February 1989 during site clearance prior to re-development, were discovered the foundations of a Tudor building directly beneath the demolished 1950s office block (whose concrete piles had been driven through the older remains). Further excavation of the site established these foundations as belonging to the original Rose theatre. The site of these foundations is about five feet below the present-day ground level. The distance between the outside perimeter wall of the Rose and the (projected) external wall of the Globe playhouse appears to be just about one hundred yards.

Various objects were found at the excavation level of the Rose theatre. They included: a half groat coin, a bone comb, shoes, rosary beads, rings, a sword hilt, and a spur. Found in two separate locations just outside the perimeter of the Rose foundations were the skull of a bear and the thigh bone of a brown bear – both of which almost certainly came from the nearby bear-baiting arena (see below). The thigh bone, which is that of an old bear, shows canine teeth marks. The explanation of this find seems to be that the bear, too old to provide any more 'sport', had been butchered and then fed to the dogs.

The Rose, constructed in 1587 for the impresario Philip Henslowe, had probably disappeared by 1606 at the latest – Henslowe's lease having expired the year before. At the theatre Edward Alleyn made his reputation as the finest actor of the age; a prestige which lead to his appointment under James I as 'Master of the Royal Game of Bears, Bulls and Mastiff Dogs' – which sports were also staged at Bankside. Alleyn's fortune enabled him to found Dulwich College as an educational establishment for poor boys. His acting, however, came to prominence through his parts in Marlowe's plays first performed at the Rose: *Tamburlaine the Great*, *Doctor Faustus*, and *The Jew of Malta*.

Works by Jonson, Dekker, and Webster were also performed at the Rose. Two of Shakespeare's early works were given their first performance here: *Henry VI* and *Titus Andronicus*, in the first of which it is believed Shakespeare himself performed.

The Rose site shows the outline of the inner and outer walls of an irregular polygonal building erected on foundations of chalk with brick inserts, together with additional chalk piles which supported the timber superstructure of the theatre. Further archaeological evidence confirms that the walls were of lath and plaster, whilst the findings of a humic layer may well derive from the remains of thatch. The diameter of the inner yard is no more than about 42 feet across, and the distance between the inner and outer walls is 11½ feet, the width of the galleries tiered above the yard.

Two phases to the history of the Rose have been established. The original Rose appears to have had a floor of mortar on which spectators stood. Though this surface was flat across the pit area furthest from the stage, the remainder of the floor area tilted down towards the stage; a design which, though clearly enhancing the sight-lines for the 'groundlings', was unanticipated by most historians.

In its second phase the Rose was enlarged, probably in 1592 – the effect of which was to increase audience-space. The stage was pushed back about 10 feet, and the theatre extended behind it. The area of the yard enclosed, excepting the stage, in the first phase was 138 square yards; and in the second, 191 square yards, an increase of almost 40% in area. In a trial conducted by Julian Bousher, the Site Director of the Rose excavation, 400 senior schoolchildren loosely packed themselves into an area equivalent to the first phase of the Rose's yard. Bearing in mind that the Elizabethan mature stature was on average below that of today's, and that the

Aerial photograph of the exposed foundations of the Rose theatre. Andrew Fulgoni Photography M.o.L.

children used in the experiment therefore provide some kind of approximation, it would have been possible to fit over 560 into the area marked out in the second stage of the Rose's extended yard – perhaps close to, or just over, 700 if the assembled bodies were tightly packed. Though the total capacity of the Rose remains conjectural, because the accommodation provided in the superstructure remains uncertain, such figures provide an interesting commentary on the potential size of an audience attending an Elizabethan playhouse.

It is possible that the extension to the structure of the Rose was achieved simply by breaking into a section on either side of the polygon and then altering the external shape by putting up new sides along the new foundation lines to match in with the existing sides. The outer shape of the Rose then resembled a closed horseshoe, the inner enlarged area now more of a mushroom shape. At this phase was laid a new yard floor of clinker and crushed hazelnut shells (though journalists rushing into print soon after the discovery were claiming that hazelnuts were the Elizabethan equivalent of today's popcorn snack for theatre-goers!). The archaeologists found that this shell and clinker surface was far harder than the first mortar surface.

The stage itself faced just a little east of south, and appears to have been between 26 and 28 feet across at its front edge, with a depth of between 16 and 20 feet.

Clearly the site carries enormous significance for what further information it might yield about the size, design, and construction of this, the smallest of the Bankside theatres – and may offer further guidance to the inferences which might be made about the staging of plays in those Elizabethan times. It must be said though that the eleven-storey office block now being erected above the site, however the remains will be displayed in the future, will limit their viewing. A sense of perspective will necessarily be lost (and as the work proceeds is visibly being lost), though an arrangement for continuing public access has been guaranteed by the developer.

***

Alongside this site, and leading off to the right from Park Street, will be found the narrow Rose Alley. Though the first naming of this throughway may well derive from its botanical reference – from medieval times there had been rose gardens on Bankside – its name calls to mind an additional association which may not be inappropriate. For the Elizabethan expression 'to pluck a rose' was an epithet for the passing of water. In the context of the facts that the surrounding playhouses appear to have had no latrines, that drink was consumed in large quantities, and that stage performances could occupy the most part of an afternoon, the epithet acquires a certain appositeness when attached to Rose Alley.

Just a few yards beyond Rose Alley, Bear Gardens leads off to the right. Just into Bear Gardens, on the right, will be found the Shakespeare Globe Museum. It covers the approximate site of the Hope theatre of Philip Henslowe. When the Globe burned down, Henslowe quickly seized the opportunity of converting an old bull and bear baiting arena to serve the second purpose of playhouse. It was designed with a moveable stage so that the animal 'sports' could still take place there. It appears that plays were staged at the Hope for a short period of three years. But during that time it is known that Ben Jonson's *Bartholomew Fair* was given its first performance there in 1614. Indeed Jonson makes specific reference to the Hope's other function when the Stagekeeper is mocked for 'gathering up broken apples for the bears within'.

From 1616 the structure seems to have been returned to its sole use as bear and bull baiting arena – visits to which were recorded by the diarists Samuel Pepys and John Evelyn.

The introduction of bear and bull baiting to England appears to have been inspired by Italian settlers during the reign of King John. The first recorded mention of these entertainments in London, at Bankside, dates from 1546. Pepys, who was accompanied by his wife on his visit, was somewhat ambivalent about these so-called sports – enjoying the spectacle but decrying the rude pleasure on which it was founded. John Evelyn, however, came to a certain conclusion in his *Diary* entry for June 1670:

> One of the bulls tossed a dog full into a lady's lap, as she sate in one of the boxes at a considerable height from the arena. Two poor dogs were killed, and so all ended with ape on horseback, and I most heartily weary of the rude and dirty pastime.

The Shakespeare Globe Museum (planned to be moved and extended: see below) occupies a Georgian warehouse on this site, and houses a fascinating collection of materials relating to the history of Elizabethan and Jacobean theatre and of the history of Bankside. There is a small entrance charge to the museum, which should certainly be visited. (Open: Monday-Saturday, 10.00am-5.00pm; Sunday, 1.30-5.30pm.)

One gallery is devoted to a Rose theatre exhibition, whilst the main exhibition room houses various materials relating to the stage of the times. The exhibits include models of playhouses, among which the re-construction of the Blackfriars theatre (see: Ludgate, St Paul's, and Aldersgate) deserves special mention.

The museum also houses a replica of the Cockpit theatre which stood in Drury Lane in the 17th century. Originally, as its name implies, a cockfighting arena, it was converted to a theatre to the designs of Inigo Jones in 1616 – was burned down the year following, and quickly rebuilt. Visitors who are used only to modern theatres will be impressed first, almost certainly, with the sense of closeness such a design generates – both for audience and for actors. Productions are staged regularly in the theatre.

Also on display in the museum is a model for the new Globe theatre to be built on Bankside, where it will be the centre of a complex of buildings which will include a new Museum, a Centre for Shakespearian Studies, and an Inigo Jones theatre. These will be known as the International Shakespeare Globe Centre, the inspiration for which has been Sam Wanamaker, the American actor and director. The complex is scheduled for opening in April 1992, though the Centre has confirmed that if further excavation of the Globe site were to be undertaken it would stop construction – so that the more exact definitions of the size, design, and construction of the original so obtained could be incorporated into the projected reconstruction. Meanwhile, for those readers who would like the detail of the scholarly research upon which the reconstruction of the 'wooden O' has so far been projected, a review of the preceding evidence will be found in *Rebuilding Shakespeare's Globe* (1989) by Gurr and Orrell.

There remain many unresolved questions about the design of the Globe, and many fascinating questions about the production and staging of plays. The recreated theatre, when it does go ahead and is completed, may resolve some of these questions. Of course it is fair comment to add that the conditions for performance will have changed. However closely the reconstruction models the physical environment of the original Globe, the audience and its expectations will be radically different; contemporary theatre-goers adopt a far more reverential attitude than their Elizabethan and Jacobean forbears – and thus the mode of acting tested in the round will be different too. What is most certainly clear nonetheless is that the new playhouse will provide its audiences with what will be, for contemporary theatre-goers, a completely novel experience.

The site for this development is located just a minute's walk away at the corner of Emerson Street with Bankside, alongside the river. Emerson Street is the next opening from Park Street beyond the turning for Bear Gardens. The site is directly opposite St Paul's cathedral. And it may be mentioned in passing that the original, narrow-fronted house where Sir Christopher Wren lived during the construction of St Paul's is just a short distance away: beyond the Shakespeare Globe Centre site, and further to the west along Bankside.

***

From Bankside one may retrace the route along Park Street towards Southwark Cathedral and London Bridge. London Bridge stations will be seen opposite the steps leading up from the cathedral grounds to Borough High Street. Alternatively, one may cross London Bridge itself, from which the length of Bankside may be viewed. At the far side of the bridge, and continuing into King William Street, will be seen the signs for the Monument tube station.

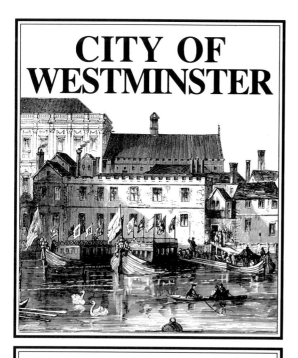

CITY OF WESTMINSTER

WHITEHALL AND WESTMINSTER
CITY OF WESTMINSTER

Though covering a comparatively limited area, the tour which follows may well occupy a good deal of time since it includes, most notably, Westminster Abbey, as well as other locations which deserve leisurely contemplation. The route itself is straightforward – beginning at Westminster underground station, proceeding along Whitehall and then returning to Westminster Abbey and locations within the immediate vicinity.

* * *

Directly facing the exit from Westminster underground station are the Houses of Parliament. To the left is Westminster Bridge.

The present bridge dates from 1854-62, replacing the first Westminster Brige which was officially opened in 1750. To this bridge the young James Boswell (1740-95) brought 'a strong, jolly young damsel' from the Haymarket in order 'to engage her upon this noble edifice'. His *London Journal* for 10 May 1763 records: 'The whim of doing it there with the Thames rolling below us amused me much.'

It might be observed that whatever other activities were conducted there, any defacing of the stone walls carried the threat of death.

Across this same bridge William Wordsworth 1770-1850) and his sister Dorothy (1771-1855) travelled in 1802. The occasion Wordsworth later commemorated in the sonnet 'Upon Westminster Bridge':

> Earth has not anything to show more fair:
>   Dull would he be of soul who could pass by
>   A sight so touching in its majesty:
> The city now doth like a garment wear
> The beauty of the morning; silent, bare
>   Ships, towers, domes, theatres, and temples lie
>   Open unto the fields, and to the sky;
> All bright and glittering in the smokeless air.
> Never did sun more beautifully steep
>   In his first splendour valley, rock, or hill;
> Ne'er saw I, never felt, a calm so deep!
>   The river glideth at his own sweet will:
> Dear God! the very houses seem asleep;
>   And all that mighty heart is lying still!

The Wordsworths were on their way to Calais where they were to spend four weeks with Marie-Anne Vallon ('Annette') and her nine-year-old daughter, whom her mother had had christened Anne-Caroline Wordsworth.

In 1791, having failed to get a good degree at Cambridge, Wordsworth had left for France. There, in Orléans, he developed an enthusiastic republicanism – and fell passionately in love with Annette Vallon. The following year Wordsworth left her, in order to return to England, stopping in Paris long enough to hear of the safe delivery of their child. Until their reunion in 1802 – during a temporary peace in the 'Coalition Wars' – Wordsworth had not seen either the child or the mother since his departure from France. Nor, after their meeting in Calais, were they ever to see each other again. Annette remained faithful to William for the rest of her life, called herself 'Madame William', and conducted an affectionate correspondence with both William and his sister Dorothy.

The facts of William's love-child were successfully concealed by the Wordsworth family from his Victorian readers (to preserve his reputation), but came to light with the scholarship of this century and the discovery in French police files, in 1923, of some of Annette's letters to William which had been confiscated during the wars with England.

Turning away from the bridge, along Bridge Street, Parliament Street opens on the right, leading into Whitehall. Some distance on will be seen the Cenotaph, and a little beyond, on the right, will be seen an impressive bronze statue in Elizabethan dress of Sir Walter Ralegh (1552-1618), poet, adventurer, and historian.

* * *

Immediately before Horse Guards Avenue, again on the right, will be found the Banqueting House of Whitehall, designed by Inigo Jones in 1619 for James I, and completed in 1622. It occupies the site of several previous halls, some of a purely temporary construction. The opening of the immediately preceding hall, in 1608, was celebrated with a performance of Ben Jonson's *Masque of Beauty*. Prior to that rebuilding, an even earlier hall may have been the venue for the first production of Shakespeare's *Othello* (1604). The present Banqueting House, all that remains of the old Whitehall Palace, was opened in 1622, again with a performance of one of Jonson's entertainments, *The Masque of Anger*. Many other masques and plays were presented here, among them works by Campion, Beaumont, and Shirley.

In 1635 the magnificent ceiling paintings of Peter Paul Rubens were installed, following which masques were no longer performed in the House itself, for fear that the smoke from the lamps would damage the ceilings.

Above the entrance to the House is a tablet, from a window close by to which Charles I stepped out on 30 January 1649 to the scaffold.

There is an entrance charge to the House which is open Tuesday to Saturday, 10.00am to 5.00pm, and Sundays between 2.00pm and 5.00pm. (Closed Mondays, Good Friday, 24-26 December, and 1 January).

* * *

From the Banqueting Hall, with Trafalgar Square and Nelson's Column away to the right, cross Whitehall and head back towards Westminster Bridge. Within a couple of minutes you will come to Downing Street, leading off on the right.

Of the original houses built here about 1680 only Nos 10, 11, and 12 still remain. From 1732, when Sir Robert Walpole was Prime Minister, No 10 has, of course, been the official residence for all succeeding Prime Ministers – though some early holders of the position have chosen not to live at the address, preferring their own town houses.

As a boy the future novelist and letter-writer Horace Walpole (1717-97) lived here with his father. Benjamin Disraeli (1804-81), twice Prime Minister – in 1868 and 1874-80 – resided here. His reputation as a novelist had been established previously with the trilogy of *Coningsby* (1844), *Sybil* (1845), and *Tancred* (1847); novels which pursued the sociopolitical theme which he had declared in 1845 as the division of England into 'two nations – the rich and the poor.'

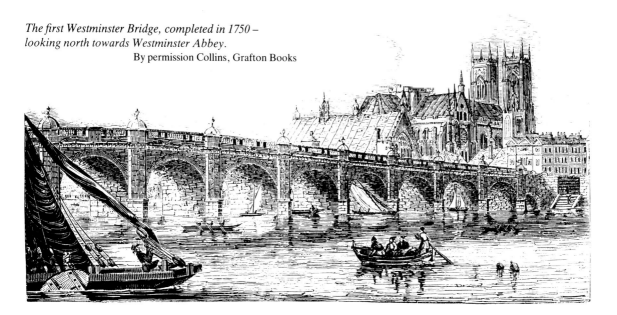

The first Westminster Bridge, completed in 1750 – looking north towards Westminster Abbey.
By permission Collins, Grafton Books

The old Whitehall Palace from the river.

Benjamin Disraeli.

Sir Winston Churchill (1874-1965), whose work as an author includes *A History of the English-Speaking Peoples*, also resided at No 10 during two periods as Prime Minister (1940-45 and 1951-2).

In the buildings which stood on the opposite side of the street James Boswell (see above) took lodgings in 1762 – 'up two pairs of stairs with the use of a handsome parlour all the forenoon.' Here much of the *London Journal* (1762-63) was composed.

Somewhere in a nearby building on the same side of the street Tobias Smollett (1721-77), novelist, set up a surgeon's practice in 1774.

* * *

Continuing to the end of Parliament Street, on the opposite side of its junction with Bridge Street and Great George Street, will be seen Parliament Square with its gardens and statues. Along the right-hand side of the square, facing into the gardens, will be found a statue of Benjamin Disraeli (see above), Earl of Beaconsfield.

Veering slightly to the right, at the far side of the Square, is Broad Sanctuary. Within a very short distance, on the left, is Westminster Abbey. Before

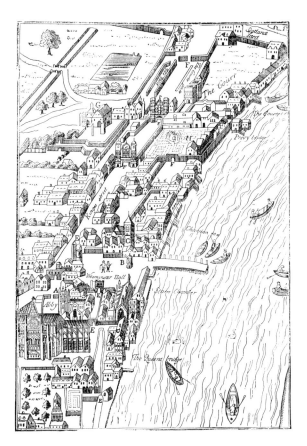

Whitehall and Westminster, from Aggas's map of 1563.

its main entrance is a small open space where stands a memorial to the Old Westminsters. There, until 1776, once stood the Gatehouse Prison, built originally in 1370. To this prison was brought Sir Walter Ralegh (see above) from the Tower of London, on the eve of his execution. Composed during that night as he awaited execution was his final poem, the Epitaph later found in his Bible:

> Even such is Time, which takes in trust
>   Our Youth, our Joys, and all we have,
> And pays us but with age and dust
>   Who in the darke and silent grave,
> When we have wandered all our wayes,
> Shuts up the story of our dayes:
> And from which Earth, the Grave, and Dust,
>   The Lord shall raise me up, I trust.

Richard Lovelace (1628-57), Cavalier poet imprisoned at the Gatehouse for his royalist sympathies, is also reputed to have penned here the famous poem 'To Althea, from Prison' – the final stanza of which achieves an impressive dignity, a statement of strength in adversity:

> Stone Walls doe not a Prison make,
>   Nor Iron bars a Cage;
> Mindes innocent and quiet take
>   That for an Hermitage;
> If I have freedome in my Love,
>   And in my soule am free;
> Angels alone that sore above,
>   Injoy such Liberty.

Samuel Pepys (1633-1703) was briefly imprisoned at the Gatehouse, in 1689, on suspicion of having been in correspondence with the exiled King James II. On the grounds of ill-health he was quickly released.

* * *

The Abbey itself traces back to ancient origins, perhaps even as far back as the 7th century if legend is accurate. Certainly a substantial church, founded by Edward the Confessor, occupied the site by the mid-eleventh century and was consecrated just a few days before Edward died and was buried in front of the high altar. During the reign of Henry III (1216-1272) work on rebuilding the Abbey began, and substantial parts were completed before the king's death. Further additions and renovations continued in successive centuries, through to the addition of the West Towers in 1745 to the design of Nicholas Hawksmoor.

In Edward the Confessor's Abbey – traces of which were discovered in the present nave and sanctuary last century – William I was crowned on Christmas Day 1066. Since that time all rulers of England and of Great Britain, with two exceptions (Edward V and Edward VIII), have been crowned in the Abbey. Here, too, were buried many of the monarchs, from Edward the Confessor onwards, a circumstance celebrated in the grim ironies of Francis Beaumont's poem 'Lines on the Tombs of Westminster Abbey':

> Mortality, behold and fear!
> What a change of flesh is here!
> Think how many royal bones
> Sleep within this heap of stones;
> Here they lie had realms and lands,
> Who now want strength to stir their hands;
> Where from their pulpits sealed with dust
> They preach 'In greatness is no trust.'
> Here's an acre sown indeed
> With the richest royall'st seed

The choir and nave of Westminster Abbey.

That the earth did e'er suck in,
Since the first man died for sin:
Here the birth of bones have cried,
'Though gods they were, as men they died.'
Here are sands, ignoble things,
Dropt from the ruined sides of kings:
Here's a world of pomp and state,
Buried in dust, once dead by fate.

Since Beaumont's time many not of royal birth have been buried in the Abbey; and memorials to others representing a wide variety of conditions and states have also been installed. Yet Beaumont's lines serve as a reminder too that from medieval times the monks of the Abbey used to put on display the effigies of the kings and queens buried there. The practice continued for centuries. Samuel Pepys recorded his visit, with a number of friends, to see the Abbey's royal effigies in February 1669:

> . . . here we did see, by particular favour, the body of Queen Katherine of Valois, and had the upper part of her body in my hands. And I did kiss her mouth, reflecting upon it that I did kiss a Queen, and that this was my birthday, 36 years old, that I did first kiss a Queen.

The effigies are now housed in the Abbey Museum located in the Norman undercroft.

Just inside the West Door entrance, however, close to the grave of the Unknown Warrior, is a memorial plaque to Winston Churchill (see above).

Proceeding further into the nave of the Abbey you will come to the entrance to the Royal Chapels – for which there is an entry charge. In the north transept, known as Statesmen's Aisle, will be found many commemoratives to those attaining high political positions – among which will be found one to Benjamin Disraeli (see above).

One of the small chapels at the eastern end of the Abbey contains the elaborate monument (designed by Le Sueur) to the Duke of Buckingham and his family – among whom was his son who, as the 2nd Duke of Buckingham (George Villiers, 1628-1687) established for himself a reputation as a poet, wit, satirist, and compulsive intriguer. The 2nd Duke lies in the chapel alongside.

In the south transept (known as Poets' Corner) congregate the graves and memorials of many distinguished poets and writers. Geoffrey Chaucer (b 1340?) was buried here in 1400; in 1556 the present tomb was erected to his memory. For perhaps the last ten or twelve years of his life Chaucer lived close to the Abbey. Just two years before his death he took out a long lease on a cottage in the garden of St Margaret's church (see below), at the eastern end of the Abbey itself.

At the burial of Edmund Spenser (1599) it is said that other poets flung into his grave manuscripts of their own unpublished works as a tribute to his memory.

The manner of interment of Ben Jonson (1637) issued from a humorous exchange with the Dean of the time, Bishop Williams. In his old age, and in impoverished circumstances, Jonson lived on the Abbey premises. The Dean asked if there was anything he could do to help him, to which Jonson replied by asking for a grave in the Abbey, and is reported to have added: 'Six feet long by two feet wide is too much for me; two feet by two feet will do for all I want.' Thus Jonson was buried standing upright. His epitaph, inscribed on a tablet on the south, or far, wall of the transept, reads simply: 'O Rare Ben Jonson'.

Also actually buried in the transept were: John Dryden; Matthew Prior; Samuel Johnson; Thomas Gray; Richard Brinsley Sheridan; Robert Browning; Alfred Tennyson; and Charles Dickens. The ashes of John Masefield were buried beneath a tablet between Browning's grave and the commemorative to W. H. Auden.

Numerous other writers are commemorated here with plaques and tablets – some of which memorials were installed many years after the death of the writer. Shakespeare's, for example, was not placed until 1740; and that of William Blake dates from as recently as 1957. Among others also celebrated here are: Gerard Manley Hopkins; Henry James; Lewis Carroll; D. H. Lawrence; Lord Byron; Michael Drayton; Thomas Gray; John Milton; Thomas Hardy; Dylan Thomas; William Makepeace Thackeray; the Brontë sisters; Oliver Goldsmith; William Wordsworth; John Keats; Percy Bysshe Shelley; Jane Austen; and George Eliot (whose floor tablet is inscribed: 'The first condition of human goodness is something to love: the second something to reverence.'). Sixteen poets of World War II are remembered in a single floor tablet inscribed with Wilfred Owen's declaration of 'The Pity of War . . .'

On leaving Poets' Corner, and turning left into the Cloisters, within a very short space will be seen the gravestone of Mrs Aphra Behn (1640-1689) set in the middle of the aisle. Aphra Behn enjoyed a reputation as a writer of witty comedies for the Restoration stage. She was also, from the age of twenty-six 'a merry widow'; became a regular visitor at the Court of Charles II; and was briefly sent to Antwerp to spy upon the Dutch – from where she reported the preparations of the Dutch to surprise the English by sending a fleet of ships up the Thames. Her news, apparently, was not believed in London. The inscription on her tablet reads:

> Here lies a Proof that Wit can never be
> Defence enough against Mortality

* * *

Following the Cloisters around will lead out into Dean's Yard. To the left, about fifty yards along, will be found the gateway entrance into Little Dean's Yard. The public is not admitted here, but from the gateway it is possible to glimpse the buildings of Westminster School which evolved from medieval times. The earliest building (the 'School'), re-built in 1959, dates from 1090-1100, with other buildings dating from the fourteenth and eighteenth centuries.

Re-founded by Elizabeth I as a school for 40 boys, Westminster has been an independent Public School since 1868. Since 1972 girls have been admit-

Mrs Aphra Behn.

ted to the sixth-form, and the total roll is now around 600.

One of the earliest headmasters of the school was Nicholas Udall (1505-56), author of the oldest extant comedy in English. *Ralph Roister Doister* (first printed 1567, but written as early as 1553) may well have been played by the boys of Westminster School.

Others, once scholars at the school, who later achieved literary distinction, include: Ben Jonson, Abraham Cowley, John Dyer, George Herbert, John Dryden, William Cowper, A. A. Milne, Matthew Prior, and Robert Southey. John Locke, philosopher, and Edward Gibbon, historian, were also scholars at Westminster. So too was John Cleland whose varied career and fortunes included his fiction of 'a woman of pleasure', *Fanny Hill*, the overwhelming success of which was to detract from the *Memoirs of a Coxcomb*. Among more recent scholars is the actor and playwright Peter Ustinov (b 1921) who has written amusingly of his days at the school in his autobiography *Dear Me* (1977).

* * *

Continuing past the entrance to Westminster School, you will come to an arched exit from Dean's Yard

Old Palace Yard at the end of the eighteenth century.

where, on the right, stands Church House. The building covers what was once No 25 where John Keats lived for some time in 1819. He moved from here to Hampstead, in order to be nearer Fanny Brawne for whom he had developed a passionate love.

***

The archway leads out into Great College Street, to the left. About 150 yards or so along Great College Street there is the junction with Abingdon Street, where one should again turn left. Almost immediately, the Parliament Buildings will be seen on the opposite side of the street. A little way along will be found Old Palace Yard, the site of the execution of Sir Walter Ralegh (see above).

Ralegh's conduct on the day of his execution was remarkable; bearing all not only with fortitude and faith, but with characteristic wit also. John Chamberlain, in a letter written on 31 October 1618 – that is, just two days after Ralegh's execution – 'set downe some few passages of divers that [he] heard'. The letter, to Sir Dudley Carleton, reads in part:

When the hangman asked him [Ralegh] forgiveness he desired to see the axe, and feeling the edge he saide that yt was a fayre sharpe medicine to cure him of all his diseases and miseries. When he was laide downe some found fault that his face was westward, and wold have him turned, whereupon rising he sayde yt was no great matter which way a mans head stoode so his heart lay right. He had geven order to the executioner that after some short meditation when he stretcht forth his handes he shold dispatch him. After once or twise putting foorth his handes, the fellow out of timerousness (or what other cause) forbearing, he was faine to bid him strike, and so at two blowes he took of his head, though he stirred not a whit after the first. The people were much affacted at the sight insomuch that one was heard to say that we had not such another head to cut of.

***

Beyond Old Palace Yard, to the right, stands the ancient Westminster Hall, all that survives of the original Palace of Westminser. The Hall dates from

110

Westminster Hall, the only surviving part of the Palace of Westminster.

1097-99, with rebuildings from the thirteenth and fourteenth centuries. Now used as the vestibule to the House of Commons, from the thirteenth century onwards (until 1882) the Hall housed the Law Courts.

One of the many tried here was Sir John Oldcastle (d 1417), condemned to death as a heretic for his support of the Lollards. Shakespeare's blustering, self-indulgent but good-humoured Falstaff of the *Henry VI* plays was based upon Oldcastle. The very different character of the Falstaff of *The Merry Wives of Windsor* – whom Shakespeare originally named Oldcastle – was changed to Falstaff following objections from a descendant of the knight.

Sir Thomas More (1478-1535) was tried here, and found guilty, on charges of treason for his opposition to Henry VIII's divorce from Catherine.

Henry Wriothesley, 3rd Earl of Southampton (1573-1624), a patron of Shakespeare, was tried in the Hall with the Earl of Essex on charges of high treason. Found guilty they, like More, were sent to the Tower of London to await execution. Southampton, however, was reprieved.

The Hall which, in addition to its main business, through many ages also housed stalls for sellers of books and other wares, was the retreat to which Charles Dickens hastened on seeing 'in all the glory of print' (in the *Monthly Magazine*) his very first literary production. In the Preface to the *Pickwick Papers* (1837) Dickens tells how he 'walked down to Westminster Hall and turned into it for half-an-hour because [his] eyes were so dimmed with joy and pride that they could not bear the street, and were not fit to be seen there'.

***

Opposite Westminster Hall, in St Margaret's Street (the continuation of Abingdon Street), is the east entrance to the church of St Margaret. Founded in the 12th century the present church dates from 1486-1523, since which time it has been restored on many occasions; including restorations carried out following bomb damage sustained during World War II. Since 1616 St Magaret's has served as the parish church for the House of Commons.

Immediately to the right upon entering the church there is the Sir Walter Ralegh memorial tablet (which may be illuminated). Ralegh's body was interred in the chancel of the church, beneath the High Altar it is thought – on the day he was beheaded, 29 October 1618. Ralegh's widow, however, kept the head; and it is not known whether head and body were ever reunited. At the far end of the church, above the west door, there is a nineteenth-century memorial window to Sir Walter Ralegh.

Also buried in the church was William Caxton (1422?-91) who, having learned the new trade of moveable-type printing on the continent, set up a press within the Almonry of the Abbey. From here in the last fourteen or fifteen years of his life he issued almost eighty separate books, including several works of his own translations. Within the church there is a memorial tablet as well as a window, in the north wall, dedicated to him.

Nicholas Udall (see above) was buried in St Margaret's. Before becoming headmaster at Westminster School, Udall had held the same position at Eton – and there had been accused of flogging boys for little or no evident reason.

Another literary man buried in the church was John Skelton (1460?-1529), who had had to seek sanctuary at Westminster in order to escape the wrath of Cardinal Wolsey. Having himself taken holy orders, Skelton made repeated attacks upon the Cardinal's power and the position of influence which he occupied. In typically vigorous, short lines, Skelton's satire and criticism were blunt indeed; as in *Why Come Ye Nat to Courte?*, in which he says of the Cardinal

> He ruleth all at wyll
> Without reason or skyll

Alongside the Ralegh window, at the west end of the church, will be seen one to the memory of John Milton (1608-74). Milton married here, in St Margaret's, his second wife Catharine Woodcock. His first marriage to Mary Powell had been far from settled or happy; within six weeks of their marriage, in 1642, she had left him to return to her parents. She did not return to her husband until 1645, during which absence he had published his pamphlet on divorce. His marriage to Catharine Woodcock, four years after the death of his first wife in 1652, lasted fifteen months only, ending with Catharine's death in childbirth. Both the mother and baby daughter, who lived only six weeks, were buried in the churchyard of St Margaret's.

Milton's marriage with Catharine, though short, was clearly founded on a happy relationship. The sonnet 'On His Deceased Wife' bears testimony to his love for her: in this he fancies that his 'late espoused Saint'

> Came vested all in white, pure as her mind:
>   Her face was vail'd, yet to my fancied sight,
>   Love, sweetness, goodness, in her person shin'd
> So clear, as in no face with more delight.
>   But O as to embrace me she enclin'd
>   I wak'd, she fled, and day brought back my night.

The poem reminds us, too, that by the time of his marriage to Catharine Woodcock, Milton had gone blind completely – a fact recognised in the memorial window which shows him dictating, the mode of composition he had to employ for the greatest bulk of his writings. Milton lived for some eight years in Petty France, just a few minutes' west of the Abbey, between the years 1652 and 1660 – 'in a pretty-garden house' which backed upon St James's Park. The house itself was demolished in 1877.

Also married in St Margaret's church was the diarist Samuel Pepys (1633-1703) who, in 1655, married the fifteen-year-old Elizabeth St Michel – ten months before they began to live with each other as man and wife.

Winston Churchill (see above) married here in 1908.

* * *

Leaving St Margaret's from the east door, and crossing over to the Houses of Parliament, Westminster underground station is just to the right, in Bridge Street.

Sir Walter Ralegh: a miniature on vellum c 1585.
National Portrait Gallery, London

THE STRAND

CITY OF WESTMINSTER

This tour will conduct the visitor the full length of the Strand itself and places immediately leading off from what was, for a long period of London's history, the main thoroughfare connecting the City of London with the City of Westminster.

From the Embankment underground station turn left into Embankment Place where, within a few yards, there is an acute right-hand turn into Craven Street. Just beyond the Playhouse which stands on that corner, on the right-hand side, will be found No 25 Craven Street. Here the American novelist Herman Melville (1818-91) stayed as a youth of about eighteen when he made a brief visit to London during his early seafaring days.

A little beyond that house, on the same side of the street, will be found No 32. A blue plaque here commemorates the stay of the German poet Heinrich Heine (1799-1856) in London from April to August 1827. It is clear, however, that he did not altogether enjoy his visit, and he never returned to England. Shortly after arriving Heine wrote to his friend Friedrich Merckel:

It is snowing outside and there is no fire in my chimney – I am very peevish and ill to boot. I have seen and heard much but have not had a clear view of anything. London has surpassed all my expectations as to magnificence, but I have lost myself . . . So far I have spent more than a guinea a day . . . It is so fearfully damp and uncomfortable here, and no one understands me, and no one understands German.

Next door, at No 33, lived Mark Akenside (1721-70) for two years from 1759. Akenside was a distinguished physician whose chief literary claim resides in the long didactic poem 'The Pleasures of Imagination'. Composed as early as 1738, and published six years later, the poem was completely re-written by Akenside and issued as 'The Pleasures of the Imagination' in 1757. Others of his shorter lyrics, such as 'The Nightingale', show him to be a forerunner of the Romantic movement in poetry.

Just opposite the Akenside house is Craven Passage, a short throughway which connects with Northumberland Street. At that junction, on the right, stands a public house, the Sherlock Holmes. Around the walls of the pub are various mementoes of Holmes, Conan Doyle's famous detective. In an upstairs room the internal furbishing recreates the sitting-room at 221b Baker Street, with a model of Sherlock Holmes sitting at the fire reading a copy of the *Times* newspaper. The display was first mounted at the offices of the Abbey National in Baker Street (see Marylebone I section) as part of the Festival of Britain celebrations of 1951.

Somewhere in the old Northumberland Street (known as Hartshorne Lane) Ben Jonson (1572-1637), playwright and poet, spent his boyhood years. From his stepfather he learned the trade of bricklaying.

* * *

Returning to Craven Street, continue to the top end of the street where it joins the Strand – which was at one time a bridle path running alongside the Thames.

To the right at this junction, within a short distance past Charing Cross station, Villiers Street opens upon the right. Almost immediately to the left will be seen York Place. Formerly known as Of Alley it is a curious reminder that George Villiers, 2nd Duke of Buckingham (1628-87), poet, dramatist and courtier, once owned this area of land upon which the original York House was sited. Upon the restoration of Charles II to the throne the house, which was

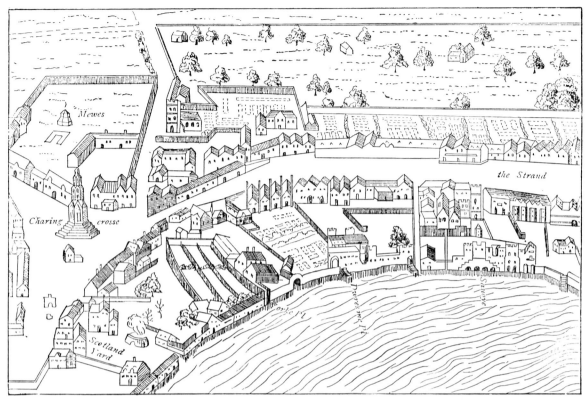

The Strand in 1560, from a map by Ralph Aggas.

formerly in the possession of his father, the 1st Duke, was returned to him. Villiers sold the house and ground in about 1670 when it was demolished for redevelopment to take place, but made it a condition of the sale that his name and title must be perpetuated in the names of the streets. Thus George Street (now York Buildings), Villiers Street, Duke Street, Of Alley, and Buckingham Street were duly named.

Some distance down Villiers Street, at No 43, on the left, will be found a blue plaque at first-floor level to commemorate the fact that Rudyard Kipling (1865-1936) took rooms here in the years 1889-91. Kipling had just returned from India where he had worked as a journalist and had already written various tales and poems. During his stay here he wrote the novel *The Light that Failed*.

Kipling's rooms, on the fifth-floor of the Villiers Street building, as he records in his autobiography, 'were above an establishment of Harris, the Sausage King, who, for tuppence, gave us as much sausage and mash as would carry us from breakfast to dinner'. Having arrived from India with very little money, one of Kipling's pleasures from this time was the music-hall:

My rooms were small, not overclean or well kept, but from my desk I could look out of my window through the fanlights of Gatti's music hall entrance, across the street, almost onto its stage.

Occasionally Kipling would have funds enough to go to the evening music-hall entertainment where 'the roar and good fellowship of relaxed humanity set the scheme for a certain sort of song'. That certain sort of song became *The Barrack Room Ballads* which began to appear during this time, and which issued in book form the year after Kipling left Villiers Street to travel again.

Somewhere on Villiers Street the diarist John Evelyn (1620-1706) spent the winter of 1682. And Sir Richard Steele (1672-1729), best-known for his essays, had two periods of residence, at different houses, on the street.

Charing Cross station, as its far end, now covers the site of the old Hungerford Stairs when the river was wider at this point – before the building of the Victoria Embankment in the 1860's pushed the river back. Here, as a boy, Charles Dickens (1812-70) was put to work in a shoe-blacking shop, his father having been imprisoned for debt. The misery of that experience in the rat-infested shop by the river was later recreated in his novel *David Copperfield*.

* * *

Shortly after the Kipling building, there is a turn to the left, down some steps, leading to a walkway alongside Victoria Embankment Gardens. About forty yards along, on the left, will be found some steps up to Buckingham Street.

Immediately on the right will be found No 15 (rebuilt), where formerly Charles Dickens (see above) took rooms on the top floor in 1833. Almost a century earlier the same residence had been lived in by another novelist, Henry Fielding (1707-54).

On the opposite side of the street are Nos 14 and 12, both of them associated with Samuel Pepys (1633-1703). Pepys, who had become secretary to the Admiralty in 1672, lived at No 12 from 1679 to 1688. Shortly after taking the lease of the house he was arrested on suspicion of being involved in the 'Popish plot' invented by Titus Oates. After a brief period of imprisonment in the Tower he was released, and all charges against him were dropped. He returned to the house in Buckingham Street which had been maintained by his clerk and friend, William Hewer. It was another five years, however, before Pepys was re-appointed to his post as secretary to the Admiralty.

From 1688 to 1701 Pepys lived in No 14, which had burned down and been re-built whilst Pepys was living next door. When Pepys moved out to go to Clapham to live with his old friend Hewer, the house was taken by Robert Harley, Earl of Oxford, whose collection of medieval manuscripts and documents compose the great treasures of the 'Harleian Library', now lodged in the British Museum. During his time at the house Harley was visited by Jonathan Swift, who was to become a friend of long-standing, and who wrote of his first visit to the house in the *Journal to Stella*.

The house which now stands on the site was rebuilt again in 1791-2.

Beyond the two Pepys's homes is No 10, the lodgings for part of 1766 of the philosopher David Hume (1711-76). Hume, a man of sceptical arguments and a mild disposition, had spent the three years prior to his return to Britain as secretary to the Embassy in Paris. There he was engaged by a number of French *philosophes*, among them Jean-Jacques Rousseau (1712-78) whose own views on the liberation of the individual were to shape important politi-

Rudyard Kipling, as featured in a 'Spy' (Leslie Ward) cartoon in an issue of Vanity Fair, *1894.*

cal and educational influences. Rousseau stayed with Hume in Buckingham Street where, prompted by Rousseau's suspicious nature (which some commentators have called persecution-mania), they quarrelled bitterly.

On the other side of the street, a little further up, will be found No 21 where Samuel Taylor Coleridge (1772-1834) stayed in lodgings for part of the year 1799, the year after the publication of his and Wordsworth's *Lyrical Ballads*, and shortly after his return from a visit to Germany.

***

Just beyond this house John Adam Street crosses Buckingham Street. At this junction, turning to the right, within a few yards will be found a modern building (No 17) which formerly was the house where Harley Granville-Barker (1877-1946) lived. Actor, producer, and dramatist in his own right, Granville-Barker's *Prefaces to Shakespeare* contain some important directions as to the 'reading' of Shakespeare – not least because their author is concerned with the stage realisations of the drama and its practical workings.

***

Continuing along Adam Street, the next but one turning to the right is Robert Street. Here, just inside the street, to the right, will be found the buildings – marked with a blue plaque – occupied at different times by Thomas Hood (1799-1845), John Galsworthy (1867-1933), and James Barrie (1860-1937).

Hood, chiefly remembered for his humorous verses, lived in this building for the two years from 1828.

Sir James Barrie, however, was in long residence – from 1911 until the year of his death. By the time he took up residence in Robert Street, on the top floor of the building, he had already achieved distinction for his dramas – three of the most enduring of which remain *The Admirable Crichton* (1902), *What Every Woman Knows* (1908) and, of course, *Peter Pan* (1904).

Galsworthy's occupation covers the years 1917-18. He and his wife had returned to England from Mantouret in the French alps where they had served as volunteers in a British hospital for wounded French soldiers; Galsworthy as masseur and bathman, his wife, Ada, in charge of the linen. During the winter following their return Galsworthy was offered a knighthood, but the letter containing the offer never arrived. The prime minister therefore hastily telegraphed Galsworthy, seeking his permission. Galsworthy declined the offer, but too late to prevent his name appearing on the published Honours List.

Among those who offered their congratulations was Thomas Hardy, to whom Galsworthy then sent a letter of explanation. Hardy's reply was wry indeed:

> I don't think that mistake about the knighthood a disaster for you exactly, and probably you don't by this time. A friend of mine who happened to be here at the time said: 'He has scored both ways. He has had the honour of being knighted, and the honour of having refused a knighthood. Many men would envy him'.

The buildings (Nos 1-3 inclusive) associated with these literary figures are the original Adam design.

***

At the foot of Robert Street, Adelphi Terrace leads off to the left. The original Adelphi (from the Greek *adelphoi*, for brothers), the complex of terraced houses built over streets and riverside vaults and designed by the Adam brothers, was completed in the early 1770s. At the far end of the terrace, set into one of the pillars of the present, modern building, there is a stone inscription to remind the reader of some of the occupants of the original Adams' homes which were demolished 1936-8.

Topham Beauclerk (1739-80) lived in the Terrace, at No 3, for the years 1772-6. Beauclerk, a scholarly, genial man, was a good friend of Dr Johnson, was indeed particularly and warmly liked by the Doctor, and was well known to the Johnsonian circle.

David Garrick (1717-79) also took out a lease on one of the houses, No 5, in the same year of 1772. The greatest actor of his age, Garrick was a lifelong friend of Johnson – the two of them having journeyed from Lichfield together, and Garrick having been a pupil at Johnson's short-lived school there. To his home at the Terrace came Johnson himself and most of the Johnsonian circle; including Boswell, Reynolds, Burney, and Burney's daughter Fanny, the novelist. Garrick died in the house, his widow surviving him by 43 years. A room from the Garrick home was reconstructed within the Victoria and Albert Museum.

The architect Sir Arthur Blomfield had offices in the Terrace in the 1860s, and for three of those years, 1864-7, Thomas Hardy (1840-1928) studied architecture there. Hardy then gladly returned to Dorchester. He liked London little, and the mud of the Thames less, claiming that his health had suffered as a result of the stench from the river.

From 1898 until 1929 George Bernard Shaw (1856-1950) and his wife had a suite of rooms at No 10 in the Terrace.

* * *

Beyond the pillars of the present building, Adam Street leads off back to the Strand where, turning to the right, within a short walk one passes the Savoy Theatre. The theatre was originally designed for Richard D'Oyly Carte (1844-1901) specifically for the staging of Gilbert and Sullivan's operas. Built in 1881, it was the first theatre in London to be lit by electricity.

One of the principal performers in these light operas at the theatre was George Grossmith (1847-1912). In addition to his role as entertainer Grossmith published two books of reminiscences and, together with his brother Walter Weedon Grossmith (1852-1919), wrote the comical *Diary of a Nobody* (1892). First serialised in *Punch* magazine, the *Diary* recounts the daily social, domestic, and business happenings of Mr Charles Pooter of The Laurels, Holloway.

* * *

A short distance past the theatre, also on the right-hand side of the Strand, there is a narrow entranceway to what was formerly Fountain Court. The entrance is marked on either side by inscriptions which recall the Fountain Tavern (frequented by Jonathan Swift) of the eighteenth century, and the Fountain Club – political opponents of Sir Robert Walpole – which met there.

In Fountain Court, however, was also located the home of William Blake (1757-1827) where he resided for the last six years of his life, and there died.

* * *

The facade of the Adelphi Terrace, photographed in 1913. Survey of London

George Grossmith, co-author of Diary of a Nobody.

A little further along the Strand, on the right, will be seen Savoy Street. A few yards into the street Savoy Hill leads off to the right, where the entrance to the Queen's Chapel to the Savoy will be found. (The Chapel is open to visitors on Tuesday to Friday each week between 11.30am and 3.30pm.)

Its title is a reminder of the manor house held here in the mid-thirteenth century by Peter, the future Count of Savoy, the uncle of Eleanor of Provence, wife of Henry III. By the middle of the following century the precincts of the Savoy were developed by Henry, 1st Duke of Lancaster, to include a mansion great hall, chapel, cloister, vegetable garden, and fish pond.

The Chapel, the whole interior of which was rebuilt in 1864-5 following a fire which left only the outer walls standing, was first dedicated in 1510. It replaced the fourteenth century Savoy Palace chapel which was destroyed in the Peasants' Revolt of 1381. Stained glass windows inside the present Chapel recall some of the history and personages associated both with the Chapel and with the Savoy Palace of which it was a part.

Among those featured are John of Gaunt and Geoffrey Chaucer. For in 1361 the palace was inherited by John of Gaunt, whose patronage Geoffrey Chaucer (1340?-1400) enjoyed, and whose sister-in-law, by Gaunt's third wife, he married, in the preceding chapel. Chaucer's *The Boke of the Duchesse* (1369) was written around the death of John of Gaunt's first wife, Blanche of Lancaster; and Gaunt himself features in Shakespeare's *Richard II*.

John of Gaunt also was a patron of John Wycliffe (1328-84), the first translator of the Bible into English, and a preacher at the chapel. Another preacher also celebrated is Thomas Fuller (1608-61), who was, for two periods of time canon and lecturer at the chapel. Fuller, author of *Church History of Britain* and *The Worthies of England* (which appeared after his death), packed the church with his sermons – though they were not to the liking of Samuel Pepys.

Richard D'Oyly Carte (see above), too, is featured in one of the stained glass windows.

It is most likely that John Donne (1572-1631) in 1601 married secretly Anne More in the Chapel Royal for which, when discovered, he was sent to the Fleet prison (see: Ludgate, St Paul's and Aldersgate).

Somewhere within the old palace precincts lived John Lyly (1554?-1606), poet and playwright; George Wither (1588-1667), Cavalier poet, whose last years were spent within the Savoy; and John Cleland (1709-89), remembered for his novel *Fanny Hill*, and for his award of an annuity from the Privy Council 'on his engaging to write nothing more of the same description'.

* * *

From the Chapel, returning to the Strand and turning right across Lancaster Place, will be seen the massive building of Somerset House, until 1973 the offices of the General Register of Births, Deaths, and Marriages, and a fine example of late-eighteenth century classical architecture. It replaced the original palace of 1547-50 in which were frequently performed masques by Ben Jonson, Inigo Jones, and others.

A little further along the Strand, leading off to the right, will be found Surrey Street. Charles Dickens's David Copperfield records that:

> There was an old Roman bath in those days at the bottom of one of the streets out of the Strand – it may

be there still – in which I have had many a cold plunge. (*David Copperfield*, ch.xxxv)

The bath is indeed still there. Down Surrey street, and off to the right, will be found Surrey Steps at the foot of which – again to the right – the bath may be viewed through a window, and may be illuminated by an external switch. The ascription 'Roman' to the bath, however, has not been universally accepted by archaeologists – and its first known mention dates only from 1784.

* * *

Further still along the Strand, more or less opposite the rear end of the church of St Clement Danes which occupies its own island in the Strand at this point, Essex Street leads off to the right. The street name is a reminder that here once stood Essex House, the great Tudor building of the Earl of Essex, favourite of Queen Elizabeth I. Essex was also the patron of Edmund Spenser (1552-99). Spenser served in Essex's household here before leaving for Ireland; and here he began composing *The Faerie Queen*.

New Essex Hall here, head church of the Unitarian movement, carries a plaque to Henry Fielding (1707-54), playwright and novelist, who resided briefly in this street as a young man.

In Essex Street itself stands the Edgar Wallace public house, so named in 1975 to celebrate the centenary of the birth of the writer of crime and detective novels. The pub occupies the site of an old inn, known as the Essex Head Tavern. In the latter years of his life the inn was regularly patronised by Dr Johnson (1709-84) and some of his associates.

In the eighteenth century this eastern end of the Strand was a popular location for coffee houses – and for thieves and prostitutes also. Here Johnson and Boswell were on one occasion accosted by one of the latter. 'No, no, my girl. It won't do', was the Doctor's rebuff. One of the notorious robbers in the area was Tom Cox (caught finally and hanged at Tyburn) – who would seek refuge in nearby St Clement Danes, disguised as an old man.

* * *

From Essex Street cross to St Clement Danes itself. The founding church of wood was replaced – probably at the turn of the tenth to eleventh century – with a stone building, the remains of the tower of which were incorporated into the present church. That stone church, pulled down in 1679, was replaced with a design of Sir Christopher Wren's.

Sir Charles Sedley (1639?-1701) was baptized in the former stone church. Sedley, renowned by the society of the day for his wit, achieved notoriety for his profligate and licentious living, and a literary reputation for some of his lyric poems and songs.

A man of very different character and attainments also baptized there was Anthony Ashley Cooper, 3rd Earl of Shaftesbury (1671-1713). His collection of essays, *Characteristics of Men, Manners, Opinions, Times* (1711), with its insistence upon respect for others, integrity, and virtue, greatly influenced the moral tone of debate for the eighteenth century.

Anne, the wife of John Donne (see above), with whom Donne had fallen in love when she was sixteen, was buried in the previous church (1617).

Buried in the Wren church was George Granville,

The Savoy in 1560, after an etching by Hollar.

Lord Lansdowne (1666-1735), a friend of Alexander Pope and himself a poet and critic.

Nathaniel Lee (1653?-1692), who turned to the writing of plays having failed as an actor, was buried here. Lee lost his reason completely and for five years was confined in Bedlam. He escaped his keepers, recovered sanity enough to produce a final play, before becoming mad once more and perishing.

Thomas Otway (1652-85) similarly began, unsuccessfully, on the stage before turning to the writing of dramas. He died a destitute, and he too was buried here.

Dr Samuel Johnson (see above) regularly attended services in St Clement Danes where his manner, as noted by Boswell on the occasion of Good Friday 1773, was 'solemnly devout'. Johnson's seat was No 18, close to the pulpit in the north (or left, on entry) gallery. A brass plate on a nearby pillar records the fact.

Outside the church at its far, or eastern, end, stands a bronze statue (1910) of the Doctor sculpted by Percy Fitzgerald. The statue certainly conveys something of the powerful build of the man, as well as the somewhat coarse ugliness of feature remarked on by his contemporaries, and represented visually by Reynolds and Barry. To the front of the pedestal on which the statute stands is a bronze plaque of James Boswell, with another of Mrs Thrale to one side.

The interior of the Wren church was gutted in the bombings of 1941, its reconstruction completed in 1958, and a new peal of bells installed in 1957. Though the rhyme 'the bells of St Clement's' is commonly associated with the church – and oranges and lemons are still handed out to children at a special service in March of each year – it is possible that the church to which the rhyme should properly be attached is actually St Clement's, Eastcheap (close by the wharves at which citrus fruits from the Mediterranean were unloaded).

* * *

The tour may be ended here, by returning along the Strand to the Aldwych underground station; alternatively one may continue on to the Covent Garden tour by crossing over the Strand towards the Royal Courts of Justice, facing St Clement Danes. Then retrace a few steps along the Strand until Aldwych opens up on the right, following this around, and crossing over Kingsway. Where Drury Lane then emerges on the right, further directions will be found in the Covent Garden section.

A riverfront view of the classical late eighteenth century Somerset House.

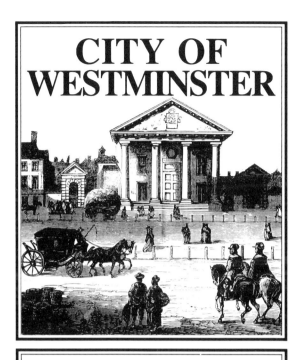

COVENT GARDEN

CITY OF WESTMINSTER

This tour of Covent Garden begins at the Aldwych underground station. There are several possibilities here. To proceed directly upon the tour of Covent Garden itself, cross the Strand from the Aldwych station exit, finding Melbourne Place, more or less directly opposite. Turn then to the left, along Aldwych, continuing just beyond Kingsway, where Dury Lane will be seen to open up on the far side of the street. Follow directions (below) from this point. Alternatively, if one intends to make this tour immediately following the tour gathered within The Strand section, cross the Strand at St Clement Danes (where that tour ends) and head back along the street until, a little distance on, the Aldwych leads off to the north and west. Within a couple of minutes' walk, circling the Aldwych and crossing over Kingsway, Drury Lane leads off to the right. Then follow the directions (below) from this point. A third possibility – again starting at the Aldwych underground station – would be to follow the later entries gathered in The Strand section (from Surrey Street onwards, p118), up to and including the visit to St Clement Danes, thereafter following the same route to Drury Lane detailed immediately above.

* * *

All three options arrive at the junction of Drury Lane with Aldwych. Here, shortly into Drury Lane, Tavistock Street opens to the left, with Catherine Street the first turning to the right.

On the right here is the Theatre Royal, the fourth playhouse on this site to carry the title. All have been known popularly as the Drury Lane theatre after the original building whose entrance actually did open upon the Lane.

The first theatre was built for Thomas Killigrew (1612-83), who had been in exile with the future Charles II. Upon the Restoration the king granted Killigrew a patent to form a company of actors to be known as the King's Men. The theatre opened in May 1663 with a performance of Beaumont and Fletcher's *The Humorous Lieutenant*. Two years later Nell Gwynn made her acting debut at the theatre in Dryden's *The Indian Queen*. In 1672 the theatre burned down, replaced by a larger design of Sir Christopher Wren.

The second theatre opened in 1674, joining forces with its London rivals, the Lincoln's Inn Fields company of actors, in 1682. Colley Cibber (1671-1757), himself an actor as well as poet and playwright – later to be attacked by Pope and made the hero of the *Dunciad* – became one of the managers of the theatre from 1711.

David Garrick (1717-79) made his first appearance on stage at the second Drury Lane Theatre in 1742, a few years later becoming one of its partners. When he retired in 1776, Richard Brinsley Sheridan (1751-1816) took over as manager, and the year following his *School for Scandal* was produced at the theatre.

The theatre, having been declared unsafe, was pulled down in 1791, its replacement opening three years later. In 1809 it, like the very first Drury Lane Theatre, burned down. News of the disaster was carried to Sheridan in the House of Commons where he was attending an important debate. Sheridan declined a suggested adjournment to the debate, observing that 'whatever might be the extent of an individual calamity, he did not consider it of a nature worthy to interrupt their proceedings on so great a national question'. When Sheridan did leave the House he went to the Piazza Coffee House in Covent

The front of the old Drury Lane Theatre.

Fielding had returned to the study of Law upon the passing of the Licensing Act of 1737 which made it impossible to stage a play unless it had first been approved by the Lord Chamberlain. The passing of this Act was in large measure consequent upon the performances of Fielding's own *Historical Register for the Year 1736*, a forceful satire of Walpole, Prime Minister of the day.

By the time Fielding, called to the Bar in 1740, took up office at Bow Street, *Joseph Andrews* (1742) had signalled his move towards novel-writing, the stage being more or less denied him. In the year of publication of that work his wife died, and four years later Fielding married her maid and children's nurse. Whilst living at Bow Street (which was home as well as office and court), Fielding completed work on *Tom Jones* (1749) – the model for Sophia being supplied by his first wife.

As a magistrate Fielding combatted crime with the same zeal and dedication that characterised his literary attacks upon hypocrisy, vanity, and pretence. He refused all bribes, produced reforming pamphlets, and established a volunteer group of six men as 'thief-takers', the originals of what were later, at the turn of the century, to be known as the Bow Street Runners. For, from its fashionable

Henry Fielding.

Garden, whence he could see clearly the flames. There he took a glass of port and, when asked how he could be so calm, replied: 'A man may surely be allowed to take a glass of wine by his own fireside'.

A new theatre, the one which stands there today, was built in the years 1811-12; the portico and colonnade added in later years.

* * *

Beyond the theatre, Russell Street crosses Catharine Street. To the left here, just a few yards along, Bow Street leads off to the right.

On the left-hand side of Bow Street, at what was No 4, stood the original Bow Stret Magistrates' Court (which later also occupied offices at No 3, alongside), a building pulled down in 1887. The location is now part of the car park alongside the Opera House.

Established by Thomas de Veil in 1740, the second magistrate of the court was Henry Fielding (1707-54) who served here from 1747 until the year of his death. After two years Fielding's blind half-brother, John, joined him as assistant at Bow Street, taking over the post upon Henry's death.

The second Covent Garden Theatre, at which both Sarah Siddons and Edmund Kean played. It burned down in 1856, to be replaced with the present building.

beginnings, Covent Garden had become notorious for its crimes of theft and murder. Of the geography of the region Fielding himself wrote of its crowded streets and narrow passageways that 'the whole appears as a vast wood or forest, in which a thief may harbour with as great security as wild beasts do in the deserts of Africa or Arabia'.

Just beyond this location, and on the same side of the street, stands the Royal Opera House, the third theatre to occupy this site. The present building, designed by E. M. Barry, opened in 1858, though it has undergone a huge extension programme in the 1980s.

The first Covent Garden Theatre opened in 1732 with a revival of Congreve's *The Way of the World*. The first owner, John Rich, had made his fortune at the Lincoln's Inn Fields Theatre where he had produced with immense success John Gay's *The Beggar's Opera* (1728). Wits declared that the opera had made Gay rich and Rich gay.

In this original theatre was first performed Oliver Goldsmith's *She Stoops to Conquer* in March 1773.

Goldsmith was himself so nervous about the reception of his play that at its premiere he invited several of his literary friends with the express command that they should clap the performance – whilst he could not bring himself to view the production until the last act.

In January 1775 Sheridan's *The Rivals* made its first appearance at the Covent Garden Theatre.

Extensively developed in 1792 the theatre burned down in 1808, its replacement opening just one year later. Among the famous actors and actresses associated with these two theatres was Peg Woffington (1714?-60). The daughter of an Irish bricklayer, her first appearance on the stage here, in 1740, was a sensational success. Her amours were numerous, and her lovers included David Garrick, with whom she lived for some time. Peg Woffington specialised in playing male roles, to the extent that she once remarked that half of the town must think her a man; to which was returned the waggish reply, 'Madam, the other half *knows* you to be a woman!' She is remembered too for the unscripted incident during a performance of Nathaniel Lee's *The Rival Queens*. Having previously quarrelled with the actress Mrs Bellamy, Peg Woffington chased her from the stage and stabbed her. Another incident from her life, in which she ended the affair between herself and a recently-married gentleman of wealth, formed the basis of Charles Reade's novel *Peg Woffington* (1853).

Charles Macklin (1697?-1797), whose most celebrated role was that of Shakespeare's Shylock, forgot the lines of that role in a production of the play in 1789. By then into his nineties, Macklin had to be led from the stage.

Mrs Sarah Siddons (1755-1831), whose reputation was that of a great tragedy queen, made her farewell stage performance at the theatre in June 1812. And in 1833 Edmund Kean (1789-1833), one of the greatest tragic actors, suffered a stroke during a performance of *Othello* and had to be carried from the stage.

The present building, home to the Royal Opera Company, is now famous throughout the world for its staging of expansive opera productions, and has been the venue for a number of premieres of the works of leading modern composers.

***

Returning to the junction of Bow Street with Russell Street, on the right-hand corner will be found No 21 Russell Street – for some part of its history also sometimes referred to as No 1 Bow Street. Once there stood here Will's Coffee House, established sometime after the Restoration. The chief attraction here was John Dryden (1631-1700), whose patronage gathered a collection of writers, critics and men of wit around him. By their presence the shop became known therefore as the Wits' coffee house. Though the first visit of Samuel Pepys (1633-1703) to the coffee house was brief – he had to leave in order to collect his wife as pre-arranged – he was impressed with the 'very pleasant and witty discourse' which he there experienced, resolving to make other returns. William Wycherly (1641-1715), out of compassion for his appearance and his circumstances, he said, introduced Alexander Pope (1688-1744) to the company at Will's; and both Sir Richard Steele (1672-1729), in the *Tatler*, and

The house in Russell Street in which Thomas Davies first introduced James Boswell to Dr Johnson.

Joseph Addison (1672-1719), in the *Spectator*, referred to Will's.

Later visitors included Dr Johnson and his friends David Garrick and Sir Joshua Reynolds.

The corner site occupied by the coffee house included No 20 Russell Street, later occupied for six years from 1817 by Charles Lamb (1775-1834) and his sister, Mary (1764-1847). Charles here composed some of the *Essays of Elia*, and wrote of this location as 'the individual spot I like best in all this great city' – for the theatres and for the variety of life surrounding them.

On the opposite side of Russell Street at this junction will be seen the entrance to the Theatre Museum (entrance to which is charged). The specialist exhibitions, of the Victoria and Albert Museum, housed here in the old Flower Market include a range of theatrical memorabilia, stage models, posters, prints and other materials. The museum covers all aspects of the stage; ballet, mime, opera, and circus, as well as theatre.

A few yards beyond the museum entrance, on

the same side of the road, is No 8 Russell Street – the original house where James Boswell (1740-95) made his first acquaintance with Dr Johnson (1709-84), unexpectedly, after having resolved with himself that he should meet the great man. On 16 May 1763 Boswell went to visit Thomas Davies, who had not long previously set up as a bookseller at the address. They were in the back parlour when the Doctor arrived in the shop:

> I drank tea at Davies's . . . and about seven came in the great Mr Samuel Johnson, whom I have so long wished to see. As I knew his mortal antipathy at the Scotch, I cried to Davies, 'Don't tell where I come from.' However, he said, 'From Scotland.' 'Mr Johnson,' said I, 'indeed I come from Scotland, but I cannot help it.' 'Sir,' replied he, 'that, I find, is what a very great many of your countrymen cannot help.' Mr Johnson is a man of a most dreadful appearance . . .

From this most unpromising beginning (as recorded in Boswell's *London Journal*), and from the simple entry 'I shall mark what I remember of his conversation', began Boswell's literary amensuensis that was to issue in the *magnum opus* of his *Life of Samuel Johnson*.

A blue plaque set at first floor level commemorates at this building one of the most significant of all literary encounters.

Two other famous coffee houses used to be located in Russell Street. On this same side of the street, a little towards the Garden, was Button's Coffee House. Daniel Button, formerly a member of the household staff at the Countess of Warwick's establishment, was set up in business by Joseph Addison (see above), who married the Dowager Duchess in 1716. Among those present at Button's literary meetings were Sir Richard Steele, Colley Cibber, Alexander Pope, Jonathan Swift and John Gay. Pope, however, quarrelled with Addison and Ambrose Philips (poet and essayist, 1675?-1749) and stopped frequenting the place; wisely, since Philips kept at the coffee house a rod with which he intended to whip Pope should he ever have turned up at Button's thereafter.

On the opposite side of the street was Tom's

Covent Garden in the middle of the seventeenth century.

Covent Garden Piazza, 1768; a view along the northern side towards the opening of Russell Street. At the extreme left of the picture is the entrance to the Shakespeare's Head Tavern, the Bedford Coffee House to its right.

Coffee House which, established in 1700, was certainly visited by Dr Johnson, David Garrick, and Sir Joshua Reynolds.

* * *

Ahead, at the end of Russell Street, opens up the square of Covent Garden itself. None of the houses built to the design of Inigo Jones now remains, and the entire character of the area is radically altered from Jones's original grand plan. In this, the central square was lined by houses, completed by 1639, whose front doors opened on to a vaulted arcade, providing a covered walkway. This walkway, rather than the square itself, was the original *piazza*, where its fashionable seventeenth century inhabitants could promenade. By the eighteenth century its residential status had declined – accelerated by the development of the market – and numerous gambling dens, taverns, and coffee houses had opened in the area.

On the east side of the square (to the right on entering from Russell Street) once stood, for example, the Bedford Coffee House – a favourite meeting-place for those who had attended performances at Drury Lane and Covent Garden theatres. Among its literary clientèle were David Garrick, Henry Fielding, Oliver Goldsmith, Richard Brinsley Sheridan, Alexander Pope, William Collins and Horace Walpole.

Next door to the Bedford, located in the corner of the square, was sited another popular gathering-place, the Shakespeare's Head Tavern. From here, his spirits and expectations having been raised, but finally disappointed after two hours in the company of a Miss Watts, James Boswell (see above) 'sallied forth to the Piazzas in rich flow of animal spirits and burning with fierce desire'. There he met 'two very pretty little girls' whom he invited to join him in a room at the Shakespeare's Head. After some 'amorous play' – toying, drinking, singing – he 'solaced [his] existence with them, one after the other, according to their seniority.'

Along the northern, or far, side of the square, in the original house sited in the corner, lived for many years the artist and engraver William Hogarth (1697-1764), whose graphic and sometimes savage works provide searing satires of the life and morals of the eighteenth century. Next door lived Charles Macklin (see above), the actor; and in the house alongside, one of several of her London addresses, lived for some time Lady Mary Wortley Montagu (1689-1762), letter-writer and one-time friend of Alexander Pope. Beyond the Montagu residence was the home of Thomas Killigrew (see above), dramatist and theatre manager.

As you walk along the northern, or top, side of the square, just beyond James Street, you will come to Bedford Chambers. Built in the last quarter of the nineteenth century, they imitate the original Inigo Jones's houses, and give a fair indicator of how the portico would have looked when it encompassed the whole square.

* * *

Further along the north side of Covent Garden you will enter King Street. On the left-hand side will be seen no.10, where Samuel Taylor Coleridge (1772-1834) lived during the years 1801-2. Coleridge's condition at this period of his life – the failing of his 'genial spirits', the disaster of his marriage, the accelerating sense of his own failure – found their poetic embodiment in that plaint of regret 'Dejection: an Ode' (1802).

On the right-hand side of King Street, at the first-floor level of No 31, there is mounted a blue plaque to Thomas Arne (1710-78), composer, who was born in this house and spent his boyhood there. Arne's literary connections include his musical composition for Milton's *Comus*, and his settings of many of Shakespeare's songs.

* * *

Shortly beyond the Arne house Garrick Street leads off to the right; and just twenty yards along here the narrow alleyway of Rose Street opens to the right, taking a dog-leg turn first to the left and then to the right.

In this alleyway John Dryden (see above) was set upon and beaten almost unconscious by three masked ruffians on the night of 18 December 1679, as he returned from Will's Coffee House (see above) to his home in Long Acre. Fortunately Dryden's cries roused some of the residents, and the assailants made off. The attack, almost certainly, was instigated and paid for by John Wilmot, Earl of Rochester (1647-80), who thought, wrongly, Dryden the author of a piece which had satirised him.

Somewhere in Rose Street Samuel Butler (1663-78), author of the long poem *Hudibras*, a satire on the Puritans, died in poverty in lodgings.

* * *

Rose Street emerges at Long Acre. Almost directly facing the exit, now occupied by No 137 Long Acre, stood Dryden's house; his home for about eighteen years from 1669.

After turning to the left, fifty yards ahead opens up on the right Upper St Martin's Lane. Another fifty or so yards along this street, West Street enters from the left. By following West Street around to the right, immediately beyond St Martin's Theatre and the Ambassadors (both of which are on the right-hand side) will be seen a blue plaque set into the wall reminding readers that on this site formerly stood the West Street Chapel. Here both John (1703-91) and Charles Wesley (1707-88) were frequent preachers; and are remembered also for their contribution to the language of some of the best-known and most-loved of English hymns.

* * *

West Street connects with Shaftesbury Avenue, which leads off to the right. Within two or three minutes' walk along the Avenue, St Giles High Street opens up on the left. Here, a short distance along, will be found the church of St Giles-in-the-Fields.

St Giles's church traces its history back to 1101 when a hospital for lepers was founded by Matilda, Queen of Henry I, at whose behest also prisoners being transported to their execution at Tyburn were given a 'Cup of Charity'. The chapel of the hospital became a parish church in 1547. The building was pulled down in 1624, to be replaced by another consecrated in 1630. A century later this church too was pulled down, the present building opening for worship in 1734. Some alterations to the interior have taken place, and the gold-leaf ceiling has recently been cleaned, restoring once more its high brilliance.

Not far from the gate of the church was 'hung and burnt hanging' Sir John Oldcastle in 1417. The leader of the Lollards he was tried for treason and heresy – the heresy being the desire to possess the Bible in the English language. Oldcastle provided the 'model' for

Shakespeare's Sir John Falstaff, whom Shakespeare had originally named Oldcastle. The reference to 'My old lad of the castle' remains in *Henry IV, Part One*, though the threat of a libel action from Oldcastle's descendents compelled Shakespeare to change the name.

To the left of the entrance to the church stands a memorial, believed to have been designed by Inigo Jones, to 'Georgius Chapman. Poeta. MDCXXXIV', who was buried in the preceding church. George Chapman (b. 1559), a contemporary of Shakespeare and very possibly the 'rival poet' of Shakespeare's *Sonnets*, was renowned as a scholar as well as a poet and dramatist. Chapman's difficult and obscure work *The Shadow of Night* (1594) lent its title to that group of advanced thinkers known as the 'School of Night', whose members included Chapman's friends Sir Walter Ralegh and Christopher Marlowe. Also celebrated were Chapman's translations of Homer's *Iliad* and *Odyssey*, the latter of which prompted one of Keats's finest sonnets 'Much have I travelled in the realms of gold . . .' ('On First Looking into Chapman's Homer').

Further along the north (left-hand) aisle of the church is mounted the memorial inscription to

George Chapman.

Andrew Marvell (1621-78) who was buried 'Near unto this place . . .' From 1659 until his death Marvell was a member of Parliament for Hull, and served as secretary to English embassies in Russia, Sweden and Denmark. His lyric verse seems to have been completed for the most part by the time he reached his early thirties, after which he produced mainly satirical verse and prose writings. The poems, whose characteristic though not sole measure of composition was the octosyllabic line, display compression, a sense of solidness, and wit. This latter quality, in his essay on Andrew Marvell (1921), T. S. Eliot described as 'a tough reasonableness beneath the slight lyric grace' – qualities evidenced in the 'Dialogue' and 'Mower' poems, 'The Definition of Love', and others, including the magnificent poem of persuasive seduction 'To his Coy Mistress'. The lengthy memorial inscription provides a summation. It speaks of the 'joining' of Marvell's 'most peculiar graces of wit and learning with a singular penetration, and strength of judgement . . .'

Beyond the Marvell memorial there stands in the aisle the top deck of the three-tier pulpit from the West Street chapel, from which John and Charles Wesley (see above) both preached regularly for well over forty years.

A number of other literary associations attach to the church of St Giles-in-the-Fields. Colley Cibber (see above), poet and playwright, was baptised in the earlier church. Cibber's pedestrian poetic and dramatic abilities incurred the jealousies and resentments of other writers upon his appointment as Poet Laureate in 1730.

John Milton's daughter, Mary, was also baptised at St Giles, in 1687. Milton (1608-74) was a parishioner of the church between the years of 1647 and 1649. Two of the children of Percy Bysshe Shelley (1792-1822) and Harriet Westbrook, together with Allegra, the illegitimate daughter of Lord Byron (1788-1824) were all baptised in the same service of 1818.

David Garrick (see above), Dr Johnson's former pupil, here married Eva Maria Violetti, a dancer, in 1749.

James Shirley (1596-1666), dramatist, was buried in the former church. He and his wife died of shock and exposure caused by the Great Fire, and were buried in the same grave.

* * *

From St Giles, returning along St Giles High Street and Shaftesbury Avenue into West Street, you will pass Litchfield Street on the right. Somewhere along this Street Thomas de Quincey (1785-1859) lodged during his early days in London.

West Steet joins with Upper St Martin's Lane where, a short distance along, there is a confluence of roads with Garrick Street opening up on the left. On the right-hand side of Garrick Street stands the Garrick Club. The Club, founded in 1831, moved to this location in 1864 from its first premises in nearby King Street. Since its inception the club has been a meeting-place for many actors, playwrights, and other men connected with the theatre. The club also houses a fine collection of theatrical portraits.

Beyond the turning into Garrick Street, continuing along St Martin's Lane, New Row turns off to the left. In not much more than a hundred yards, Bedford Street opens on the right. Fifty yards into the street, opposite the entrance to Henrietta Street, stood the house of Thomas Sheridan (1719-88), elocutionist, and father of the playwright Richard Brinsley Sheridan (see above). On the corner of Bedford Street and Henrietta Street – the left-hand corner looking along Henrietta Street – was formerly sited in Castle tavern. Here Richard Brinsley Sheridan completed the duel with Captain Matthews which had begun in Hyde Park, and then had transferred to this location, where it ended with Sheridan's disarming of Matthews, after the two duellists had badly cut each other. The duel was occasioned by a remark which Matthews had passed on Elizabeth Linley, a singer, and daughter of Thomas Linley, composer for the Drury Lane Theatre. It was one of several duels Sheridan fought over the lady, with whom he eventually eloped. Much of the experience was later fashioned by Sheridan as the material for his comedy *The Rivals*.

***

In Henrietta Street itself, on the right-hand side, will be found No 10. Formerly the premises of the bankers Austen, Maunde and Tilson, here Jane Austen (1775-1817) stayed for several months from 1813 into the following year whilst visiting her brother, Henry.

Two doors beyond, at No 8, once resided the actress Frances Maria Kelly – to whom Charles Lamb (see above) sent a letter proposing marriage. He received from her a letter, by return on the same day, refusing his offer.

On the left-hand side of the street there is a gateway entrance into the gardens of St Paul's Church, Covent Garden. The church itself, associated from its earliest days with the theatre, is now often referred to simply as 'the actors' church'.

Jones's original church, completed in 1633, underwent major renovations towards the end of the eighteenth century, most of which work was destroyed by fire in 1795. The church was restored once more, and underwent some alterations in the nineteenth century.

Baptised in the church were Lady Mary Wortley Montagu (see above), letter-writer, one-time friend of Alexander Pope, and a noted wit in her own right; and W. S. Gilbert (1836-1911), author of the *Babs Ballads*, and renowned as the librettist of the Savoy comic operas.

Buried just outside the church (his feet 'touching the wall', it is recorded) was Samuel Butler (see above). Also buried in St Paul's were: William Wycherley (see above), dramatist, whose comedies trade in the stage manners and morals of the Restoration period; Charles Macklin (see above), actor; Thomas Arne (see above), composer; and Thomas Davies (1712-85), actor and bookseller, who introduced Boswell to Dr Johnson.

Around the walls of the church will be found many scores of memorials to famous actors and actresses, playwrights, and others who have been associated with the theatre – and many celebrated too for their work in film and television.

The ashes of Ellen Terry (1847-1928) are housed in a silver urn on the south wall of the church, at the altar end; also on the south wall will be found the monument (most frequently described in the epithet 'gruesome') of Charles Macklin (see above).

***

Returning to Henrietta Street from the church and continuing towards the square of Covent Garden, the front (portico) end of St Paul's comes into view.

In his design, Jones intended the church to face the square of Covent Garden; but that would have meant placing the altar in the west end of the church, a design which was not permitted. So the east end of the church, beneath the columned portico, is actually a blind wall. George Bernard Shaw (1856-1950) made this portico the setting, in the opening act of *Pygmalion*, for the encounter between Eliza Doolittle and Professor Higgins. Subsequently, both in the filmed version of *Pygmalion* and of *My Fair*

Lady (the musical derived from Shaw's play), the church portico was featured.

The Earl of Bedford, who had commissioned Inigo Jones to design the church, told the architect that he would not, however, 'go to any considerable expense', adding, 'In short, I would not have it much better than a barn'. Jones, in his reply, promised that Bedford would have 'the handsomest barn in England'. From the square one can clearly see there is indeed some truth in that so far as the external design goes.

* * *

David Garrick.

Beyond the church, Southampton Street turns off to the right. On the left-hand side of the street, at No 17, stood the house which was the birthplace of W. S. Gilbert (see above).

A little further into Southampton Street, on the opposite side, will be seen No 27, with a plaque at first-floor level to remind viewers that this was the home of David Garrick (see above). He lived here from 1749, the year of his marriage to Eva Marie Violetti, until 1772. His wife wrote of the house, the lease to which cost 500 guineas, that '*Dirt* and all, 'tis reckoned a very good Bargain'. During all of this residency Garrick was himself involved in the management of the Drury Lane Theatre.

A few yards beyond the Garrick House, Maiden Lane opens on the right where, a little way in and on the left-hand side, will be found a plaque recording the lodging 'near this spot' of the French writer and *philosophe* Voltaire (François Marie Arouet, 1694-1778). Exiled from Paris, having been twice imprisoned in the Bastille, Voltaire spent the three years from 1726 in England. For part of 1727 and of the following year Voltaire stayed at the White Whig Inn, at approximately this site, No 9. Here he was visited by a number of literary persons, including Alexander Pope and William Congreve.

The same site was earlier the location for the house where Andrew Marvell (see above) lived for the last year or so of his life. At this house he received a visit from Charles II's Lord Treasurer offering him patronage on behalf of the King. Marvell, though he needed financial support, refused the offer in order to hold true to his parliamentary convictions.

* * *

Continuing along Maiden Lane, crossing Bedford Street into Chandos Place and bearing to the right, is William IV Street. Just ahead stands the statue (1910) of Sir Henry Irving (1838-1905), the first actor to receive a knighthood. To Irving's acting is attributed a good measure of the revival of popular interest in Shakespeare. Stage manager to Irving for a number of years was an Irishman, Bram Stoker (1847-1912), the author of *Dracula* – the horror story which has spawned dozens of cinematographic versions borrowing from his creation.

On the far side of the road (St Martin's Place) is the entrance to the National Portrait Gallery. The present building, housing some nine thousand portraits, was opened in April 1896. Founded forty years previously, to display 'the most Eminent Persons in British History', among those portraits on show are many of literary interest.

The gallery is now arranged chronologically, from the top floor down, from the Tudor age through to the twentieth century. The selection criteria have always concentrated on the significance of the person portrayed, rather than on the excellence of the painter – though there are many instances where the two have united. These include the portrait of Sir Thomas More by Holbein; Disraeli by Millais; Sir

Winston Churchill by Sickert; T. S. Eliot by Epstein.

Other portraits, by lesser or unknown artists, are of no less significance. Here, for example, may be seen the 'Chandos portrait' of William Shakespeare. Thought to have belonged at one time to the poet and playwright William D'Avenant (who himself probably fostered the notion that he was Shakespeare's illegitimate child), the portrait dates from about 1610. It is the only portrait of Shakespeare to have any credible claim to having been painted from life.

Similarly the uncompleted drawing of Jane Austen, by her sister Cassandra, is the only portrait of her to have been made from the life.

The full list of literary persons represented in the Gallery is far too extensive to cite here – but the visitor's appetite may be whetted at mention of just a few from the total. These would include: John Milton ('drawne very well and like when a Cambridge schollar'); Samuel Pepys (of the sittings for which he recorded: 'I . . . do almost break my neck looking over my shoulders to make the pose'); Alexander Pope (a profile view); Dr Samuel Johnson (by James Barry – a powerful and arresting study); James Boswell; William Blake (whose 'rapt poetic expression' Thomas Phillips's portrait is said to have captured well); John Keats; the three Brontë sisters (by their brother Branwell); Henry James; Thomas Hardy (made when Hardy was in his fifties, this portrait by William Strang strongly expresses a downcast melancholy); James Joyce (who at his own insistance was not portrayed full face).

Since quite clearly the Gallery cannot display at any one time all of its acquisitions – which now include a large photographic collection – any portrait may be seen on request.

* * *

On leaving the Gallery, to the right and opposite will be seen the church of St Martin-in-the-Fields. One of a succession of churches to have stood on this site, the present church dates from 1722-4. Christened in the preceding church was Francis Bacon (1561-1626) – who would appear to provide the one direct literary connection here. The church's history supplies other references at a remove; for among those buried in the church were Nell Gwynn (1687) and Sir Joshua Reynolds (1762).

Alongside the church, running back to the Strand, is Duncannon Street, where a subway entrance leads to Charing Cross station and the Embankment underground.

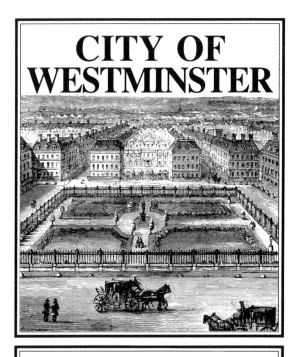

CITY OF WESTMINSTER

SOHO

CITY OF WESTMINSTER

Until well into the seventeenth century this area of London was still open hunting fields. Its naming remains something of an unresolved mystery. The most usual explanation argues that its name derives from the hunting-cry 'Soe Hoe' – denoting that the fox had been found. Variations of 'So Ho' appear in rate books of the early seventeenth century. An inscription of 'Souhou', however, found on a fourteenth century seal, is also argued to be the origin of the name.

Towards the end of the seventeenth century the open spaces had begun to be filled in. Development and building proceeded rapidly – led by established landowners and by speculators alike.

By Victorian times the cramped streets of Soho had established its reputation for prostitution – a reputation, or notoriety, which it has retained. Many prostitutes then lived in comfortably furnished apartments, whilst in the small courts around Leicester Square the trade was offered in less reputable surrounds. Here gaslights burned dimly through the drawn blinds, and notices over the doors carried the legend: 'Beds are to be had within'.

The area also suffered from the insanitary conditions of the times, and epidemics of cholera were frequent. By the mid-nineteenth century the middle classes of Soho began to organise themselves to make public their anxieties. The following letter, carrying fifty-four signatures, appeared in *The Times* of 5 July 1849:

> Sur,
>   May we beg and beseech your proteckshion and power. We are Sur, as it may be, livin in a Wilderniss, so far as the rest of London knows anything of us, or as the rich and great people care about. We live in muck and filthe. We aint got no privez, no dust bins, no drains, no water splies, and no drain or suer in the whole place. The Suer Company, in Greek Street, Soho Square, all great rich and powerfool men, take no notice watsomedever of our complaints. The Stenche of a Gullyhole is disgustin. We al of us suffur, and numbers are ill, and if the Colera comes Lord help us . . .

Five years after this letter was written there was indeed a serious outbreak of cholera, after which most of the remaining wealthy families moved away from the district.

Contemporary Soho has become a centre for a variety of entertainments, hosting theatres, cinemas and film companies, eating-houses by the score, public houses and clubs (including jazz clubs), shops and street markets – a crowded precinct of cosmopolitan hustle and bustle harbouring within the City of Westminster. It has long been a place of settlement for immigrants to London: French, Greeks, Germans, Italians, Cypriots, Chinese and Vietnamese, among others, have all at various times settled in the area. Here they could continue their various trades – making for a history which is manifestly reflected everywhere one looks today.

Soho also has its 'Bohemian' character and history – its pubs and clubs and regular haunts of innumerable writers and artists for several decades of this century. Among the pubs which can claim an especial place in this context is 'The French House' in Dean Street, opposite St Anne's church. Known formerly as 'The York Minster' it was referred to for many years simply as the 'French' or 'French's' after its owners, the Berlemonts, father then son (the latter having himself just retired). The most famous club is almost certainly 'The Colony Room', also in Dean Street. It, and its former owner Muriel Belcher, have passed into the literary and artistic folk-lore of the country. For one set of reminiscences, which includes these venues amongst others, readers might like to refer to Daniel Farson's *Soho in the Fifties* (1987).

And in Daniel Farson's phrase Soho remains what it always has been – 'a state of mind', not simply a location: an area of London where visitors will find something of interest wherever they wander.

* * *

From Leicester Square underground station (taking the Leicester Square exit) turn right into Cranbourn Street. Within a very short distance you will arrive at a corner of Leicester Square itself – its north-east corner.

In the middle of the gardens in the Square stands a statue of William Shakespeare; though much-photographed it is, one must say, wholly unconvincing. At the four corners of the gardens will also be found busts to four famous men who lived in the Square. Sir Joshua Reynolds (1723-92), painter and regular companion of Dr Johnson and his circle, lived at No 47 for the last thirty years of his life. Since demolished, his residence was on the right-hand (or west-side) of the Square as one faces the Shakespeare statue; the site of the house is marked with a commemorative plaque. (The site of another of Reynolds's houses will be found at No 5 Great Newport Street, at the confluence of six streets where Long Acre joins St Martin's Lane – just two minutes' walk away.) William Hogarth (1697-1764), whose engravings in particular have a very literary and emblematic design to them, lived in what was the second house on the left-hand (or east-side) of the Square. The surgeon Dr Hunter (1728-93) lived in the house which was alongside Hogarth's.

Sir Issac Newton (1642-1727) occupied a house just off the Square. On the far side of the Square (to the south) will be found St Martin's Street where, a little way in on the left, the site of his house is marked by a plaque. During the seventeen years he occupied the house he received many literary figures at his meetings there: they included Jonathan Swift, William Congreve, John Arbuthnot and Matthew Prior.

The genius of Newton as scientist has been attested to by every succeeding generation. Alexander Pope made him the following epitaph intended for

Sir Isaac Newton's house, later occupied by the Burneys.

the great man's memorial in Westminster Abbey:

Nature and Nature's Laws lay hid in Night.
God said, *Let Newton be*! and All was *Light*.

From 1774 to 1789 the house was rented by Dr Charles Burney, musician and music-teacher, for whom Dr Johnson always retained a very warm affection. During their time there the fourth of his nine children published anonymously her fiction *Evelina: or a Young Woman's Entrance into the World* (1778). Fanny Burney (1752-1840) wrote copiously throughout adolescence; but on her fifteenth birthday she made a bonfire of her writings. Among the papers was the draft of a novel which she later re-cast from memory to form the basis of *Evelina*. She confessed to the authorship of the book only after her father had heard it praised by his friends – including Dr Johnson. The contemporary reception of the work made it a huge success. It was a work which greatly delighted Dr Johnson himself as well as other critics of the day. Though her subsequent novels lack the liveliness of the original, her *Early Diary* (1768-78) has a freshness of observation, and a vivid portrayal of character. The recording of her first impression of Dr Johnson when he called upon the Burney household shows well her characteristic sense of detail:

> He is, indeed, very ill favoured; is tall and stout but stoops terribly; he is almost bent double. His mouth is almost continually opening and shutting as if he was chewing. He has a strange method of frequently twirling his fingers and twisting his hands. His body is in continual agitation, see-sawing up and down; and, in short, his whole person is in perpetual motion. His dress, too, considering the times, and that he had meant to put on his best becomes, being engaged to dine in a large company, was as much out of the common road as his figure; he had a large wig, snuff-colour coat, and gold buttons, but no ruffles to his shirt, doughty [dirty] fists, and black worsted stockings . . .

Despite this initial impression Fanny and the Doctor established a very warm relationship. Indeed she was one of the many friends who waited upon the Doctor in his final illness.

For five years, from 1786, Fanny Burney attended Queen Charlotte at court, a position she did not enjoy in the least. Shortly after her time at court she married a French nobleman, with whom she shared a happy companionship.

The building which presently occupies the site of the Newton house and Burney residence is the Central Reference Library of Westminster City Libraries, and is open to the public. On the second floor is housed a collection of books on the life and works of William Blake who for some years lodged at a house in Poland Street, just off Oxford Street (see later entry).

* * *

From Leicester Square, directly opposite the corner where one first entered (past the Swiss travel centre), Wardour Street leads off to the north. Within a few yards along here, on the right, Lisle Street opens up. Something like fifty yards into the street, on the left-hand side, used to stand the house (No 9) where Edmund Kean (1787-1833), who became the Shakespearian actor of his age, spent his boyhood. Here he was brought up by an uncle, his mother having deserted him.

Almost opposite this location, at the corner of the junction with Leicester Street, stand the buildings which previously formed the German Hotel, where Karl Marx (1818-83) first stayed on his arrival in England. The consequences of Marx's political philosophy have, of course, subsequently had their influence upon many areas of intellectual life and debate, including the literary-critical.

* * *

Returning to Wardour Street and a little further on in the same direction, heading north, will be found Gerrard Street. Today the street is filled with the restaurants, bakers, and supermarkets of London's 'Chinatown'. Though there are a number of literary associations with the street, only two are actually celebrated with a formal plaque.

A little way into the street, on the left-hand side, stands No 22 where James Boswell took lodgings in 1775-76. For the 'very neat' first floor he paid 'sixteen shillings per week'.

Further along the street, on the same side, occupied by No 16, there was a tavern at which a group of writers met prior to the First World War. Among them were John Masefield, W. H. Davies, Ford Madox Ford, Hilaire Belloc, G. K. Chesterton, Edward Thomas – and, occasionally, John Galsworthy and Joseph Conrad.

At No 10 Charles Dickens's uncle, Thomas Barrow, once lived in the upper part of the house. Though in the fiction Dickens transposed the house to the south, or opposite, side of the street, this is almost certainly the one which he had in mind for the residence of the lawer Mr Jaggers – whose habit was to wash 'his hands with scented soap' as he 'washed his clients off' . . . 'in the halo of scented soap which encircled his presence':

> Rather a stately house of its kind, but dolefully in want of painting, and with dirty windows . . . we all went into a stone hall, bare, gloomy, and little used. So, up a dark brown staircase into a series of three dark-brown rooms on the first floor . . .
>
> (*Great Expectations*, ch.xxvi)

The former No 9, next door, housed the Turk's Head Tavern. There under the aegis of Dr Johnson, met the 'Literary Club' founded by Sir Joshua Reynolds and whose original members included most prominently Oliver Goldsmith and Edmund Burke. Later, proposed by Dr Johnson, Richard Brinsley Sheridan was elected a member: 'He who has written the two best comedies of the age', said Johnson of him, 'is surely a considerable man.' James Boswell was elected a member in 1773. The formal letter proposing his membership, written by Dr Johnson, is on display in one of the rooms at 'Dr

Johnson's House', Gough Square. (See section: Fleet Street.)

The Club met here once a week for supper, and conversation (its express purpose) from 1764 until 1783.

Towards the far end of the street, and on the right-hand side, will be seen, above No 43, a plaque inscribed: JOHN DRYDEN POET LIVED HERE B.1631 D.1700. In fact the plaque is mis-placed, and was erected in error, for Dryden lived next door, at No 44, and died in the house, of gout and gangrene, having lived at the address for fourteen years. During these years he had to survive almost solely by the income from his pen – his habit being to do his writing in the room at ground level facing the street.

Just how pressed he was for money is shown by his contracting with the publisher Tonson for the work *Fables Ancient and Modern* for just 250 guineas. This large collection of Dryden's versions of tales found in Ovid, Chaucer and Boccaccio, together with original poems of his own, appeared just two months before Dryden's death.

During this last period of his life Dryden also produced his translation of the *Satires* of Juvenal and Persius and, between 1693 and 1697, his translation of the whole of Virgil. Having been deprived of all his official titles (including the Poet Laureateship), and the income therefore, Dryden was committed to the continuous toil of literary production – in the face of deteriorating health and, so his letters of the time reveal, the malice of his enemies.

Dryden had made enemies both by his espousal of causes and by his changing of sides in those causes. He had eulogised Cromwell; and welcomed the Restoration of Charles II. A supporter of the Anglican faith (*Religio Laici*, 1682), he became a convert to the Catholic faith in 1685 and its apologist in *The Hind and the Panther* (1687). The opportunism charged to him by his contemporaries for his change of church may not be wholly justified. It is true that his acceptance of Catholicism dated from the year of accession of James II, Catholic brother to the late Charles II. But it is also true that it was his refusal to swear allegiance to James's successor, the protestant William of Orange, which resulted in his loss of all official titles.

Though his last years were spent mainly in translation, Dryden's status as the foremost poet of his age rested upon a large and varied corpus of work. For thirty years he had written for the theatre;

comedies, tragedies and heroic dramas. His essays established him as the founder of modern criticism; and his poetry extended through a range of subjects and styles. Dryden's poetry was founded upon public themes and issues. And he was also, as W. H. Auden reminded us, 'the poet of Common Sense'. The mode of poetry which made him most feared by his contemporaries was that of satire. And the style of which he perfected, that of the heroic couplet, became the model for verse composition adopted by the succeeding century. From that perspective Dr Johnson wrote of Dryden: 'To him we owe the refinement of our language, and much of the correctness of our sentiments.'

Dryden endowed the heroic couplet with a vigorous, swift movement which sustained the capacity for sinuous thought – where many in the later generations of poets would often reduce the measure to a mechanical plod. As a small sample of these qualities of verse, and of Dryden's sharp-edged satire, here are a few lines from *Absolom and Achitophel* (1681) in which is presented his word-portrait of 'Zimri', that is, George Villiers (1628-87), the second Duke of Buckingham:

> A man so various that he seemed to be
> Not one, but all mankind's epitome:
> Stiff in opinions, always in the wrong,
> Was everything by starts and nothing long;
> But in the course of one revolving moon
> Was chymist, fiddler, statesman, and buffoon;
> Then all for women, painting, rhyming, drinking,
> Besides ten thousand freaks that died in thinking
> ....
> Railing and praising were his usual themes,
> And both, to show his judgement, in extremes:
> So over violent or over civil
> That every man with him was God or Devil.
> In squandering wealth was his peculiar art;
> Nothing went unrewarded but desert.
> Beggared by fools whom still he found too late,
> He had his jest, and they had his estate.

Dryden was himself proud of this portrait and thought it 'worth the whole poem'.

The last composition made by Dryden was *The Secular Masque*, written for a benefit performance of *The Pilgrim* given on his behalf in April 1700. It contains poetry of real vigour whose compact lines seem to reflect Dryden's final, considered reflection on his times. Chronos carries the globe of the world on his back:

Weary, weary of my weight,
Let me, let me, drop my freight,
   And leave the world behind.
I could not bear
Another year
   The load of humankind.

Venus, goddess of love, offers herself:

Take me, take me, while you may;
Venus comes not ev'ry day.

But there is no consolation for Chronos:

The world was then so light,
I scarcely felt the weight;
Joy rul'd the day, and Love the night.
But since the Queen of Pleasure left the ground,
   I faint, I lag,
   And faintly drag,
The pond'rous orb around.

The masque closes with the final lines of the Chorus:

'Tis well an old age is out,
And time to begin a new.

The Secular Masque is an astonishing achievement with which to close a long poetic career. For it is not only a commentary on Dryden's time, but also perhaps an old man's adieu to the world.

Returning along Gerrard Street, on the same side of the street as the Dryden house, will be seen the locations of Nos 37 and 35.

At No 37 Edmund Burke (1729-97), statesman and philosopher, was living in the 1780s.

At No 35 once lived Charles Kemble (1775-1854), actor, who took lodgings there with his daughter Frances ('Fanny') Kemble (1809-93) in 1820. Where the father made his reputation for comic roles, the daughter was pre-eminent for her portrayal in roles such as those of Lady Macbeth and Portia. Henry James, in his *Essays in London*, wrote warmly in appreciation of her acting.

* * *

From Gerrard Street return to Wardour Street and turn to the right, crossing over Shaftesbury Avenue. Fifty yards beyond that junction, on the right, will be seen the tower of St Anne's Church – all that remains of the building following an air raid of 1940. The St Anne's site is currently being developed, and in 1991 there is scheduled to open here an Exhibition Room for the Soho Society.

At St Anne's was buried William Hazlitt, the essayist and critic, with two mourners only in

St Anne's, Soho, as it appeared in a sketch of 1840.

attendance (Charles Lamb and P. G. Patmore).

In a chapel at the base of the church's tower were placed the ashes of Dorothy L. Sayers (1893-1957), the writer of many detective fictions and the creator of Lord Peter Wimsey.

* * *

Continuing along Wardour Street you will come to the turning, on the right, of Old Compton Street. Just ahead, and off to the left, is Brewer Street. David Hume (1711-76), the Scottish philospher and historian, lived on this street for four years: first in lodgings at No 67 (1765-7), then at No 7 (1767-9).

By turning into Old Compton Street, however, you will arrive at Dean Street at the next junction, just a few yards ahead. Off to the right at this point you will be able to see 'The French House' referred to in the opening part of this section – though all the following references are to be found in that part of Dean Street running off to the left at this junction.

Along the left-hand side of the street you will come to No 67, the home formerly of Anthony Chamier (1725-80) during the years 1764-7. Stockbroker, and for a period Deputy Secretary of War, Chamier was highly-regarded by Dr Johnson as a friend and was one of the original members of the Literary Club. Johnson had a genuine regard for Chamier's conversational abilities, and was a frequent visitor to Chamier's country house at Streatham – celebrating there, in fact, his seventieth birthday.

Another of Johnson's friends, Hester Lynch Salusbury (1741-1821, who became Mrs Hester Thrale) lived somewhere on Frith Street – at which house is not known – prior to her marriage.

A little beyond the Chamier house stands No 73 – now known as Royalty House (a recent building from the late 1950s). Here, destroyed in the Blitz, was Miss Kelly's Theatre and Dramatic School which opened in 1840. The theatre itself in fact stood in the garden of the large Georgian residence; entry to it was via some public rooms and a staircase in the house. In 1845 there was staged in the theatre a production of Ben Jonson's *Every Man in His Humour*, with Charles Dickens (1812-70), taking a leading role – together with his friend Douglas Jerrold (1803-57), dramatist and regular contributor to *Punch* magazine.

In 1850 the theatre became the Royal Soho Theatre, and in 1861 was re-launched as the New Royalty Theatre, where were hosted the first English productions of Ibsen's *Ghosts* and *The Wild Duck*. And in this theatre at 10.00pm on 25 March 1875 more theatrical history was made when the curtain went up on the first production of what was to prove a unique theatrical partnership: the first of Gilbert and Sullivan's comic opera masterpieces, *Trial by Jury* – which ran for 300 performances in Dean Street.

A few yards further along, on the same side of the street, stands No 78 where lived the Irish actress Peg Woffington (1714?-60), whose fame as an actress was established at the Drury Lane theatre, and whose notoriety was established by her amours – which were numerous, and included that with David Garrick.

Charles Dickens in Every Man in His Humour.

Continue along Dean Street until the small entrance to Carlisle Street opens to the left. In this recess, facing towards Soho Square, stands No 12. This site, now occupied by a modern building, is commonly presumed to be the one which Charles Dickens had in mind as the location for Dr Manette's house, as described in his *A Tale of Two Cities* (ch.6):

> The quiet lodgings of Doctor Manette were in a very quiet street-corner not far from Soho Square . . .
>
> A quainter corner than the corner where the Doctor lived, was not to be found in London. There was no way through it, and the front windows of the Doctor's lodgings commanded a pleasant little vista of street that had a congenial air of retirement on it.

From Carlisle Street, return along Dean Street, on its opposite side, until you come to No 21, now the West End Street Synagogue. Between the years 1748-63 this site was occupied by Caldwell's Assembly Rooms, where the young Wolfgang Amadeus Mozart stayed with his sister ('Nannerl') and their father for a part of their time in England.

On the way back to Old Compton Street you will pass by on this side of the street No 28 – now a part of one of Soho's famous restaurants, the Quo Vadis.

Karl Marx.

At second-floor level is mounted a blue plaque to commemorate the stay there of Karl Marx (see above). In fact Marx and his large family occupied just two small rooms on the top floor of the building – both of them, by report, always in an untidy and dirty state. Throughout the family's stay there, 1851-6 (the date ascribed on the plaque is not accurate), three of his young children died in the house.

No 33 was once Walker's Hotel (where Lord Nelson spent his last night before leaving for Trafalgar), and before that was Jack's Coffee House – patronised by Johnson and Goldsmith and other friends within their circle.

* * *

Having returned to Old Compton Street, turn left, and within a few yards, you will be at the junction with Frith Street. Turn left at this point.

Some distance along, on the left, you will come to No 64. Here lived William Charles Macready (1793-1873) in 1816, a few years before he established his reputation as a leading actor of his day. Macready subsequently went on to become manager of the Drury Lane Theatre and also of the Covent Garden Theatre.

Though replaced now by a modern building, a few yards further on, at No 67, there used to stand a café-restaurant which, prior to the First World War, provided a regular meeting-place for artists and writers. Among those known to have attended these sessions were: T. E. Hulme, philosopher; the sculptor Jacob Epstein; and the writers Middleton Murray, Ezra Pound, Edward Marsh, and W. W. Gibson.

On the other side of Frith Street, and returning to the junction with Old Compton Street, you will come to No 6, a house built in 1718 – at which William Hazlitt (1778-1830) spent the last six months of his life. The house is marked with a plaque.

Critic and essayist, Hazlitt died broken and dispirited, financially straightened, and separated from his second wife, a widow. He had met Mrs Bridgewater whilst travelling in a coach, and had married her in 1824, though it was not long before Hazlitt deserted her. 'Worn by sickness and thought', as one of his contemporaries expressed it, Hazlitt died with one of his staunchest friends, Charles Lamb, in attendance. Lamb had been best man, and Mary Lamb had been bridesmaid, at Hazlitt's first marriage to Sarah Stoddart in 1808. That marriage had his reputation as a professional critic remains high.

Beyond the Hazlitt house, though all trace of the original has gone, at No 20 (now the stage entrance for the London Casino) lodged the Mozart family for a part of their stay in London.

Continue beyond the junction with Old Compton Street until, on the far side of the entrance of Romilly Street, you find No 28 Frith Street – in 1801 the home of Arthur Murphy (1727-1805), actor, and author of comedies which were very successful during his time.

* * *

At this point turn left into Romilly Street which leads, within a short distance, to Greek Street, off to the left. Along this street Thackeray chose to locate the home for Becky Sharp of *Vanity Fair*.

On the right-hand side of the street stands No 12, where there is a plaque to the pottery designers and manufacturers, the Wedgwoods. But this number was also the boyhood address of Coventry Patmore (1823-96), whose poetry was to espouse the cause of married love, as gathered in *The Angel in the House*.

Not far from here, on the same side of the street, stands The Pillars of Hercules public house. It was from the doorway of an earlier public house (of the same name) on this site, that Francis Thompson was rescued by Wilfred Meynell. Thompson (1859-1907), starving and addicted to opium, was nursed back to health by the Meynells: Wilfrid, editor of the Catholic journal *Merry England*, and Alice, his wife, a poet. Thompson, whose long poem *The Hound of Heaven* was to record his flight from God, the pursuit, and his capture, had been living as a virtual beggar – sleeping in the alleyways and door ways around Covent Garden and elsewhere.

To No 61 Greek Street, on the other side of the street, Thomas de Quincey (1785-1859), at the age of seventeen, ran away from his school in Wales.

Here, on the one guinea a week allowed him by his mother, the young de Quincey would have starved, had it not been for the friendship of Ann, a young prostitute just a year or two older than himself, whom de Quincey met in Soho Square. One day Ann disappeared into a London crowd, and was never seen again by de Quincey – except in his dreams, which she inhabited until the end of his life. Though the author of numerous essays, de Quincey is best-remembered for his autobiographical *Confessions of an Opium-Eater* (1822, revised and extended 1856).

William Hazlitt.

not survived Hazlitt's developed penchant for falling repeatedly in and out of love. They divorced in 1822 after some years of separation.

The critical essays are marked by Hazlitt's enthusiasms, a characteristic very much of a piece with the man himself. His writings on *Characters of Shakespeare's Plays* (1817, 1818) are incisive and contain many sharp perceptions – a sharpness not always so evident when he wrote of his contemporaries, as in *The Spirit of the Age* (1825). Though he championed Keats he misrepresented Coleridge – despite an acknowledgement that Coleridge was 'the only person I ever knew who answered to the idea of a man of genius.' Nonetheless, and despite Hazlitt's own confession that he had 'loitered [his] life away'

The frontispiece illustration by 'Phiz' (H. K. Browne) to Dickens's A Tale of Two Cities, *of the courtyard of the house where Dr Manette lived. The illustration is taken from the frontispiece of Dickens's favourite edition of his own works, and the last to be published in his own lifetime.*

This location faces the Gay Hussar, another of Soho's best-known restaurants, which is alongside No 1, the House of St Barnabas in Soho. Now a refuge for women, it is very probably the *model* for the house of Charles Dickens's Dr Manette, though transposed to another location (see earlier entry):

> The Doctor occupied two floors of a large still house, where several callings purported to be pursued by day, but whereof little was audible any day, and which was shunned by all of them at night. In a building at the back, attainable by a court-yard where a plane-tree rustled its green leaves, church-organs claimed to be made, and silver to be chased and likewise gold to be beaten by some mysterious giant who had a golden arm starting out of the wall of the front hall . . .

The goldsmith's sign, the golden arm of the giant, may be seen today at the Dickens House in Doughty Street (see Bloomsbury I section). Manette Street, from which Dickens undoubtedly derived the Doctor's name, you will have passed on your way along Greek Street. The plane-tree which is referred to in Dickens's description may be seen still in the courtyard garden of the House of St Barnabas – as it is featured also in the frontispiece by 'Phiz' (H. K. Browne) to the Oxford Illustrated Edition of Dickens's works. The house is open to the public on Wednesdays, 2.30-4.15pm, and Thursday, 11.00am-12.30pm.

* * *

At this house Frith Street opens into the south-east corner of Soho Square. The square, once a very fashionable area in which several noble families chose to live, was the location selected by Sir Richard Steele (1672-1729) for the London residence of his comic creation, Sir Roger de Coverley, whose experience and opinions were recorded in the *Spectator*.

To the right-hand of this point of entry, where No 22 now stands, William Beckford (1760-1844) was born and spent most of his boyhood. His father, a rich Alderman and a Lord Mayor of London, there had the family home for almost twenty years from 1751. Beckford, the son, achieved notoriety for the conduct of his life, and a lasting reputation largely on the strength of one work, the Gothic novel *The History of the Caliph Vathek* written originally in French in 1782, but translated into English and published six years later without Beckford's permission.

Just beyond this point, at the corner with Sutton Street on the site now occupied by St Patrick's Roman Catholic Church, once stood Carlisle House. From 1760 Carlisle House was the venue for Mrs Cornelys's Assembly Rooms, where she provided various entertainments for her guests; dancing, masques, concerts, and even card-playing. The rooms were known for their sumptuous décor and expensive furniture. Mrs Cornelys (real name Imer), a Viennese opera singer and courtesan, was one of the innumerable lovers of Casanova, by whom she had a daughter. (About four years after Mrs Cornelys opened the Rooms Casanova was himself staying in lodgings in Greek Street.) Tobias Smollett refers to the Assembly Rooms in *Humphrey Clinker*, Laurence Sterne and Hugh Walpole were both visitors, as was Emma in Charles Dickens's *Barnaby Rudge*; so, too, was Fanny Burney, who left her own recorded impression of 'the magnificence of the rooms, splendour of the illuminations and embellishments, and the brilliant appearance of the company . . .'

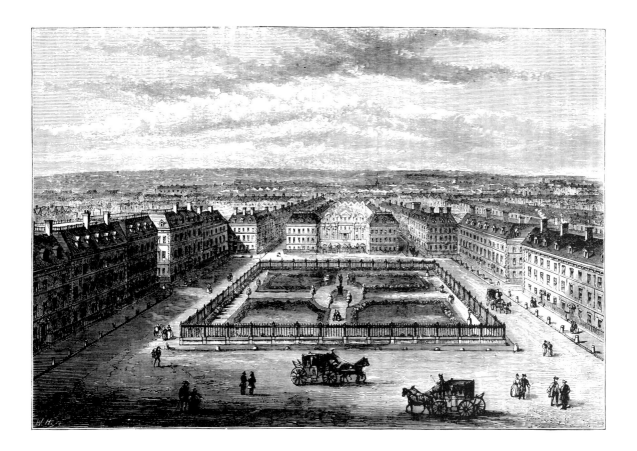

Soho Square, around 1700, looking south. The building which housed Mrs Cornelys's Assembly Rooms is immediately beyond the opening along the left-hand flank.

To the left of the point of entry to the Square, on a site now covered by the New Hospital for Women, once stood No 29, the home between the years 1822-5 of Charles Kemble and his daughter Fanny (see above).

On the opposite (north) side of the Square, at No 10 – an original house of the late seventeenth century – two doors to the right of the *Église Protestante Française de Londres*, lived Lady Mary Wortley Montagu (1689-1762) in 1734, one of several London addresses she inhabited at different times. Read still for her letters, Lady Mary was celebrated as a wit, and was notorious for her slovenliness. She was for some time a friend of Alexander Pope, and it is possible they were once romantically attached. Later they became enemies and she was satirised by him in several of his poems, as in 'To a Lady' where she is depicted in the character of Sappho, contrasting her:

> . . . at her toilet's greasy task
> With Sappho fragrant at an evening mask:
> So morning insects that in muck begun,
> Shine, buzz, and flyblow in the setting sun.
>
> [generate]

* * *

From that (north) side of Soho Square, Soho Street leads out into Oxford Street. Turning left here, and a few hundred yards along Oxford Street will be found Poland Street opening to the left. A short way into this street, where No 28 stands on the left-hand side, William Blake (1757-1827) lodged for six years from 1785. The son of a hosier (whose shop was in nearby Golden Square) Blake was born at what was then No 28 Broad Street – now Broadwick Street, No 74, incorporated into a modern office block. Formally uneducated, Blake was apprenticed to an engraver at the age of fourteen. In this trade he earned his living, sometimes precariously, throughout his life. After the appearance of his first conventionally-produced book (*Poetical Sketches*, 1783) Blake engraved all his subsequent writings, adding illustrations which were hand-coloured.

From a very early age Blake claimed to experience visions; including the face of God peering through his father's window, and a host of angels in the branches of trees. For his prophetic writings – and Blake conceived of himself very much in the Old Testament sense of a prophet such as Ezekiel – he claimed merely to have acted as an amenuensis to these spiritual visitations, writing down the words without any alterations or intrusion on his part.

For Blake the supreme reality, what indeed was the essentially human (and not merely a quality or ability) was the Imagination, a power of perception by which alone true understanding could be achieved. As poet and artist Blake may be best described as a revisionist in various codes – social, political and religious – whose writings create their own complex myths as a means of embodying the vision.

Whilst at Poland Street, Blake produced *Songs of Innocence* (1789), lyrics of a profound simplicity which lend themselves to extensive exegesis. In the same year Blake issued *The Book of Thel*, the first of his 'prophetic' books to appear, and in 1790 *The Marriage of Heaven and Hell*. In rhythms close to the King James translations of the Bible, this prose work contains the seventy 'Proverbs of Hell' – sayings which through the opposition of 'contraries' (in Blake's own term) serve both to shape perception and induce dialetic. By turns these proverbs subvert comfortable habits of thought, are sometimes riddling, and are sometimes antinomian – as in: 'As the catterpiller chooses the fairest leaves to lay her eggs on, so the priest lays his curse on the fairest joys.' A few others taken from the whole sequence include these provocations to reflection:

> The road of excess leads to the palace of wisdom.
> The hours of folly are measur'd by the clock, but of wisdom: no clock can measure.
> Prisons are built with stones of Law, Brothels with bricks of Religion.
> The lust of the goat is the bounty of God.
> What is now proved was once, only imagin'd.
> The eagle never lost so much time, as when he submitted to learn of the crow.
> The head Sublime, the heart Pathos, the genitals Beauty, the hands & feet Proportion.

Considered a little mad by some of his contemporaries, but admired by others (including Wordsworth and Coleridge) Blake has now been accorded his proper status as a wholly original artist.

Further along the left-hand side of Poland Street,

Cast of the head of William Blake, taken from life.

immediately beyond the junction with Noel Street, will be found No 15 – a building dating from the first decade of the eighteenth century. The building carries a plaque noting that Percy Bysshe Shelley once lived there. The whole of the facing flank of the house has very recently acquired a painted mural, sponsored by the Soho Society, of a depiction of Shelley's 'Ode to the West Wind'.

In fact Shelley (1792-1822) lodged there for a few weeks only, in the spring of 1811, with his friend Thomas Jefferson Hogg (1792-1862) after they had been expelled from University College, Oxford. There they had met and, influenced by the radicalism of William Godwin, had produced and circulated a pamphlet, *The Necessity of Atheism*. Given that membership of the University depended upon subscribing to the Thirty-Nine Articles of the Church, and given that the two young men sent copies of the pamphlet to bishops, heads of the Oxford colleges, and to University professors, the authorities had little option but to expel them in March 1811.

In a letter to his father, a country squire and Member of Parliament in Sussex, Shelley claimed with a characteristic mixture of naïvety and sweet reasonableness that since he and Hogg

> ... found to our surprise that (strange as it may appear) the proofs of an existing Deity were as far as we observed, defective. We therefore embodied our doubts on the subject, & arranged them methodically in the form of 'The Necessity of Atheism', thinking thereby to obtain a satisfactory, or an unsatisfactory answer from men who had made Divinity the study of their lives.

In the August following his expulsion from Oxford Shelley, just nineteen, eloped with sixteen-year-old Harriet Westbrook, one of the daughters of a man who had made a substantial amount of money as a coffee-house proprietor. But to Shelley's father, one of the landed gentry and heir to a baronetcy, the match was wholly unacceptable. He cut off his son's allowance, so that Shelley both borrowed and drew up debts against his future inheritance as he and Harriet travelled through England, Wales, Ireland and Scotland in search of their ideal cottage to rent.

Many years after Shelley's death by drowning whilst crossing the gulf of Spezia, Italy, in a small boat Hogg published his *Life of Percy Bysshe Shelley* (1858), though its narrative goes as far only as 1814. At this point Shelley was about to leave Harriet for Mary Godwin, daughter of William Godwin and Mary Wollstonecraft, campaigner for women's rights, who had died giving birth to Mary. Hogg conceals also in this memoir his own attempted seduction of Harriet. The picture of the young 'mad Shelley' (the nickname he acquired whilst at Eton) which he draws shows the developed scientific curiosity of the young poet; his rooms at Oxford full of electrical apparatus and chemical substances – books, furniture and carpets burned with acids. At Eton he had alarmed his schoolmates by his experiments with gunpowder and the subsequent explosions he caused. Science throughout his life retained an intense interest for Shelley, one which was transmuted into some of his poetry, and one which undoubtedly enabled him later to provide Mary with so much of the detail to simulate the scientific credibility of *Frankenstein* (written 1816, published 1818).

The character of Shelley has always been difficult to appraise. To some, and perhaps especially to some of the later Romantics, Shelley was the apotheosis of the sensitive, artistic spirit struggling towards liberation of self and others; and a major proponent of the cult of Love. But he can be seen too in an opposite light: as one who was self-absorbed and grossly insensitive – as shown most starkly in his treatment of Harriet. He abandoned Harriet when she was pregnant, having proposed a *ménage-à-trois* in which she would live as a sister to himself and Mary Godwin. She subsequently drowned herself in the Serpentine. And yet where Shelley's behaviour is judged brutish, there is the fact that many testified also to his kindness, his gentleness and benevolence.

Shelley's political, religious and sexual views opposed the orthodoxies of his day. And just as analyses of his character differed so widely, so it is true that critical opinions as to the estimation of his poetry remain divided today.

* * *

From Poland Street return to Oxford Street where, some distance along to the left, will be found the nearest underground station at Oxford Circus.

> THE
> NECESSITY
> OF
> ATHEISM.
>
> A CLOSE examination of the validity of the proofs adduced to support any proposition, has ever been allowed to be the only sure way of attaining truth, upon the advantages of which it is unnecessary to descant; our knowledge of the existence of a Deity is a subject of such importance that it cannot be too minutely investigated; in consequence of this conviction, we proceed briefly and impartially to examine the proofs which have been adduced. It is necessary first to consider the nature of Belief.

Shelley's pamphlet The Necessity of Atheism, *sent to all heads of the Oxford colleges, to the Vice-Chancellor, and to every bishop in the country, was on sale for just twenty minutes at Slatter's bookshop, Oxford, before being removed and burned. Only three copies of the original have survived. The reduced facsimile page, above, shows the opening of the argument.*

By courtesy Bodleian Library, Oxford

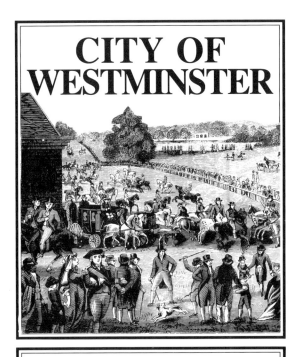

CITY OF WESTMINSTER

MARYLEBONE I

CITY OF WESTMINSTER

From the second of the churches built for this parish derives the title St Marylebone. St Mary-by-the-bourne was constructed around 1400 at the top end of what is now Marylebone High Street (see later entry). The bourne in question was the Tyburn, a stream which flowed south from Hampstead, through Regent's Park, following the approximate line of the High Street and Lane to St James's Park.

The large area enclosed within the two tours Marylebone I and Marylebone II extends north to south from Marylebone Road to Oxford Street; and will take the visitor west, on a line with Marble Arch, and as far as Cavendish Square to the east. The tours may be undertaken consecutively, as one extended tour – but have been divided for the convenience of the visitor who, having undertaken the first tour, may wish to stop at Oxford Street: either to go on a shopping trip there or to go to Marble Arch and thence into Hyde Park. The second tour may then be undertaken, from Oxford Street, beginning either at Marble Arch or at Bond Street underground stations.

Viewed as a single, extensive tour, the area marked out will take the visitor from the bustle of Marylebone Road and Oxford Street through many quiet backwaters. And although the inclusive tour has been made more or less circular – beginning and ending at Baker Street underground station – some backtracking will be involved if all the locations cited are to be inspected.

* * *

The first part of the tour begins at Baker Street underground station. At the station take the Baker Street North exit, and cross to the other side of Baker Street, heading to the right. Fifty yards ahead stands an Abbey National office block. On the side of the building will be seen a bronze plaque, inscribed with the following quotation: 'We met next day and inspected the rooms at 221b Baker Street . . . and at once entered into possession'.

Thus begins, in *A Study in Scarlet* (1887), the legend of the great amateur detective, Sherlock Holmes, created by Sir Arthur Conan Doyle (1859-1930). And at this site begins also the mystery of the exact whereabouts of the famous detective's lodgings. Here, without question, you are standing at the closest possible *address*; though scores of Holmes buffs – following the descriptions of the rooms offered by Conan Doyle – have placed them elsewhere. Nos 109 and 111 Baker Street are among the favourites to have emerged to carry the title of the originals of the rooms.

In 1951, to mark the celebrations for the Festival of Britain, Holmes's sitting room was re-created in the Abbey National building. Later it was transferred and re-assembled within a public house off the Strand (see section: The Strand).

* * *

Turn about and return down Baker Street to the junction with Marylebone Road where you should cross the road and turn to the right. Something like a hundred yards along Marylebone Road, Gloucester Place opens up on the left. Now continue along Gloucester Place, beyond its junction with York Street. On the right-hand side of the street, immediately before the next junction (Crawford Street), will be seen No 99. The house carries a plaque to Elizabeth Barrett Browning.

At the time of her residence here, for three years from 1835, Elizabeth Barrett (1806-61) lived with her family – this address being their first London home. She had already published volumes of poetry and a translation from the Greek of Aeschylus, and in the year when the family moved from here she published a third collection. Already she was establishing a reputation which, in her own lifetime, would surpass that of her future husband, Robert Browning (see later entry).

* * *

A further hundred yards along Gloucester Place, Montagu Place leads off to the right, and Dorset Street leads off to the left. Turn into Dorset Street.

William Wilkie Collins.

'As a doctor he does not practice, and as a novelist he does not preach' – concluding remarks of a review of The White Company *alongside this caricature of Conan Doyle in the December 1895 issue of* The Ludgate.

Just on the left will be found No 22 where lived Algernon Charles Swinburne (1837-1909). He lived here for five years from 1865, the year in which he published *Atalanta in Calydon*, a drama in the classical Greek tradition – a work which first brought him to attention. During his stay at Dorset Street Swinburne went on to publish the first of those poems and ballads which, defying conventions, are most frequently described as pagan in spirit. Certainly they display a rich, sometimes lush, melodiousness – a masterly euphony.

A good way further into Dorset Street, beyond its junction with Baker Street used to stand the house (now gone) where Robert Browning (1812-89) and Elizabeth Barrett Browning (see above) stayed during the year 1855, during which time Elizabeth was working on *Aurora Leigh*, published two years later.

* * *

From Dorset Street return to Gloucester Place, turning to the left, and crossing the street. There will be found No 65, marked with a blue plaque to William ('Wilkie') Collins (1824-89). Collins lived here for a total of nearly twenty years (1866-80 and 1883-8), with one of his permanent mistresses. By these women he had a number of children – and supported them all.

Wilkie Collins trained as a lawyer, having first been apprenticed to a firm of tea importers, and was called to the Bar in 1851, but turned to literature as a profession. He became a friend of Charles Dickens, with whom he collaborated on many stories in the latter's periodicals *Household Words* and *All the Year Round*. In the second of these Collins first published *The Woman in White* (1860) – the initial conception of which seems to have started out of an actual experience. For walking one evening with friends near Regent's Park, a young woman dressed in flowing white robes ran out of a garden gate, quite clearly in some agitation and fear. Collins followed her, and for some years he and the woman, Caroline, lived together. Though it appears she had been held captive in the house by Regent's Park, the final details of the mystery have not been resolved.

Whilst at Gloucester Place, however, Collins worked on what T. S. Eliot described as 'the first and greatest of English detective novels' – *The Moonstone* (1868), in which Collins created the detective Sergeant Cuff.

A few doors beyond the Collins house stands No 57 where Charles Dickens (1812-70) stayed for a while a couple of years before Collins took up residence in the street.

* * *

Now retrace steps, and turn to the left into Montagu Place where, somewhere along the right-hand side, at which house is not known, lived Sir Arthur Conan Doyle (see above) when he first came to London and set up practice as a doctor in Devonshire Place (see Marylebone II).

Fifty yards along Montagu Place, on the left, Montagu Square opens up. Taking its second opening – that is, its western flank – and a short way down this side of the square will be seen No 39. The house is marked with a plaque to commemorate the residence of Anthony Trollope (1815-82) who lived there for eight years from 1872.

During his time here, his reputation as a novelist having steadily increased from the publication of *The Warden* in 1855, Trollope made visits to South Africa and to Iceland, whilst continuing his considerable output of fictions. His writing habits he described in his own *Autobiography* (1883): 'Three hours a day will produce as much as a man ought to write. It is still my custom to write with my watch before me, and to require myself 250 words every quarter of an hour.' Every day, therefore, Trollope wrote from

Anthony Trollope photographed around 1864.

eight in the morning until eleven, when he would lay down his pen no matter what stage of writing he had arrived at – his three thousand words for the day, a prodigious output for a single sitting, achieved. By such sustained discipline Trollope produced altogether more than fifty works.

For more than thirty years Trollope had also been an official with the General Post Office, first as a clerk and later rising to the rank of Inspector. His chief recreation had been to ride with the hounds twice a week. When settled in London his major amusement appears to have the playing of whist at the Garrick Club. By his contemporaries Trollope was viewed as a man of bluff and sometimes loud contention, given to outbursts and an angry manner – whilst at the same time being tender-hearted, genuinely fond and solicitous of his friends.

Several doors beyond the Trollope house stands No 46, one of the London homes of John Forster (1812-86), a friend of Charles Dickens and his first and most authoritative biographer (1872-4), though glossing some of the facts of Dickens's life now established. Forster also produced a biography of Walter Savage Landor, another friend, and of Goldsmith.

Turn about, returning to Montagu Place and head to the left. A little way on Bryanston Square now opens to the left. A short way down this flank of the square may be found No 17 (though it is not in fact numbered) – where C. P. Snow (1905-80) located the home of Mr March in *The Conscience of the Rich* (1958).

Returning to Montagu Place, and almost immediately opposite, will be seen Wyndham Place. Thirty yards into the Place, on the right-hand side, stood No 2 where lived William Somerset Maugham (1874-1965), novelist, short-story writer, and dramatist, from 1920-23.

Continue to the next opening into Bryanston Square, its western edge. At its far end stood No 43 (now replaced) – to which Maugham moved from the above address. At this address he stayed too for a period of three years.

* * *

This side of Bryanston Square leads to the junction with George Street. At this point there is a location some two or three minutes' walk away which some will wish to visit.

At George Street turn to the left and continue until the major junction with Gloucester Place is reached. On the far side of this crossroads, on the right and just past the corner, will be seen No 85 George Street. Here, at first-floor level, will be found a plaque commemorating the stay in this house of Thomas Moore (1779-1852), Irish poet and musician.

Upon his first arrival in London, in 1799, Moore had taken lodgings for a short time at another house in George Street – further to the east, and now gone – before transferring here.

Moore, just twenty, had come from his native Ireland – he was born in Dublin – in order to study law, for which he was enrolled at Middle Temple. Soon after his arrival in London, however, Moore's gaiety, wits, and good looks established him as a favourite among gatherings of fashionable society. At twenty-two he published his first collection of *Poetical Works*, under the pseudonym of 'Thomas Little' – and as quickly as 1803 he had secured an appointment as admiralty registrar at Bermuda; which appointment he immediately transferred to a deputy, whose embezzlement of funds produced a debt of £6,000. Moore left England for several years but returned when the debt had been repaid.

Moore's lyrics, frequently slight in theme (though sometimes subversive of 'correct' moralities, as judged by some contemporaries), convey nonetheless a lilting lyricism, a genuinely rhythmic organisation – qualities which promoted him to one of the acknowledged lyricists of Ireland.

In later years Moore became an intimate friend and confidant of Lord Byron. To Moore Byron gave the manuscript of his memoirs – which Moore, presumably out of loyalty and a wish to avert the damage they might have caused, destroyed.

* * *

From the Moore house return along George Street to Montagu Street, on the left. For those proceeding directly from Bryanston Square, Montagu Street will be found, facing, just a little to the left on exiting from the square.

Some distance into Montagu Street, on the right-hand side, stands No 21, one of the many short-stay addresses of George Borrow (1803-81), whose books reflect the nomadic quality of much of his own life, interfusing autobiography with fiction.

Beyond here, and on the same side of the road, stood No 35 (now incorporated into a block of flats) where Olive Schreiner (1855-1920) lived for most of the two years 1888 and 1889. A writer, later in her career, in the feminist cause, she is most widely remembered as the author of *The Story of an African Farm* (1883) – a work which she published originally under the pseudonym 'Ralph Iron'.

* * *

Montagu Street leads to the junction with Upper Berkeley Street, with New Quebec Street directly opposite. This in turn leads to Seymour Street running across at right angles. Just around the corner here, to the left and on the left-hand side, will be seen No 18 Seymour Street. Here lived Thomas Campbell (1777-1844) for most of the 1820s.

A Scotsman by birth and education, Campbell's poetic reputation was established with the long didactic poem *The Pleasures of Hope* (1799). He is remembered as one of the principal activists for the founding of London University, and for his shorter songs. Among these are: 'Hohenlinden', 'The Soldier's Dream', 'Lord Ullin's Daughter' – and of course 'Ye Mariners of England'.

A few steps beyond this house is No 10 where the novelist Edward Bulwer-Lytton (1803-73) spent a good deal of his boyhood.

Return now to the junction with New Quebec Street and go beyond it. Just a few doors past this junction, and on the same side of Seymour Street, you will come to No 30. The building is marked with a blue plaque to Edward Lear (1812-88). Lear lived here as a young man, before he had established his reputation either as an artist or as the writer of nonsense verse.

He lived here so as to be close to Regent's Park Zoo, where he had a commission from the Royal Zoological Society to undertake a series of drawings – his first real success.

* * *

Opposite the Lear house, and a little way back along Seymour Street, Old Quebec Street leads off south. Just the other side of its junction with Bryanston Street, on a site now occupied by an apartment block to the left, stood No 14. J. M. Barrie (1860-1937), playwright, lived at this address for most of 1889.

Retrace the few steps to Bryanston Street, taking the section to the right. Just around the corner used to stand No 13 where John Buchan (1875-1940), diplomat and author, lived for the two years 1910-12.

Further into the street, at No 26, George Borrow (see above) took lodgings in 1926; and J. M. Barrie (see above) lived briefly at No 14, now gone.

* * *

At the end of Bryanston Street, just across and a little to the right of its junction with Portman Street, will be seen Granville Place. Its left-hand flank is now almost wholly occupied by the Savoy Court Hotel. Formerly in the mansions here once lived the Meynells: Alice (1847-1922), poet, and Wilfrid (1852-1948), editor. And here they were visited by the Catholic poet Francis Thompson, whom they had befriended, having rescued him from virtual starvation and from advanced drug-addiction (see Soho section).

* * *

Continue along Portman Street until it meets with Oxford Street. At this point there are several options. Some may wish to break off their touring to go on a shopping trip along Oxford Street itself. Alternatively, one may proceed directly to the Marylebone II tour by turning to the left here to find, about a hundred yards ahead, Orchard Street leading off to the left – at which location that tour opens with further directions.

A third option would be to turn to the right, where Portman Street enters Oxford Street. Within a couple of minutes' walk away at the junction of Bayswater Road (continuation of Oxford Street) with Edgware Road, may be found the approximate site of the Tyburn gallows. This, from towards the end of the fourteenth century until the last decades of the eighteenth, was the principal place of public execution in London. A round, stone marker set into the traffic island at this junction indicates one probable location of the gallows; one of several locations in the immediate area – since the gallows were certainly moved through the centuries.

By Henry Fielding's time, execution days had long been public holidays, festive occasions attended by tens of thousands. (The execution day of Jack Shepherd was calculated in contemporary records to have been attended by as many as 200,000 people!) Such crowds, and the encouragement which they offered to the condemned, served to embolden the criminal to seek a glorification in his dying:

> The day appointed by law for the thief's shame is the day of glory in his own opinion. His procession to Tyburn and his last moments there are all triumphant; attended . . . with the applause, admiration and envy of all the bold and hardened.

Fielding's report (. . . *the Late Increase of Robbers*, 1751), written in his capacity as magistrate, had already been preceded by his fiction *Jonathan*

Robert Southwell.

Wild the Great (1743), a satire on the 'greatness' achieved by a hardened rogue in the progress of his career towards, and final moments at, Tyburn. Based to some extent upon the real Jonathan Wild who had been executed at Tyburn in 1725, there is an irony in the fact that Wild is thought to have lived at one time just yards away from the Old Bailey.

In 1595 Robert Southwell (b.1561?) was executed at Tyburn on a charge of treason. For under a law of Elizabeth I a native Englishman ordained a catholic priest was guilty of treason if he remained in England for more than forty days. And Southwell, who had been received into the order in 1580 in Rome, returned to England six years later – at his own request. Though kept under surveillance he was not arrested – for another six years travelling the country as a missionary for his faith. Almost all of Southwell's poems were composed whilst he was in prison. Of his most famous poem, 'The Burning Babe', Ben Jonson once declared that he would gladly have destroyed a number of his own poems to be the author of that one poem of Southwell's.

* * *

The first section of the Marylebone tour may be ended here – the Marble Arch underground station is just a few steps back along the Oxford Road; or, having reached this point, some visitors may wish to take the underpass leading into Hyde Park, emerging at Speaker's Corner – where the British right of free speech is exercised, mainly on Saturday and Sunday evenings, by speakers as diverse as the subjects which they declaim or denounce.

Hyde Park, the largest of the London parks, was opened to the public by Charles I in 1635. Almost at once it became a fashionable area in which to ride. Within twenty years of that date, however, by order of parliament the park was sold off in three lots. One result was that the private landowners could then charge for allowing carriages to pass through the parkland. John Evelyn (1620-1706) the diarist, noted bitterly that 'the sordid fellow' who had bought one of the lots charged him entry of 1s for his coach, and 6p for each horse.

The park was taken back into royal possession at the restoration of Charles II to the throne in 1660, and the fashion of parading a fine equipage became even more firmly established, the King himself frequently on display. Away to the right at Speaker's Corner runs the Ring, a road running off to the west before heading south towards the Serpentine lake.

Richard Brinsley Sheridan.

It was at the Ring where began the duel between Richard Brinsley Sheridan and Captain Matthews over Elizabeth Ann Linley – who subsequently became his wife (see Marylebone II). The crowds which gathered here forced a postponement of the fight, which later transferred to Hyde Park Corner, where the continuation was again interrupted – ending finally, at the third attempt, at Henrietta Street (see entry: Covent Garden).

The present Ring, very roughly, marks out a part of the route of the enclosure followed by carriages in the latter half of the seventeenth century – though the Tour, as it was first called, would have been inside of the present line of the roadway.

May Day celebrations in the park became great public festive occasions. In 1663 Samuel Pepys (1633-1703) decided to cut a figure at such an entertainment in the hope of being noticed by the King and thus furthering his prospects. The clothes which he bought new for the occasion were 'all the mode', and he thought himself to look 'mighty noble'. Unfortunately the horse which he hired for the day was far too high-spirited for him to handle and Pepys had to withdraw from the parade without having come to the royal attention he coveted.

A fashionable venue for persons of quality (or of aspirations to that degree), the Park was also a notorious haunt of highwaymen and footpads. Horace Walpole (1717-97), letter-writer and author of the Gothic novel *The Castle of Otranto*, was robbed by two highwaymen whilst crossing the Park. They threatened him with a blunderbuss, taking his watch and eight guineas.

In 1814, to mark the Peace Celebrations, the battle of Trafalgar was re-enacted on the Serpentine lake as part of the Great Fair of arcades, drinking-booths, and other amusements. Charles Lamb (1775-1834) reported: '. . . the stench of liquors, bad tobacco, dirty people and provisions conquers the air and we are stifled and suffocated in Hyde Park.'

Two years after these celebrations Harriet Westbrook, Shelley's distraught and pregnant wife whom he had deserted, drowned herself in that part of Hyde Park's lake known as the Long Water.

With so many footpaths crossing the Park the visitor is free to wander at will – returning to Hyde Park underground station or going on to the Hyde Park Corner station at the south-east end of the Park. The following suggestion, however, would provide the visitor with a particular route. From Speaker's Corner, take the footpath which will converge upon Serpentine Road skirting the lake. Here turn to the right, following the edge of the lake until one comes to a bridge crossing the water – into Kensington Gardens. And on the far side of the lake there is a footpath, heading off to the right, which follows that continuation of the lake known as the Long Water.

Some way ahead will be seen the statue of Peter Pan, the character in J. M. Barrie's play of that name. Beyond that you will come to the Fountains and Marlborough Gate leading out of the Gardens into Bayswater Road. On the far side of Bayswater Road, which must be crossed with care, will be found Lancaster Gate underground station.

Hyde Park on a Sunday, from a print of 1804.

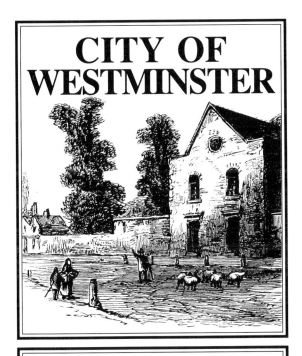

CITY OF WESTMINSTER

MARYLEBONE II

CITY OF WESTMINSTER

This tour may be undertaken independently by starting either at Marble Arch or Bond Street underground stations. From Marble Arch turn left into Oxford Street, continuing ahead for a couple of minutes until arriving at Orchard Street, opening on the left. From Bond Street turn left along Oxford Street where, again within a couple of minutes' walk, on the far side of Oxford Street you will see the entrance to Orchard Street.

For those undertaking this tour as a continuation of the Marylebone I tour (and not ending in Hyde Park), at their point of issue into Oxford Street from Portman Street a turn to the left will bring them, after about a hundred yards, to this junction with Orchard Street.

* * *

Though all trace has gone, it was to a house on Orchard Street that Richard Brinsley Sheridan (1751-1816) brought his wife, Elizabeth Linley, the singer. Sheridan, politician and playwright, had fought duels over her – a good part of which experience went into the making of his play *The Rivals*, written whilst at Orchard Street and first acted at Covent Garden in 1775, just two years after the marriage. *The Duenna* was also composed whilst at Orchard Street. (See also: Covent Garden.)

* * *

A short walk ahead Orchard Street empties into the south-east corner of Portman Square. At the diagonally opposite corner of the square, and itself at an angle to the open space before it, formerly stood Montagu House, bombed out during the Second World War. The house was built for Mrs Elizabeth Montagu (1720-1800), cousin by marriage to Lady Mary Wortley Montagu, letter-writer and friend, later enemy, of Alexander Pope. Mrs Montagu, however, was herself a lady of critical discrimination and one of the leading hostesses of her times. To her house came most of the leading literary figures of her day, including: Dr Johnson, Boswell, Burke, Walpole, and Cowper.

Mrs Montagu's soirées gave rise to the term 'bluestocking', an epithet which subsequently represented a woman with literary tastes or pretensions. For such evening assemblies at Mrs Montagu's, 'where the fair sex might participate in conversation with literary and ingenious men, animated by a desire to please' – in the description offered by Boswell in his *Life of Samuel Johnson* – attracted the title Blue Stocking Club. Admiral Boscawen so nicknamed them after the habit of one of the regular guests, Benjamin Stillingfleet, who regularly wore blue stockings instead of the more usual black silk.

* * *

Continuing along the right-hand (east) side of Portman Square and at its topmost end, Fitzhardinge Street opens to the right. This street leads into Manchester Square where one turns to the left. Along this northern edge of the square will be seen Hertford House, since 1900 a national museum for the Wallace collection of art. This distinctive collection, which includes works by Boucher, Fragonard, and Watteau among many others, was begun by the first Marquess of Hertford and continued by the line. As a passing note it may be mentioned that the 3rd Marquess, whose flamboyant life-style made him a noted London figure, features as the Marquis de Steyne in Thackeray's *Vanity Fair*.

Visitors will almost certainly want to take time to view this important collection. (Admission free: open Monday to Saturday, 10.00am to 5.00pm;

Mrs Elizabeth Montagu of whom Dr Johnson remarked: 'That lady exerts more mind in conversation than any person I ever met with.'

Sunday, 2.00pm to 5.00pm; closed New Year's Day, Good Friday, May Day Bank Holiday, Christmas Eve, Christmas Day, Boxing Day.)

Just beyond Hertford House, Spanish Place leads off to the north. A few steps into this narrow street, on the right-hand side, will be found No 3, marked with a blue plaque, where lived Captain Frederick Marryat (1792-1848). Marryat's tales of the sea have been immensely popular with generations of readers and were much admired by fellow novelist and sailor Joseph Conrad. Easily the best-known among his many titles remains *Mr Midshipman Easy* (1836).

Later the same house was occupied by George Grossmith Jnr. (1874-1935), actor and theatre-manager. Grossmith made a considerable reputation for himself at the Gaiety theatre in the Strand in the years before the First World War. Tall, rather thin, and with a deliberately languid manner, he was the model (at least in good part) for P. G. Wodehouse's marvellously comic creation of Bertie Wooster.

* * *

Beyond Spanish Place, Hinde Street leads off from the far side of Manchester Square. Hinde Street becomes Bentinck Street, and a little way in will be seen No 18 where stood a house in which Charles Dickens's family lived. At the time of their occupation Dickens had just begun to pen the first of those impressions which were later to be gathered as the *Sketches by Boz.*

On the left-hand side of Bentinck Street stands No 7. At first-floor level there is a plaque to Edward Gibbon (1737-94) who lived in a house on that site for ten years from 1773; together with six servants, a lapdog, and a parrot. During this time Gibbon completed a good deal of the work for his *magnum opus, The Decline and Fall of the Holy Roman Empire*, of which the first three volumes appeared in 1781. From Bentinck Street Gibbon retired to Lausanne for five years, there completing the huge undertaking (volumes 4 to 6 appearing in 1788).

* * *

At the end of Bentinck Street there is a junction with Welbeck Street. To the left here, and some distance along, will be seen No 29, an original house from the 1720s, which carries a blue plaque to Thomas Woolner (1825-92), sculptor and poet, who lived for some time at this address. Woolner remains one of the lesser-known figures of the pre-Raphaelite movement of the 1850s, though he was in fact one of the original Brotherhood of seven. Woolner's very moderate success prompted him to leave for and spend time in the Australian goldfields, from which he returned to London. His poems appeared in the short-lived periodical of the movement, *The Germ*; and two of his statues are on display in public places within London (a seated bronze figure of J. S. Mill in the Victoria Embankment Gardens, and a stone bust of John Hunter, physician, in Leicester Square Gardens).

A little past this location and on the same (right-hand) side of the street, replaced now by more modern buildings, were located Nos 33 and 34. At No 34 lived Anthony Trollope (b.1815) during the last couple of years of his life, and here died, in November 1882, in the nursing home at this address.

Mrs Hester Lynch Thrale (1741-1821), Dr Johnson's dearest woman friend, came to No 33 following her second marriage to the Italian musician Gabriel Piozzi. This marriage, of which Johnson heartily disapproved, estranged him from Mrs Thrale. Two years after the Doctor's death Mrs Thrale published a collection of *Anecdotes* on her former friend; and two years after that published her correspondence with him.

Now turn about, heading back to the point of entry into Welbeck Street, and continue past that entrance.

On the site now covered by an hotel, on the right, formerly stood the house (No 58) at which Robert (1812-89) and Elizabeth (1806-61) Barrett Browning stayed in 1852 on one of their return visits from Italy. A few doors beyond, close to Wigmore Street which opens on the right, was located the home (No 64) of Lord George Gordon of Dickens's *Barnaby Rudge*. From the balcony of this house he addresses the mob.

* * *

Beyond these locations Henrietta Place leads off to the left. Within a minute's walk along here, Old Cavendish Street will be seen to the right. Though all trace of the building has gone, J. M. Barrie (1860-1937) once had a home on this short street.

Another resident was Thomas Campbell (1777-1844), poet, who moved to the street following the death of his wife.

George Grossmith Jnr, the model for P. G. Wodehouse's Bertie Wooster.

A short distance further along, Henrietta place emerges at the south-west corner of Cavendish Square. Directly to the right of this point – that is, along the south face of the square before Holles Street which will be seen opening up to the right – once stood one of the London homes of Lady Mary Wortley Montagu (1689-1762), letter-writer and wit. As in the case of most of her homes her residence in Cavendish Square was by no means continuous.

Holles Street itself carries several literary associations, though all traces of the locations to which they belong have gone. George Gordon Byron (1788-1824), who came into his title at the age of ten, was born in a house on this street. Anthony Trollope (see above) lived for a short time on the street. Maria Edgeworth (1767-1849), the Irish-born novelist whose novels, including *Castle Rackrent*, in great part depict Irish life of the times, also lived briefly on Holles Street.

Immediately to the left of the corner of Cavendish Square to which Henrietta Place issued, there may be seen a blue plaque commemorating the residence there, at No 20, of Herbert Henry Asquith (1852-1928), prime minister 1908-16, and his second wife, Margot (1864-1945) – both of whom were writers of various memoirs, Margot's more outspoken and self-centred than the cautiously-reserved style displayed by her politician husband. Though Margot Asquith also wrote novels – fictional variants not far from biographical fact – it is largely for their place within the social and political world of the times that the Asquiths retain the interest devoted to them.

* * *

Continue along the left-hand flank of Cavendish Square, heading north. At the top end of the square Harley Street leads off straight ahead, with Wigmore Street opening to the left. A few doors into Harley Street, on the right-hand side, stands No 12. Here Wilkie Collins (1824-89) lived with one of his permanent mistresses for the five years from 1859.

Now retrace your steps and turn into Wigmore Street – where, at No 12, T. S. Eliot (1888-1965) twice took temporary lodgings (one might say refuge), from June to August 1921, and March to June of the following year. The second turning to the right along Wigmore Street will take you into Wimpole Street.

On the left, a very short way into the street, you will pass by No 82 (rebuilt), to which Wilkie Collins (see above) moved in the last year of his life and there died in 1889.

Further on, Queen Anne Street crosses Wimpole Street. Along Queen Anne Street lodged James Boswell (1740-95) in the year 1788; and Edmund Burke (1729-97) had lodgings on the street 1764-5. Richard Cumberland (1732-1811), playwright and novelist – caricatured by Sheridan as Sir Fretful Plagiary in *The Critic* – also lived along Queen Anne Street.

Beyond the junction with Queen Anne Street, and on the left-hand side, stands No 67. Here lived Henry Hallam (1777-1859), historian, author of *The Constitutional History of England* (1827), from 1819 to 1840. Alfred, Lord Tennyson was engaged to be married to his daughter when Hallam's son, Arthur Henry (1811-33), Tennyson's intimate friend, died. The death, whose melancholic after-effects persisted with Tennyson for many years, occasioned his *In Memoriam*, the poem which Tennyson worked on for a space of fifteen or sixteen years.

Alfred, Lord Tennyson, aged 22, depicted in the year before he and Arthur Henry Hallam travelled on the continent in 1832.

Elizabeth Barrett Browning: Gordigiani's portrait of 1858.　　　　　　　National Portrait Gallery, London

Continuing along Wimpole Street, and a little way past the junction with New Cavendish Street, you will arrive at No 50, on the left. From 1838 here lived 'The Barretts of Wimpole Street' – to adopt the title of the 1930 play made by Rudolf Besier – and here was enacted one of the most famous of literary romances.

Elizabeth Barrett's father was a jealous, suspicious, and tyrannical guardian. Demanding and exercising total control over his children, he had also an intense, almost pathological, objection to his daughters marrying. His daughter Elizabeth (see above) was an invalid confined to her bedroom and sitting-room in Wimpole Street. She had to be carried from bed to sofa where, because she was often so weak, she had to be propped up. Her bedroom, which had been 'sealed up' on doctor's orders, was stuffy and confining.

Elizabeth was shy and, conscious of her spinal deformity, did not welcome the prospect of meeting new people. Her poems, however, had achieved a considerable public notice, and had attracted the attention of Robert Browning (see above), who admired them greatly. Elizabeth's reputation was already high, and Browning's own poetic status was

Robert Browning: Gordigiani's portrait of 1858.
National Portrait Gallery, London

steadily increasing. Browning wrote to Elizabeth Barrett expressing his admiration for her work and asking to meet her. She refused: 'If my poetry is worth anything to any eye, it is the flower of me . . .', she wrote to him, and all else about her was 'fit for the ground and dark'.

Nonetheless Browning persisted in his requests to meet her, and finally she relented. They met at Wimpole Street for the first time in May 1845. Browning was then thirty-three, and Elizabeth was six years his senior. They contrived other meetings, often with the complicity of Elizabeth's sisters, in order to circumvent the undoubted objections of Elizabeth's father. Browning confessed his love for her and proposed marriage: Elizabeth replied that her father 'would rather see me dead at his feet' than consent to the match.

The wooing continued in secret, and led to Browning's proposition that they must elope. For the first time for many years, on the day that she had decided whether to assent or not to this bold move, Elizabeth tested her strength by travelling with a sister in a hired carriage to Regent's Park. Then, on 12 September 1846, Elizabeth walked out of the house at Wimpole Street to marry Robert Browning in nearby Marylebone Church (see below). After the ceremony Mrs Barrett Browning returned to the home in Wimpole Street, where she remained for the next seven days, unvisited by Browning.

Finally, in the afternoon of 19 September, Elizabeth Barrett Browning left the family home to join her husband, together travelling immediately to France and then on to Italy. There they settled in Florence, though travelled widely – making several return visits to London in the next fifteen years.

The story of Elizabeth Barrett's 'recovery' from sickness through the power of love has lead to readings of her character which have been variously described as hypochondriacal, hysterical, and sexually frustrated. The genuineness of her ailments has been commonly doubted. Such a view has been recently challenged, however, and from a strictly scientific point of view. Following an examination of the doctors' letters of the time, Dr David Young (in an issue of *The British Medical Journal*, 1989) has argued the following case: at the age of fifteen Elizabeth contracted a form of poliomyelitis which led to curvature of the spine, a dropped left shoulder, and serious bronchitis. Having lived in the cleaner air of Torquay for three years her doctor recommended the sealing of her rooms as a protection against the damp and polluted air of London. This, Dr Young argues, brought about a gradual restoration of her health some three years before Elizabeth Barrett met Browning; an improvement which continued upon her removal to the more beneficial, warmer and cleaner atmosphere of Florence, staving off the bronchitis. The return trips to the smog of London's air perhaps brought on once more the breathing difficulties and a deterioration of health so that by 1857, four years before her death, she was once more an invalid.

The meeting of Elizabeth and Robert, their courtship and marriage, remains nonetheless a history of courage, trust, and evident and sustaining love.

***

From this point retrace steps along Wimpole Street to the junction with New Cavendish Street. Turn to the right here. A little way on Westmoreland Street opens on the right. (A short distance further on into New Cavendish Street stood the house, now gone, where Wilkie Collins was born.)

Just yards into Westmoreland Street you will come to Wheatley Street at whose right-hand corner (No 1, now a public house) is displayed a plaque to

The fashionable Marylebone Gardens in the eighteenth century.

Charles Wesley (1707-88), who lived and died in a house on this site. With his brother John, Charles was one of the leaders of the Methodist movement and a prolific hymn-writer. Among the thousands of hymns he composed are some of the best-known in the English language.

* * *

Westmoreland Street leads on past Weymouth Street and becomes Beaumont Street which in turn leads on to the junction with Devonshire Street. Beyond this meeting-point, Beaumont Court stands on the left-hand side of Beaumont Street.

There, at the former No 38 the poet Walter Savage Landor (1775-1864) took lodgings in the year 1794 following his expulsion from Oxford University for having fired a pistol at the window of a man whose politics he disliked.

The area covered by Beaumont Street, Devonshire Street and eastwards to Devonshire Place (see below) was once occupied by Marylebone Gardens, opened in 1660 and closed in 1778. They contained bowling greens and provided the venue for cock-fighting, dog-fighting, bull and bear-baiting, and boxing matches; and quickly became a setting for the activities of gamblers and thieves. Pepys thought the gardens themselves 'a pretty place', though they were used also as the haunt for the highwayman Captain Macheath in John Gay's *Beggar's Opera* (1728). In the late 1730s the Gardens were extended, 'persons of ill repute' were forbidden entrance, and they became a fashionable promenade with assembly rooms and an orchestra playing there each evening.

* * *

Turn right at this crossroads along Devonshire Street, then first left into Devonshire Place, terraces of tall houses built in the early 1790s. Just into this street, on the right-hand side, stands No 2 where Conan Doyle (1859-1930) had his consulting-room when he tried to set up in practice as a consultant ophthalmist in 1890, having spent six months, and a good deal of money, specialising in that field.

Of his months spent in a front room of the Devonshire Street practice Conan Doyle wrote: 'Every morning I walked from the lodgings at Montague Place, reached my consulting room at 10 and sat there until three or four with never a ring to disturb my serenity'. Since not *one* patient arrived during the whole of his time here, Conan Doyle therefore took up writing as a means of occupying the days. Thus were born the Sherlock Holmes stories; the first two of which appeared in the *Strand Magazine* of 1891.

Two doors on, at No 4, lived for some time William Beckford (1760-1844), the dissolute and extravagant son of a Lord Mayor of London. The author of *Vathek* (written originally in French and published 1784; published in English 1786), Beckford retired in 1796 to his mansion of Fonthill, where he continued to live in almost total seclusion.

A little further on will be seen No 9, the home between the years 1803-5 of the novelist Matthew 'Monk' Lewis (1775-1818), remembered for and nicknamed after his book *The Monk* (1796) – a mixture of the horrific and the supernatural.

* * *

Having continued to the end of Devonshire Place, turn to the left along Marylebone Road where very quickly you will come to Marylebone High Street.

On the right-hand side at this turning stands a yellow-brick office block. It covers the site of the former No 1 Devonshire Terrace, demolished in the 1950s. 'A house of undeniable situation and splendour' it faced into the Marylebone Road and was the home for the years 1839-51 of Charles Dickens (1812-70). Before Dickens moved in, the family of George du Maurier (1834-96) had occupied the house. Du Maurier, who wrote three novels from his late fifties on, spent some part of his very early boyhood here, having been brought back from Paris, the place of his birth.

Dickens, however, was in the full maturity of his writing at this place. Here he wrote: *The Old Curiosity Shop*, *Barnaby Rudge*, *Martin Chuzzlewit*, *A Christmas Carol*, *David Copperfield*, and part of *Dombey and Son*. In the porch of the present build-

No 1 Devonshire Terrace.

ing, facing the Marylebone Road, may be seen a fine bas-relief panel (by Eastcourt Clark, 1960) of Dickens and various of the characters from the novels written at this address.

Just into Marylebone High Street itself, and located at ground level on the flank of the office block, there is a tablet inscribed with Dickens's own words: 'I seem as if I had plucked myself out of my proper soil when I left 1 Devonshire Terrace and could take root no more until I returned to it'.

About a hundred yards into Marylebone High Street, and on the right-hand side, will be seen some gardens. These mark the site where stood, from about 1400 until 1740, the second of the parish churches, the one from which the parish of St Marylebone derived its title. In this church Francis Bacon (1561-1626), statesman and philosopher, married Alice Barnham in 1606.

In 1740 the parish church was rebuilt. This is the church which is featured in the fifth scene in the series of eight paintings by William Hogarth, *The Rake's Progress* – in which the Rake marries a rich but one-eyed woman. (On view at Sir John Soane's Museum: see Holborn section.) In this church Richard Brinsley Sheridan (see above) married Elizabeth Linley in 1773. Lord Byron (see above) was baptized in the church – in the same year (1788) in which Charles Wesley (see above) was buried in the churchyard. Though Wesley's grave has now been moved from the gardens, an obelisk marks the former burial-place.

In 1813-17 a new parish church was built, the church of 1740 being demoted to the status of chapel. Severely damaged during the Second World War, the parish chapel was pulled down in 1949. The entrance to the present church may be reached via a footpath, to the side of the building, from the gardens. In this church Elizabeth Barrett (see above) and Robert Browning (see above) married in 1846. Within the church there is a Browning Memorial Chapel, containing memorabilia of the couple.

* * *

From the church turn left along Marylebone Road. On the right you will see, and may wish to visit, Madame Tussaud's Waxworks – housed at this site from 1884. Originally a touring spectacle, Madame Tussaud's permanent show from 1835 was in Baker Street; and by 1850 Charles Dickens was already describing the exhibition as 'an institution'.

Almost opposite the exhibition you will pass Luxborough Street where Thomas de Quincey (1785-1859), essayist and author of the *Confessions of an English Opium Eater*, had lodgings in 1806-7. No trace of the house remains.

Beyond Madame Tussaud's, and on that side of the road, stands the massive, light stone-faced construction of Chiltern Mansions (1911). H. G. Wells (1866-1946), novelist, took a flat in this building in 1930. And late in the same year Arnold Bennett (1867-1931) moved in to another apartment here; and here, attended by his mistress, he died.

* * *

A short way further along Marylebone Road, at the junction with Baker Street, there is a subway crossing to the other side of the Marylebone Road. And on that far side of the road, with entrances in the Chiltern Mansions building, will be found the Baker Street underground station.

The Marylebone parish church of 1740.

CAMDEN

HOLBORN

CAMDEN

The following tour will include both Gray's Inn and Lincoln's Inn of Court, among other locations, and is designed to begin and end at Holborn underground station.

Directly opposite the Holborn underground station exit issuing into Kingsway stands the church of Holy Trinity (1909-11) which replaced an earlier church of 1829-31. The church occupies the site of the house where Mary Lamb (1764-1847), in a fit of madness, stabbed her mother to death in 1796. Committed to an asylum, she was released into the guardianship of her brother Charles (1775-1834). Charles Lamb continued to care for his sister for the rest of his life and, despite making one proposal of marriage, he remained single so as the better to discharge his responsibility to Mary.

***

From this location, cross High Holborn into Southampton Row leading away to the north. A short distance into Southampton Row, Fisher Street turns off to the right and crosses Proctor Street to lead into Red Lion Square – much of the northern side of which has changed character with recent re-development.

In the small central garden of the square, facing Conway Hall, there is a bronze bust of Bertrand Russell (1872-1970), philosopher, who was connected with many of the literary and intellectual members of the Bloomsbury Group, and others. His relationships with them are substantially recorded in his own *Autobiography*, though some details of his own presentation have been challenged by biographers working on the lives of other subjects.

On the right-hand side of the square will be found No 17. A plaque there commemorates two literary and artistic connections. Dante Gabriel Rossetti (1828-82) lived at this house during the year 1851; his landlord imposing a condition that 'the models are to be kept under some gentlemanly restraint, as some artists sacrifice the dignity of art to the baseness of passion.' Rossetti's stay here followed shortly upon the forming of the Pre-Raphaelite Brotherhood. Among the seven members who formed the original group of painters were Rossetti, William Holman Hunt, and John Everett Millais. Though his first reputation was for art, and he was indeed known only as a painter for some years, Rossetti began his writing of poetry from about the age of eighteen or nineteen.

A few years after Rossetti's stay at No 17 it became the home of another painter-poet, William Morris (1834-96). Morris was a young man at the time of his occupancy (1856-9), and was at the beginning of that varied career which would bring him recognition as writer, painter, designer, and prominent socialist. The house was shared with Morris's lifelong friend Edward Burne-Jones (1833-98), a painter also associated with the pre-Raphaelites, and Richard Watson Dixon (1833-1900), poet and writer, whose friendships included members of that artistic movement together with Gerard Manley Hopkins and Robert Bridges.

***

At the far end of Red Lion Square, Princeton Street leads off to join, at its second junction, Bedford Row. Turning to the right here, Bedford Row continues for some little distance before turning to the left. Immediately ahead will be seen a gateway entrance with a few steps down into the gardens and precincts of Gray's Inn. One of the four remaining London Inns of Court, whose functions include the preparation of its students for the practice of Law as Barristers, Gray's Inn dates back to the fourteenth century.

Among literary persons, poets and dramatists, who have had connections with Gray's Inn, either as students or residents, and are not referred to later in the text of this section, are: Sir Philip Sidney (1554-86); George Chapman (1559-1634); Thomas Middleton (1570?-1627); James Shirley (1596-1666); Sir John Suckling (1609-42); Dr Samuel Johnson (1709-84); Oliver Goldsmith (1730?-74); Robert Southey (1774-1843); Hilaire Belloc (1870-1953).

To the left of the entrance will be seen a long flank of buildings. Beyond the first of these, the Aitkin Buildings, stretches the Raymond Buildings. At No 5, for almost 40 years from 1903, lived Edward Marsh (1872-1953). Marsh is remembered today chiefly as the editor of a series of anthologies of *Georgian Poetry*, of which five collections appeared between 1912 and 1922. Included in these collections, among others, were: Rupert Brooke, John Drinkwater, W. H. Davies, W. W. Gibson, James Elroy Flecker, John Masefield, Walter de la Mare, Ralph Hodgson, Siegried Sassoon, Robert Graves, Edmund Blunden, and D. H. Lawrence. And many of these poets visited Marsh at one time or another at this residence. Though the term 'Georgian' as applied to English poetry has come to stand, dismissively, as an epithet for a certain decorative preciousness, one lacking an intensity of substance (featured certainly in the slightest poetry of the period), the actual range of the poetry of the period covers a variety of styles and accomplishments – as the shortlist of names, above, confirms.

Directly facing are the gardens, laid out in 1606 to the design of Sir Francis Bacon (1561-1626). Sir Walter Ralegh (1552?-1618) walked these gardens in company with Bacon, and Bacon wrote an essay 'On Gardens' praising the beauties and contemplative virtues of gardens such as these. In addition to all the literary men, above, who would certainly have taken advantage of its walks, Gray's Inn gardens were much admired by Samuel Pepys, Joseph Addison, and Charles Lamb. They were used also, as a Sunday refuge, by Percy Bysshe Shelley (1792-1822) where he could meet Mary Godwin (1797-1851) and be free of arrest for debt.

From the gateway entrance the main pathway (around the gardens) leads off to the right, followed by a bearing to the left. The pathway comes to an arched entrance which is signed for Gray's Inn Square.

To the immediate left, No 1 marks the location of the chambers held by Sir Francis Bacon for a period of some fifty years of residence at the Inn. In the middle of the left-hand wing of buildings stands No 7, occupied for the last few years of the nineteenth century by Lionel Johnson (1867-1902), poet of the *aesthete* group and a member of the Rhymer's Club (see section: Fleet Street).

The building a few feet away and just to the right of the archway from which you emerged into the square, is Gray's Inn Hall, restored to its original designs after the bomb-destruction of 1941.

Two of the plays of George Gascoigne (1525?-77), a member of the Inn, were first performed in this Hall in the year 1566. They were: the tragedy, *Jocasta*, an adaptation from an Italian play (and ultimately from Euripides); and *Supposes*, a prose comedy – adapted again from the Italian (of Ariosto).

Almost thirty years later (1594) the *Comedy of Errors* of Shakespeare (1564-1616) was first performed at the Gray's Inn Hall.

Beyond the Hall, to the right, opens up South Square, surrounding a lawn and a statue of Sir Francis Bacon (see above).

Thomas Babington Macauley (1800-59), historian of England and the poet of *Lays of Ancient Rome* lived for some time at No 8 in the square. Charles Dickens (1812-70) worked as a youth of fifteen and sixteen at No 1, where he was employed as a junior clerk to an attorney in the firm of Ellis and Blackmore. Known then as Holborn Court not South Square, Dickens later sited somewhere in the square the chambers of Mr Phunky in the *Pickwick Papers*; and alongside the office where he had worked he located the address for Traddles in *David Copperfield*.

W. S. Gilbert (1836-1911), author of the *Babs Ballads* and the librettist of the Savoy comic operas, took chambers at No 3 South Square in 1866 or 1867.

* * *

Alongside No 1 will be seen a squared exit which will lead directly to a gateway issuing into High Holborn. On the far side of the road stands the large, half-timbered construction of Staple Inn – to which this tour will return.

Turn to the left where, within a few yards High

Holborn comes to the junction with Gray's Inn Road, beyond which Holborn continues. A short distance ahead, on the left, is Brooke Street. The street name is a reminder that here stood the house, until about 1680, of Sir Fulke Greville, Lord Brooke (1554-1628). The epitaph which he composed for himself and which is inscribed on a monument to him in a Warwick church reads: 'Servant to Queen Elizabeth, Councillor to King James, Friend to Sir Philip Sidney'.

The epitaph itself merely points to the public life of the man who attained high office, and knew from boyhood Sir Philip Sidney – of whom he wrote a biography which, like almost all of his works, was not published in Fulke Greville's own lifetime. A patron of Shakespeare and of Ben Johnson, Fulke Greville himself composed plays and poems – some of the latter of which deserve to be more widely appreciated. For in the best of them there is a sureness of control and an easy movement of line – as in, for example, this sonnet from the collection *Caelica*:

> In night when colours all to black are cast,
> Distinction lost, or gone down with the light;
> The eye a watch to inward senses plac'd,
> Not seeing, yet still having power of sight,
>
> Gains vain alarums to the inward sense,
> Where fear stirr'd up with witty tyranny [imagined]
> Confounds all powers, and thorough self-offence,
> Doth forge and raise impossibility:
>
> Such as in thick depriving darknesses,
> Proper reflections of the error be,
> And images of self-confusedness,
> Which hurt imaginations only see;
>   And from this nothing seen, tells news of devils,
>   Which but expressions be of inward evils.

Just within Brooke Street, on the left-hand side, formerly stood the house in which Thomas Chatterton (1752-70) committed suicide by taking arsenic. A plaque set at first-floor level in the present building locates the site.

Chatterton had arrived in London that year from Bristol where, in a remarkable feat of precocious literary mimicry, he had fabricated poems supposed to have been written by an imaginary fifteenth century monk, Thomas Rowley. With these he hoped to make his reputation in London. Though the fraud was discovered, some of the pieces – and other 'non-Rowley' compositions of Chatterton's – clearly display a remarkable poetic talent; one acknowledged in Wordsworth's famous description of him as the

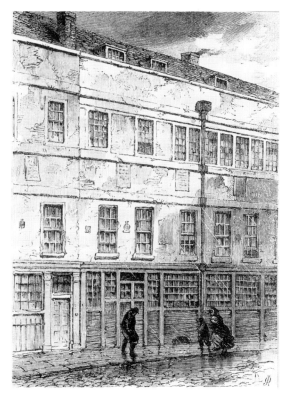

The house of Chatterton's lodgings, Brooke Street. Here the boy-poet occupied the garret – a square, largish room in the attic with two dormer windows. When his room was broken into on 25 August 1770 he was found lying on his bed, stiff and cold, with the remains of arsenic between his teeth.

'marvellous boy'. The story of Chatterton and his last days at this site have recently (1987) been made into the fiction and imaginatively-turned fact of Peter Ackroyd's novel *Chatterton* – a work which interweaves past with contemporary present, and which proposes an alternative theory of the boy-poet's death.

* * *

Beyond Brooke Street stands the enormous Victorian construction designed for the Prudential Assurance Company. A plaque at the entrance to this building reminds the reader that this was formerly the site of Furnival's Inn, one of the Inns of Chancery.

The function of the Inns of Chancery was the preparatory training of students wishing to be called to the Bar by one of the Inns of Court (the Chancery Inns themselves having no power to do so). The derivation of their title remains uncertain, but may well refer back to medieval times when Chancery clerks were responsible for drawing up all writs for the King's courts.

The original buildings which comprised Furnival's Inn were demolished in the first quarter of the nineteenth century, and the replacement building (which retained the title Furnival's Inn) was demolished in 1897. Sir Thomas More (1478-1535), whose brilliant legal career and parliamentary achievements led to the Lord Chancellorship (in 1529), was for some time a reader at Furnival's Inn.

In the replacement building Charles Dickens (see above) lived whilst working as a reporter,

A part of the terrace of the replacement Furnival's Inn, showing No 15 where Dickens lived.

'Boz', from the drawing by S. Lawrence, made the year after Dickens left Furnival's Inn.

mainly of debates in the House of Commons, for the *Morning Chronicle* during the years 1834-7. During this period he also contributed to a number of periodicals those pieces which were later gathered as the *Sketches by Boz*. Here too he worked on the *Pickwick Papers*, as they are known in their collected and short title. Appearing in twenty monthly instalments, the first of the *Posthumous Papers of the Pickwick Club* appeared in April 1836, when Dickens was just twenty-four.

Inside the entrance of the Prudential building there is a bust of Charles Dickens.

* * *

Crossing to the other side of Holborn, opposite the entrance to the Insurance Company's building, there is a narrow entrance to Dyer's Buildings. To the left of that entrance used to stand the house where Mrs Anne Radcliffe (1764-1823) was born. Anne Radcliffe, author of the 'Gothic' novel *The Mysteries of Udulpho* (1794), remained always a London resident.

Returning along Holborn towards its junction with Gray's Inn Road, within a few yards is the façade of the restored sixteenth century shops and houses which front Staple Inn.

Staple Inn itself, another of the Inns of Chancery, was originally a wool warehouse – from which the term 'staple' derives – purchased by Gray's Inn in 1529. Dating from the last quarter of the sixteenth century, its buildings have been restored on several occasions; substantial re-building in the mid-eighteenth century, most notably, and in the 1950s, most recently, following bomb damage sustained in World War II.

There is a central archway entrance, through the half-timbered houses, into the first of the two courtyards surrounded by the premises of the Inn. In Charles Dickens's unfinished *Edwin Drood* will be found the following description of the instant change experienced on stepping from Holborn into the courtyard; an experience with which the visitor will certainly agree:

> Behind the most ancient part of Holborn, London, where certain gabled houses some centuries of age still stand looking on the public way, as if disconsolately looking for the Old Bourne that has long run dry, is a little nook composed of two irregular quadrangles, called Staple Inn. It is one of those nooks, the turning into which out of the clashing street, imparts to the relieved pedestrian the sensation of having put cotton in his ears, and velvet soles on his feet. It is one of those nooks where a few smoky sparrows twitter in smoky trees, as though they called to one another, 'Let us play at country' . . .

In one of the houses (destroyed in the bombing) which made up Staple Inn Dr Samuel Johnson (see above) took attic lodgings during the years 1759-60. Here, in Boswell's account of the Doctor's life, Johnson wrote his moral fable *Rasselas, Prince of Abysinnia*

> that with the profits he might defray the expense of his mother's funeral, and pay some little debts which she had left. He told Sir Joshua Reynolds, that he composed it in the evenings of one week, sent it to the press in portions as it was written, and had never since read it over.

Johnson received one hundred pounds for the manuscript, with a further payment of twenty-five pounds on its reprinting. More than twenty years after its publication Johnson did re-read *Rasselas* and 'eagerly', when accidentally he came across a copy of the work.

Facing the entrance from Holborn stands the

The Hall of Staple Inn.

Hall of the Inn, restored, but dating from 1580. To the left of the Hall is another archway, leading into the second courtyard of the Inn. It was to this inner courtyard and its attractive gardens that Nathaniel Hawthorne was referring in this description of his discovery:

> . . . in a court opening inwards from [the first courtyard], there was a surrounding seclusion of quiet dwelling-houses, with beautiful green shrubbery and grass-plots in the court, and a great many sunflowers in full bloom. The windows were open; it was a lovely summer afternoon, and I have a sense that bees were humming in the court, though this may have been sug-

163

gested by my fancy, because the sound would have been so well suited to the scene . . .

To the left, on emerging into the second courtyard, will be seen No 10, and over the 'ugly portal' of its doorway 'the mysterious inscription', as Dickens referred to it in *Edwin Drood*:

> Neither wind nor sun favoured Staple Inn . . . one December afternoon towards six o'clock, when it was filled with fog, and candles shed murky and blurred rays through the windows of all its then occupied sets of chambers; notably from a set of chambers in a corner house in the little inner quadrangle, presenting in black and white over its ugly portal the mysterious inscription:
>
> P
> J T
> 1747
>
> in which set of chambers, never having troubled his head about the inscription, unless to bethink himself at odd times on glancing up to it, that haply it might mean Perhaps John Thomas or Perhaps Joe Tyler, sat Mr Grewgious writing by his fire.

Once inside the inner courtyard, visitors may notice an equally 'mysterious' (and also restored) legend over the doorway to one of the houses which is to the left of the archway leading back to the first quadrangle (T L P 1753).

* * *

Having explored the courtyards, return to Holborn turning to the left on leaving Staple Inn. Holborn soon becomes High Holborn, and within a short walk will be found Southampton Buildings opening on the left.

A number of literary associations attach to this street, though none of the buildings now remains. Charles Lamb (1775-1834), essayist, lived in one of the houses here during the years 1810 until 1817. The year after he moved in one of his house-guests was Samuel Taylor Coleridge (1772-1834), who stayed with Lamb for a period of several weeks.

Another resident was Thomas Love Peacock (1785-1866), novelist and poet. Peacock was an intimate friend of Shelley (see above), who stayed with Peacock at the Southampton Buildings address whilst he was in hiding from his creditors and meeting Mary Godwin on Sundays in the Gray's Inn gardens.

On the left-hand side of the street there is a modern office block, Hazlitt House, covering the site of a house which once stood there and was occupied by the critic and essayist during 1829. William Hazlitt (1778-1830) almost ten years earlier had lived in a house on the opposite side of the road. There, whilst still married to Sarah Stoddart, he fell in love with the landlady's daughter. *Liber Amoris* (1823) records the dejection and misery of this unsuccessful love-affair.

* * *

Southampton Buildings turns to the right and enters Chancery Lane, almost directly opposite one of the gateway entrances to the precincts of Lincoln's Inn, an Inn of Court founded in the middle of the fourteenth century.

The collection of buildings which comprise Lincoln's Inn date from the late fifteenth century through to the middle of the nineteenth. While building work was proceeding during the last stages of the sixteenth century Ben Jonson (1572-1637) was at work on the constructions, as a bricklayer – the trade he had learned from his stepfather. The fact was noted by John Aubrey (in his *Lives*), and confirmed by Thomas Fuller, historian and churchman – in whose words Jonson 'having a trowel in one hand, he had a book in his pocket'.

A number of literary men have been associated with Lincoln's Inn either as members, law students or simply as residents. Sir Thomas More (1478-1535) was a member of the Inn as, in a later age, was another philosopher, Jeremy Bentham (1748-1832). The poets George Wither (1588-1667) and John Denham (1615-69) studied at the Inn. Novelists connected with Lincoln's Inn include Benjamin Disraeli (1804-81), who enrolled as a student in 1824; Horace Walpole (1719-97); and Charles Reade (1814-84) – whose studying here, in the words of George Williams, 'seems to have consisted mostly of dining the required number of times in the Hall'.

On entering the precincts of the Inn, there will be seen ahead, and running off to the right, the classically-styled Stone Buildings of the 1770s. A little way along the flank of these buildings is No 5, where John Galsworthy (1867-1933), novelist and dramatist, had chambers for four years from 1890.

By turning to the left here, away from the Stone Buildings, you will enter Old Square. Ahead is the Chapel, easily distinguished by the open arches of its undercroft; an unusual feature of its design intended to serve as an informal meeting-place for students. Much restored and renovated, the Chapel

The undercroft of Lincoln's Inn Chapel.

dates from 1619-23, and is usually attributed to Inigo Jones. The foundation stone was laid by John Donne (1572-1631) who by that time had been made Dean of St Paul's. Donne had himself been admitted to membership of the Inn in 1592. Upon the completion of the Chapel Donne, appointed also as the Inn's Divinity Reader, returned to deliver the sermon at the consecration service held on Ascension Day 1623.

It became the custom then, as it has remained to this day, to toll the bell for a half-hour between 12.30 and 1.00pm when a Bencher of the Inn dies. This, it has long been argued, suggested the theme out of which emerged Donne's famous reflection gathered in his *Devotions*:

> No man is an island, entire of itself; every man is a piece of the continent, a part of the main; if a clod be washed away by the sea, as well as if a promontory were, as well as if a manor of thy friend's or of thine own were; any man's death diminishes me, because I am involved in mankind; and therefore never send to know for whom the bell tolls; it tolls for thee.

Adjoining the chapel is Old Hall, dating from the last decade of the fifteenth century. From the middle of the eighteenth century until the opening of the new Law Courts in 1882, the Old Hall of Lincoln's Inn was often used, after term-time, as the High Court of Chancery; during term-time transferring to Westminster Hall.

Here, in the Old Hall, maunders on the unending case of Jarndyce v. Jarndyce in Charles Dickens's *Bleak House*, for which it provides the opening setting: 'London, Michaelmas term lately over, and the Lord Chancellor sitting in Lincoln's Inn Hall. Implacable November weather . . .' From this develops the wonderfully atmospheric 'fog' of the novel's first chapter – a fog which provides too a working metaphor for the legal complexities of the case in question.

In one of the houses surrounding the Chapel and Hall, Dickens located the office of Serjeant Snubbin (*Pickwick Papers*, chap. xxxi). At No 13 lived for some time Sir Henry Newbolt (1862-1938), and at a later period a part of the same house was occupied by Richard Church (1893-1972) – poets of widely dissimilar intents and attainments.

On leaving Old Square there will be seen, away to the right 'the new garden which they are making and which will be very pretty', as Pepys recorded the progress on 27 June 1663. Almost two centuries later Dickens's Miss Flite (in Bleak House, ch. v) spoke of the garden of Lincoln's Inn:

> I call it my garden, It is quite a bower in the summer-time. Where the birds sing melodiously. I pass the greater part of the long vacation here. In contemplation.

The Gardens, since towards the end of the last century, have been open to the public.

***

To the left on exiting from Old Square and the Hall, however, are the three sides of buildings comprising New Square, rows of houses dating from the 1680s and 90s. On the left-hand, nearest side of the square are Nos 1 and 2; in the far, top left-hand corner are Nos 7 and 8.

At No 1 lived Arthur Murphy (1727-1805), in his day a successful dramatist – during the Garrick era – whose plays seem now very much to belong merely to the period. Murphy was a friend of Garrick and Garrick's circle, including Dr Johnson.

John Galsworthy (see above) had rooms at No 2 whilst he was studying law. At the opposite side of the square, at No 7, William Wordsworth (1770-1850) is known to have stayed on occasion with one of his friends, Basil Montagu, for periods of time during 1795 and 1796. For part of 1827 Charles Dickens was employed as a law clerk in the chambers next door, at No 8; whilst just before the end of the nineteenth century Lionel Johnson (1867-1902), poet of the 'Aesthetic' movement and a member of the Rhymers' Club, had lodgings in the same house.

***

Beyond the far flank of houses comprising New Square there is an archway exit into Serle Street. Turn to the left here, and about a hundred yards on, on the left-hand side of the junction with Carey Street, stands a building with a statue of Sir Thomas More (see above) mounted at first floor level. The stone figure (of 1866) of More is inscribed to 'The Faithful servant both of God and the King. Martyred July 5th 1535'.

At this junction turn to the right along Carey Street which circles back towards Portugal Street where, facing, stretches a long, unbroken flank of tall brickwork. The wall is part of the rear of the museum of the Royal College of Surgeons (see later entry), but marks the former location of the Lincoln's Inn Fields Theatre which stood on this site.

The first Lincoln's Inn Fields Theatre opened in 1661, converted from a covered tennis court. It was occupied by the company of Sir William D'Avenant (1606-68), playwright and Poet Laureate, and rumoured – almost certainly falsely – to have been the natural son of William Shakespeare. Two innovations to this theatre were: the first use of a proscenium arch, and the use of movable scenery on stage.

Ten years later, the Duke's company having moved elsewhere (to Dorset Garden theatre), it was used by the company of Thomas Killigrew (1612-83) for just two or three years, before it reverted once more to being a tennis court.

Towards the end of the century the building was again converted into a theatre. This time the company was led by William Congreve (1670-1729) and Thomas Betterton (1635?-1710), the latter of whom had been formerly a member of D'Avenant's company at the Lincoln's Inn Fields theatre. The leading female members of this new company were: Elizabeth Barry (1658-1713), to whom the dramatist Thomas Otway was devoted, but from whom he received no encouragement; and Anne Bracegirdle (1663?-1748), Congreve's constant friend and, perhaps, lover too – of whom Colley Cibber flatteringly remarked that 'on the stage few spectators that were not past it could behold her without desire'.

The new company opened with Congreve's *Love for Love* in 1695, and in 1700 staged the first production of his *Way of the World*. Four years later the company moved out to another theatre in the Haymarket.

After another ten years the theatre was re-opened by John Rich (1682?-1761) in 1714. In 1728 he staged at Lincoln's Inn theatre John Gay's *Beggar's Opera*, a production which met with such overwhelming success that it was said to have 'made Rich gay and Gay rich'. In 1732, however, Rich transferred his theatrical ventures to the Covent Garden theatre. Thereafter the buildings of the Lincoln's Inn theatre were put to a variety of purposes before their eventual demolition in the middle of the nineteenth century.

***

At this junction Portugal Street runs off to the right to join Serle Street. Turning left here will bring you to the south-east corner of Lincoln's Inn Fields. The original fields enclosed by the square had been, from the fourteenth century, the playground for students from the adjoining Lincoln's Inn. Not until the 1630s, however, were these open spaces enclosed by residential buildings. It soon became a fashionable area in which to live. The fields themselves, however, were still a place of execution, and the daily setting for brawling and robbery. The danger of the open space was clearly detailed by John Gay (1685-1732) in his *Trivia; or, the Art of Walking the Streets of London* (1716):

> Where Lincoln's Inn, wide space, is rail'd around,
> Cross not with venturous step; there oft is found
> The lurking thief, who, while the daylight shone,
> Made the walls echo with his begging tone,
> That crutch, which late compassion moved, shall wound
> Thy bleeding head, and fell thee to the ground . . .

To the immediate left of the corner entered from Serle Street stands the Royal College of Surgeons' building, covering the site of a house once occupied by Robert Sidney, 2nd Earl of Leicester. To his daughter, Dorothy, Edmund Waller (1606-87) paid court, after the death of his first wife, addressing her in a series of love poems as 'Sacharissa'. Some of the love-lyrics display a fine compression and an elegant simplicity.

Beyond these and the adjoining buildings, at the south-west corner of the square, the narrow Portsmouth Street leads off. Within a very short distance along here, on the left, will be found *The Old Curiosity Shop*. The building, of 1567, is certainly worth inspecting in its own right, for there can be little doubt that it is the oldest of its kind still remaining in London. It is certainly not, however, the original for the home of Dickens's Little Nell, despite the claims of the shop-front legends. (*That* Old Curiosity Shop was located in the area of the National Portrait Gallery – either in front of the gallery, in St Martin's Place, or just beyond and behind the gallery, in what is now Orange Street.)

The building in Portugal Street, formerly the Lincoln's Inn Theatre.

Stepping back to the square, about half-way along the left-hand (west) flank of Lincoln's Inn Fields, will be found No 58. This was the home of John Forster (1812-76), critic, and author of the first biography, a three-volume work, of his friend Charles Dickens. To Forster and other friends Dickens first read at this house the then unpublished story *The Chimes*, in 1844. Dickens returned from a trip to Italy especially for the purpose.

Dickens reading to his friends, on 2 December 1844, 'The Chimes', at 58 Lincoln's Inn Fields. The drawing, by Maclise, shows (left to right): Forster, Jerrold, Blanchard, Carlyle, Dickens, Frederick Dickens (brother), Maclise, Fox, Stanfield, Dyce and Harness. Three days later, at the insistence of the Rev R. H. Barham (author of the Ingoldsby Legends)*, Dickens gave a second reading with, in Barham's own diary words, 'remarkable effect'.*

Dickens also chose No 58 in which to locate the residence of Mr Tulkinghorn, Sir Leicester Dedlock's lawyer in *Bleak House*:

> Here, in a large house, formerly a house of state, lives Mr Tulkinghorn. It is let off in sets of chambers now; and in those shrunken fragments of its greatness, lawyers lie like maggots in nuts. But its roomy staircases, passages, and ante-chambers still remain; and even its painted ceilings . . .

At the house alongside, No 59, Charles Sackville, 6th Earl of Dorset (1638-1706), lived for a year or two around 1700. After youthful dissipation, Sackville attained distinction in public affairs. His verses, admired by many of his contemporaries, are frequently light, and sometimes playful in tone – as in his best-known *Song; Written at Sea, in the first Dutch War* . . .

> To all you ladies now at land
>   We men at sea indite;
> But first wou'd have you understand
>   How hard it is to write;
> The Muses now, and Neptune too,
> We must implore to write to you,
>   With fa, la, la, la, la . . .

The same house, No 59, was later occupied by Dante Gabriel Rossetti (see above) in 1862, shortly after the death in that year of his wife, Elizabeth Siddal (b.1829), who had been the model for Rossetti and other painters of the pre-Raphaelite Brotherhood. She and Rossetti had been lovers for years before Rossetti married the beautiful Elizabeth in 1860. They lived at Rossetti's house (now gone) just off Victoria Embankment, close to Blackfriars Bridge. In the year after their marriage she gave birth to a stillborn daughter. And in the year following she took an overdose of laudanum, by accident or design will not finally be established, and died the next morning. Distraught and perhaps even distracted, Rossetti caused to be buried with her a collection of his own manuscript poems, sonnets written to his wife, which were laid across her body. Subsequently, after much persuasion from friends, Rossetti had the poems disinterred. Some appeared in *Poems* (1870), and the completion of the sonnet-sequence 'The House of Life' of which they were a part, appeared in the collection of *Ballads and Sonnets* (1881).

Along the far, northern, side of the square stand Nos 12, 13, and 14, the façades to which present a symmetrical composition balancing around the central house. Somewhere before these houses stood a former residence, facing *away* from the Fields, which was occupied by John Milton (1608-74) for a couple of years or so during that period of something like twenty years in which the only poetry he wrote was the occasional sonnet. Where the present houses stand there was formerly a house where John Dryden (1631-1700) lived briefly.

The present houses were designed by Sir John Soane (1753-1837), and now comprise the Museum named after him. Here are exhibited a diverse, fascinating, and crowded miscellany of antiquities and curios collected by Sir John. A number of paintings are held here; among them works by J. M. W. Turner, Canaletto, Fuseli, and Sir Joshua Reynolds. For those interested in the eighteenth century, and the compositional interaction between art and literature, there is on display in the Picture Room some of William Hogarth's most important paintings. There is the set of eight paintings representing *The Rake's Progress* of Tom Rakewell, the eight phases of his career from inheritance to the mad-house. There is also the savagely satirical series of four scenes depicting political greed and corruption, *The Election*.

Entrance to the Museum is free. It is open 10.00am until 5.00pm Tuesday to Saturday (closed Sundays, Mondays, and Bank Holidays).

***

Upon leaving the Museum and turning to the right, straight ahead will be seen the narrow Remnant Street which connects with Kingsway. To the right here, a little distance ahead, will be seen the entrance to Holborn underground station.

BLOOMSBURY I

CAMDEN

The boundaries of Bloomsbury are usually defined by the large area drawn within Euston Road (to the north), Gray's Inn Road (to the east), Theobald's Road and its continuations of Bloomsbury Way and New Oxford Street (to the south), and Tottenham Court Road (to the west).

Because the area bounded by these limits is so extensive the following guide to Bloomsbury has been divided into two tours. They have been designed in such a way that, since the first of them ends at Russell Square underground station and the second begins at the same place, it would be possible for the energetic to cover the whole territory within a day – perhaps making separate visits on other occasions to the Dickens House (Bloomsbury I) or the British Museum (Bloomsbury II).

* * *

The title of Bloomsbury itself derives from the thirteenth century *Blemondisberi*, the 'bury' (or manor) of Blemond – after William Blemond, who first acquired the land. The development of the squares within the area began in the seventeenth century with Bloomsbury Square (then known as Southampton Square), followed by the building of grand houses, most notably Montagu House (now the British Museum). Subsequent developments largely derived from the Russell family who came to own much of the estate. Through into the eighteenth century the area retained a rural quality, the hills of Hampstead and Highgate still visible. In the nineteenth century Bloomsbury began to lose much of its appeal to families of quality and fashion, though retaining its respectability – and its residences became increasingly popular with lawyers, artists, and writers.

* * *

Starting at Holborn underground station, cross to the far side of High Holborn, heading left, beyond Southampton Row. Some fifty yards or so beyond this junction, Southampton Place opens on the right.

On the left-hand side of Southampton Place, immediately at the corner with Bloomsbury Square, stood the house in which Colley Cibber (1671-1757) was born. Poet and playwright, he became Poet Laureate in 1730, for which he was fiercely attacked by other writers; most notably Alexander Pope, who made Cibber the 'hero', and the butt of his satire, in *The Dunciad*.

On the opposite corner of Southampton Place, facing into Bloomsbury Square, stands the residence which was formerly the town house of the Earls of Chesterfield. The building carries a plaque to their memory. The 4th Earl (Philip Dormer Stanhope, 1694-1773) did not make the house his regular residence – though he certainly stayed there on occasion. And it is this Earl of Chesterfield who is remembered on two particular counts – one to literature itself, and one to literary history. There are his *Letters*, written for the education of his natural son; and there is the history of his 'patronage' of Dr Johnson, and the latter's scheme for his *Dictionary*.

* * *

In the houses which formerly occupied Bloomsbury Square three authors resided. Charles Sedley (1639?-1701), poet and dramatist, achieved his contemporary position as much for the locution of his wit and the profligacy of his living as for the quality of his plays and light lyricism of his songs. Sedley lived in the Square throughout his last ten years.

Mark Akenside (1721-70), author of the long philosophical poem *The Pleasures of Imagination*, lived at Bloomsbury Square from 1750, for almost ten years. A man who seems to have been almost universally liked, Akenside was also a physician of high reputation.

Sir Richard Steele (1672-1729) lived in the Square for the three years up to 1715, the year in which he received his knighthood. A man whose career and accomplishments were many and varied, his place in literature now records his role as essayist rather than as poet and playwright. His house was somewhere on the east (right-hand) side of the Square covered by the extensive London Victoria Insurance buildings.

* * *

Sir Richard Steele, whose profligacy led him to take on a large, grand residence in Soho Square, though clearly he could not afford it. At one of the entertainments which he there hosted six queer-looking individuals waited at table. Steele himself announced to the distinguished guests that 'His lacqueys were bailiffs in disguise to a man'.

On the far side of Bloomsbury Square, leading northwards to Russell Square, is Bedford Place – an avenue of terraced houses built in the first years of the nineteenth century. Visitors who wish to explore Bedford Place will find, about a hundred yards into the street, on the left-hand side, No 30, the house where Richard Cumberland (1732-1811) died. Cumberland, dramatist and novelist, provided Sheridan with the model for Sir Fretful Plagiary in his play *The Critic*.

No 34 was the home, briefly, of Richard le Gallienne (1866-1947), poet and critic, and member of the Rhymers' Club.

* * *

Returning to Bloomsbury Square, and taking the right-hand side of the square, you will pass No 12, about half-way down that flank. Here lived one of the Rossettis' aunts, and here Christina Rossetti (1830-94) frequently stayed.

Beyond this house, at the bottom (south) end of the Square, Bloomsbury Way leads off to the west. Within a short walk along here, to the right, is Bury Place; and shortly into Bury Place, Little Russell Street opens on the left. Just into this latter street, on the right-hand side, stands No 18, where W. H. Davies (1871-1940), poet, lodged in 1914. Some six years prior to taking up this temporary residence he had already recounted the direction of his life with the *Autobiography of a Super-Tramp*.

A hundred yards or so beyond here Museum Street crosses Little Russell Street. By turning right at this junction the visitor will emerge at Great Russell Street, just a few yards on, and directly opposite the British Museum (which this tour passes by – incorporating a visit within Bloomsbury II).

Turn to the left here. A short distance along Great Russell Street you will come to No 38 – on the left and immediately beyond the turning into narrow Willoughby Street. At this address, for twenty years until 1930, lived Harold Monro (1879-1932), poet, and founder of the *Poetry Review* (1911), through which he exercised a considerable influence upon English poetry of the times.

Just beyond this place, and on the opposite side of the street, at first-floor level of No 91, will be seen a plaque to George du Maurier (1834-1896), artist and writer, who lived at this house 1863-68. His three novels were all written in the last six years or so of his life, the last (*The Martian*) published posthumously. The best-known of the novels is undoubtedly *Trilby* (1894) for two reasons: for the creation of Svengali, the musician with almost magical powers of hypnosis; and for the hat worn by Trilby O'Ferrall. For the felt hat with the indented crown worn by him came to be known, through association, by the

171

name of its wearer. In addition to his writings many of du Maurier's satirical drawings appeared originally in the magazine *Punch*.

Continuing along Great Russell Street, beyond its junction with Bloomsbury Street, you will come to No 14, on the left. Here lived Mr Charles Kitterbell, 'one of the most credulous and matter-of-fact little personages that ever took *to* himself a wife, and *for* himself a house in Great Russell Street . . .' A blue plaque commemorates the association of this place with the story of Charles Dickens (1812-70), 'The Bloomsbury Christening'. Collected in his *Sketches by Boz*, it was the third or fourth fictional sketch written by Dickens for *The Monthly Magazine* in 1832; and therefore one of the pieces which effectively launched the young writer upon his career.

W. H. Davies (see above) later stayed in this house for six years from 1916.

On the opposite side of the street, and heading back towards the junction with Bloomsbury Street, stands No 109. The essayist and critic William Hazlitt (1778-1830) stayed at this, his brother's house, for the three years up to 1807 – the year before his marriage to Sarah Stoddart, to whom he had been introduced by his friends Charles and Mary Lamb.

A few yards further on will be seen the house, at Nos 100-101, of Topham Beauclerk (1739-80), always thought of with affection by Dr Johnson, and one of the founding members of his Literary Club. Though the front of the house was re-designed in 1821, the house itself dates from the 1680s. When Beauclerk, a scholar and bibliophile, took over the building in 1778 he installed there a library of some 30,000 volumes.

* * *

Having retraced steps as far as Bloomsbury Street, turn left. Within a short walk Bedford Square, the only entirely Georgian (of 1775-80) square of terraced houses remaining in Bloomsbury, opens on the left. Around the square will be found located the offices of several publishing houses.

Along its southern flank, the first to be entered, will be found No 44. Here, for part of the 1920s lived the Asquiths. Herbert Asquith (1852-1928), who had been Prime Minister between the years 1908 and 1916, and his wife Margot (1865-1945) were both authors of several memoirs, Margot's the more

One flank of the Georgian houses of Bedford Square.

spontaneous and therefore the ones causing greatest social reaction.

The same house had earlier been occupied by the Morrells, Philip and his wife Ottoline, before moving to a nearby house in Gower Street (see Bloomsbury II). Lady Ottoline Morrell (1873-1938), as she became, was acquainted with many – and intimately with some – of the Bloomsbury Group as they subsequently came to be known, though she was herself not a member of the Group.

Three doors beyond, at No 41, lived Sir Anthony Hope Hawkins (1863-1933) between the years 1903 and 1917. As Anthony Hope, though his plays are largely forgotten, he is read still for his adventure stories *The Prisoner of Zenda* (1894) and *Rupert of Hentzau* (1898).

By continuing around the Square, along its opposite (northern) flank stands No 25, where lived Bryan Waller Proctor (1787-1874), friend of Leigh Hunt, William Hazlitt, Charles Lamb, and Charles Dickens. As Barry Cornwall he had a considerable contemporary reputation – mainly for his poetry, most of which was composed as lyric songs. He was also a playwright, and the author of biographies of Edmund Kean and of Charles Lamb.

* * *

Almost directly opposite the exit from this northern flank of the square will be seen the entrance to Montague Place which passes by the rear of the British Museum to lead into Russell Square. This large square was first formally laid out in 1800, was popular with professional people, but has undergone much alteration. A few of the original houses remain. Thackeray took the square for the residences of the Sedleys and the Osbornes in his *Vanity Fair*.

Some way along the row of houses on the south side of the square (the flank to your right as you emerge into the square) is No 56 where lived Mary Russell Mitford (1787-1855), novelist, dramatist, and author of some *Sketches of rural life, character, and scenery*, which are still very readable. In her *Recollections of a Literary Life* (1852) she recorded her observations on various guests attending a dinner at the house in Russell Square in 1836. Among those who attended were William Wordsworth, Walter Savage Landor ('exceedingly clever'), Bryan Proctor, Robert Browning . . . 'and quantities more of poets'.

Across the square, on its far side, stands the Imperial Hotel. The hotel covers the site of the former houses there which included Nos. 61 and 62. At No 62 lived William Cowper (1731-1800), poet, whilst a day-student at Westminster School. And at No 61 lived Mrs Humphrey Ward (1852-1900) and her husband. The granddaughter of Thomas Arnold, of Rugby School, and a niece of Matthew Arnold, Mrs Humphrey Ward was novelist, translator, and social campaigner.

Along the western flank of the square and further on from the point where one entered, stands the building of the Royal Institute of Chemistry. Formerly there stood here No 30 where Henry Crabb Robinson (1775-1867) lived for the last twenty-five years of his life. As a young man Robinson had travelled in Germany, where he had met both Goethe and Schiller. His extensive diary and correspondence, first published two years after his death, reveal a good deal of interesting fact and opinion on the character and personality of many of the literary persons with whom he was acquainted; including Wordsworth, Coleridge, and Lamb.

Beyond this building, and just to the right of the narrow Thornhaugh Street which leads off from the corner of the square, stands No 24. A plaque here celebrates T. S. Eliot (1888-1965), poet, playwright, and author of criticism which continues to exercise a profound influence. At this address were the editorial offices of Faber and Faber (formerly Faber and Gwyer) where Eliot worked as editor and director in the publishing-house business from 1925 until his death.

His office was on the second floor at the rear of the building and looking north, towards Woburn Square. In 1943 Eliot, who was spending Tuesday and Friday of every week in London, frequently stayed in a small flat within the offices – principally because he had taken up fire-watching duties. In June of the following year a 'flying bomb' fell upon the building, rendering the small flat uninhabitable.

At this office he was harassed by his first wife from whom he was estranged. To escape Vivienne he left messages to say he was engaged, and on other occasions took flight on the fire escape in order to avoid her.

* * *

By continuing along this northern side of the square you will come to Woburn Place with exits on the left. Within a short distance along Woburn Place, Coram Street opens on the right.

Though all trace of the house has gone (No 13 Great Coram Street, as it then was), William Makepeace Thackeray (1811-63) lived here for six years upon his return from Paris, in 1837, having married Isabella Shawe the year previously. Here, despite the 'modest' rent, they struggled financially whilst Thackeray worked hard to establish himself as a writer – accepting every commission which came his way. His wife sadly never recovered from the mental breakdown which assailed her following the birth of their third child, and in 1840 they separated.

During the last year of his occupancy of the Coram Street residence Edward Fitzgerald (1809-1903), translator of the *Rubaiyat* of Omar Khyyam and Thackeray's friend from Cambridge days, stayed with Thackeray for several months.

* * *

Coram Street takes a turn to the right to join with Bernard Street, where you turn to the left. Bernard Street leads into Brunswick Square. The square has been completely re-developed, so the locations of the following literary associations no longer exist, though the 'airy' aspect noted by Isabella in Jane Austen's *Emma* may still be to some extent witnessed (by turning one's back on the intrusive concrete greyness of Brunswick Centre which occupies the whole of the west side):

> Our part of London is so very superior to most others . . . The neighbourhood of Brunswick Square is very different from all the rest. We are so very airy . . . Mr Wingfield thinks the vicinity of Brunswick Square the most favourable as to air.

Several members of the Bloomsbury Group (see further details: Bloomsbury II) shared a four-storey house, at what was No 38, in the square. Virginia Stephen and her brother Adrian, together with Duncan Grant, John Maynard Keynes, and Leonard Woolf all lived at the same address, before Leonard Woolf and Virginia left to get married in 1912.

Another member of the Group, E. M. Forster (1879-1968) had a home in the square for ten years from 1929.

Others who have lived on the square include: Bryan Waller Proctor (see above); and A. E. (George William Russell, 1867-1935), whose poetry was so much admired by W. B. Yeats.

On the north flank of the square (to the left at the

William Makepeace Thackeray.

point of entry) stands, at No 40, the offices of the Coram Foundation – and beyond that Coram's Fields (open to children, and adults accompanied by children). In those fields once stood the Foundling Hospital established in the first part of the eighteenth century by Captain Coram, a retired sea-captain, as a response to the horror of so many abandoned small children fending for themselves in the streets of London.

In those early days William Hogarth was a patron of the charity, donating some of his works as a means of attracting guests to the house so that they too would support the foundation. Handel, likewise, was a patron, presenting to the chapel an organ. This, and Hogarth's paintings, may be seen on display in the present headquarters.

In the nineteenth century Charles Dickens was a strong supporter of the charity, attending quite regularly its Sunday chapel services. The name of the foundling child Tattycoram, in Dicken's *Little Dorrit*, quite clearly evokes the charity.

***

The left-hand side of Brunswick Square leads directly into Hunter Street. In a house, of which no trace remains, a little way into this street (at what was No 54) John Ruskin (1819-1900) was born and spent the first four years of his boyhood. The writings of Ruskin, the Victorian moralist and critic of art, were subsequently to be held up as models of 'style' for generations of schoolchildren.

A short distance on, Tavistock Place crosses Hunter Street. A turn to the right here will bring you, within a hundred yards or so, to Regent Square on the left. Now completely re-developed as blocks of flats, in a former house in the square Aldous Huxley (1894-1963), novelist, essayist, and social critic, lived briefly in 1921.

***

Continuing past the square, and no more than a couple of minutes' walk ahead, Sidmouth Street leads to Gray's Inn Road. Turning to the right here, fifty yards along Gray's Inn Road, Heathcote Street emerges on the right. Mecklenburgh Street immediately opens up to the left, with Mecklenburgh Square just ahead.

A little to the right of the corner of the square at which you emerge stood No 37, now covered by a more recent building, to which Virginia Woolf (1882-1941) and her husband Leonard (1880-1969) moved in 1939 from Tavistock Square (see Bloomsbury II).

Leonard Woolf stayed on at this address for a year following Virginia's suicide.

A little further along this (northern) flank of the square can be seen No 44 where D. H. Lawrence (1885-1930) stayed for two months towards the end of 1917. Lawrence and his wife, Frieda, had been living in a cottage at Zennor in Cornwall. The activities there of Lawrence and Frieda had attracted the attentions of the authorities. Lawrence was known to be passionately anti-war; his writings were an unambiguous proclamation of his views. Frieda von Richthofen, born in Germany, was of aristocratic Silesian descent, and cousin to the famous Red Baron, the air ace. She was also in contact with her family, via Switzerland – such affiliations which she once described as 'the little bit of German in me'. Additionally, whilst at Cornwall, the Lawrences had entertained many visitors, some of them foreign. The whole consequence was that on the 11 October the Lawrences had been visited by a captain, two detectives, and a constable, and ordered to leave within three days.

At such short notice, and as always with very little money, the Lawrences had to rely upon the generosity of friends to house them. An invitation from Dorothy Yorke, a young American woman, brought them to her rooms in Mecklenburgh Square, in which house lived also Richard Aldington (1892-1962), poet, critic and novelist – at that time serving in the army – with his wife Hilda Doolittle (1886-1961), the American Imagist poet 'H.D.'. At the instigation of his wife who, following a miscarriage, wished to avoid further sex with him, Aldington had taken Yorke as a mistress – subsequently leaving Doolittle in order to marry her. After the Lawrences had been at No 44 for some weeks Aldington, in his own words, 'most inconsiderately turned up on long leave'. In the December the Lawrences left Mecklenburgh Square in order to take up yet another temporary accommodation, at a farm in Berkshire.

After the First World War, Dorothy L. Sayers (1893-1957), creator of the Lord Peter Wimsey detective fictions, moved into one of the apartments in the same No 44. The impulse to the writing of the first Wimsey novel was Sayer's financial problems. The success of her writing enabled her to move to Great James Street (see below) within three years.

Continuing straight ahead from the corner where you entered the square, along the eastern side of the square consisting of terraced houses – a little beyond

No 21 where there is a blue plaque to R. H. Tawney, historian and political writer – will be seen No 18. This was the home of John Masefield (1879-1967), poet, playwright, and novelist, for the three years from 1932. By the time he took up residence here he had already published most of that work upon which his reputation persists, and had been made Poet Laureate (1930) in recognition.

***

Beyond the square, Doughty Street leads away, crossing Guilford Street. A little way past this junction, on the left-hand side of the street, will be found No 48, The Dickens House.

To this house Charles Dickens (1812-70) moved with his wife Catherine and their first-born child Charles, then but a few weeks old, from chambers in Furnival's Inn on the last day of March or the first days of April 1837. By then the Dickenses had been married for a year, and were to stay at this address until the end of 1839. It is the only one of Dickens's London homes still standing.

Whilst at this address Dickens completed work on *The Pickwick Papers*, and *Oliver Twist* (the first few instalments of which had been begun at Furnival's Inn). Here he wrote too the whole of *Nicholas Nickleby*, a project he had had in mind for some time, but which took firm shape following a trip to Yorkshire (accompanied by 'Phiz', the illustrator H. K. Browne) in January 1838 to investigate the scandalous conditions of some of the cheap boarding-schools. Before leaving Doughty Street Dickens had also begun work on the first sections of *Barnaby Rudge*.

Dickens's prodigious output demanded sustained periods of work and a quite remarkable ability to concentrate on the work-in-hand, whatever distractions might be around him. And yet he was a gregarious man – as the list of visitors to this house would demonstrate. His ability to get on with the work, *and* to enjoy company simultaneously reminds one of the same energies of composition which Mozart was able to bring to his music. For just as Mozart was able to continue his scoring whilst engaging in the conversation around him, so was Dickens able to continue his writing and engage with his company.

Dickens was also a sentimental man who felt deeply. Within a month of moving in to Doughty Street Mary Hogarth, his wife's younger sister and a regular visitor to the house, collapsed of a heart seizure. She died the following day, in Dickens's arms, in her bedroom at the house. Dickens was extremely fond of the seventeen-year-old girl and her death 'left a blank which no one who ever knew her can have the faintest hope of seeing supplied'. Three years later Mary's death found its fictional embodiment in the illness and death, at the same age, of Little Nell in *The Old Curiosity Shop*.

The Dickens House is a museum, administered by the Dickens Fellowship, for which there is a small entrance charge (open weekdays, 10.00am to 5.00pm, closed Sundays and Bank Holidays). It should certainly be visited, for it contains a fascinating collection of materials and objects, many of them unique, displayed to advantage and in a way which will almost certainly demand the lingering perusal of the visitor.

The Dickens House at 48 Doughty Street.

There is not space here, obviously, to attempt to catalogue the exhibits, but mention of just a few random items here may serve to arouse interest and curiosity. In the Morning Room on the ground floor, for example, is displayed the desk at which Dickens sat and worked as a junior clerk in the offices of Ellis and Blackmore, Gray's Inn. In the same room can be seen the pantry window, from a house in Chertsey, through which Oliver was supposed to have been pushed by Bill Sikes in *Oliver Twist*.

In the first floor Study can be seen the writing-desk at which Dickens worked in his Gad's Hill home – and nearby is the death-bed sketch made of Dickens by Millais.

On the landing between the first and second floors there is the original Goldbeater's Arm from No 2 Manette Street, Soho, referred to in *A Tale of Two Cities* (ch.6).

Dickens's life-long passion for theatre is amply evidenced in exhibits collected in Mary Hogarth's Room and the Suzannet Rooms on the second floor. In the former can be seen some of the original play-bills which Dickens had printed for productions which he staged at Tavistock House (see Bloomsbury II). In the Suzannet Rooms are displayed several of the author's personal prompt-copies which he prepared for readings of various of his works. They show not only a meticulous preparation but very clearly too a sense of the theatrical with which he animated his public readings.

Since the museum has been restored to its contemporary conditions, it should be mentioned too that the geography of the house will itself be of interest to visitors, as a reminder of early Victorian conditions.

* * *

On leaving the Dickens House turn left along Doughty Street which becomes John Street. Within a minute's walk will be seen to the right narrow Northington Street which emerges at the northern end of Great James Street, a stylish file of houses – most of them the originals of the 1720s.

Some way down the street, on the left-hand side, will be found No 15. Here, in the years 1872-3, lived Walter Theodore Watts-Dunton (1832-1914) who, trained as a solicitor, gave up that profession in order to engage with literary criticism. In 1872 he met George Borrow (then nearly seventy and living just off Gloucester Road, South Kensington), later editing re-publications of Borrow's two best-known

Charles Dickens, his wife, and her sister, from the pencil drawing by Maclise (1843).

works, *Lavengro* and *Romany Rye*. And in the same year of 1872 Watts-Dunton met Algernon Charles Swinburne (1837-1909), whom he befriended. Swinburne was living further along the same side of Great James Street, at No 3. He lived there for two periods: for three years from 1872, and then from 1877-8.

Swinburne's lush and pagan poetry had shocked Victorian readers, as would his life-style of debauchery have scandalised, had it been public knowledge. Even whilst at Great James Street his health was not good. And when, the year after his second occupation of the house in Great James Street, he was living in nearby Guilford Street, his health was in actual decline. In that year Watts-Dunton rescued the poet, transferred him to his home in Putney, and looked after him from that time until Swinburne's death. It is a commonplace of criticism to note that after his removal from that former life of dissipation, Swinburne never again produced verse of the intensity of the earlier poems and ballads, though the sureness of euphony persists.

Before the Swinburne house will be seen No 5, where E. V. Lucas (1868-1938), novelist and essayist (and biographer and editor of the works and letters of Charles and Mary Lamb), lived in the last decade of the nineteenth century.

Alongside, at No 4, lived Frank Swinnerton (1884-1972), novelist and man of letters; and author of several memoirs recalling many of the famous literary persons with whom he was acquainted during his long life.

On the other side of the street, back towards and nearly opposite the point of entry from Northington Street, will be seen No 26, the home in the 1840s of George Meredith (1828-1909) where he lived with his father, having been articled to a solicitor. He abandoned that career for journalism and literary writing, and at the end of the decade through which he lived here he married a widowed daughter of Thomas Love Peacock.

Alongside, at No 24 (rebuilt) Dororthy L. Sayers (see above) lived from 1921 for more than twenty years. Known most widely for her detective stories, Sayers was also a scholar, and produced a verse translation of Dante's *Divina Commedia*.

Arthur Waley (1889-1966) lived at the house next door, No 26, for the last several years of his life. To Waley's translations of Chinese poems, more so than to the work of Ezra Pound, the vast majority of English-speaking readers owe whatever knowledge they have of Oriental poetry and its distinctive modes.

* * *

Though Great James Street proper stops at this northern end, there is a paved pedestrian area which one may cross directly into Millman Street – somewhere along which George Borrow (1803-81), as a young man of twenty-one, stayed upon his first arrival in London.

Fifty yards ahead Great Ormond Street leads off to the left. Some distance along here on the left (beyond the building carrying the plaque to John Howard, social reformer) it will be possible to locate No 41 – an early eighteenth century building. At this address lived William Morris (1834-96) for a year or so following his marriage. By this time (1859) Morris had already produced a collection of poems, though then known mostly as a painter. Shortly after leaving Great Ormond Street he would set up in a

Algernon Charles Swinburne, as depicted in an 'Ape' (Carlo Pellegrini) cartoon which appeared in a Vanity Fair *issue of 1874 – at which time Swinburne was residing in Great James Street.*

manufacturing and decorating business (in partnership with Marshall, Burne-Jones, Rossetti and others) which would substantially alter public perceptions of design.

Re-development has covered over the locations of two other literary associations. Along the right-hand side of the street, for example, was *The Rebel Art Centre* established by Wyndham Lewis (1884-1957) in 1914. Both as artist and as writer Lewis was idiosyncratic and restlessly experimental, though his novels have acquired, and still maintain, their own partisan readership.

Thomas Babington Macaulay (1800-59), historian and poet, lived from 1823-31 with his father, Zachary, in a house now occupied by the Royal London Homeopathic Hospital. Macauley left the family home to take chambers in Gray's Inn.

To the Hospital for Sick Children, which you will pass on the right, Sir James Barrie (1860-1937), dramatist and novelist, made in 1919 a gift of the copyright of *Peter Pan* – to cover all book, film, and stage productions. Robert Bridges (1844-1930), poet, practised medicine for some time at the Hospital before turning full-time to writing.

* * *

Great Ormond Street leads to Queen Square, which dates from the time of Queen Anne and was named after her. None of the original buildings remains.

At one time a fashionable part of town in which to live, its northern aspect was open, giving a vista as far as the hills of Highgate and Hampstead.

Just to the left of the entry to the square from Great Ormond Street used to stand the house occupied by Dr Charles Burney (1726-1814) – musician and a dear friend of Dr Johnson – and his daughter Frances (1752-1840), known in the family and ever since as Fanny, the novelist. They lived here during the years 1771-2, during which time (and for several years after) Fanny continued to keep the diary which she had started as a sixteen-year-old. First published towards the end of the nineteenth century it contains some interesting character sketches, including one of Dr Johnson.

On the far (west) side of the square will be seen the Art Workers' Guild, one of whose founders was William Morris (see above). Morris was also a long-time resident in the square (his house was on the opposite, or east, flank) between the years 1865-82.

* * *

Ahead of the place where you entered the square will be seen the Church of St George the Martyr, alongside which is the narrow entry to Cosmo Place, leading to Southampton Row. By turning to the right here, the eastern side of Russell Square will be reached very quickly. Beyond the Hotel Russell, just into Bernard Street which is off to the right, will be found Russell Square underground station – where one may end the tour of this section of Bloomsbury. Alternatively one may proceed directly to the Bloomsbury II tour by continuing straight ahead into Woburn Place, and following the directions gathered in the next section.

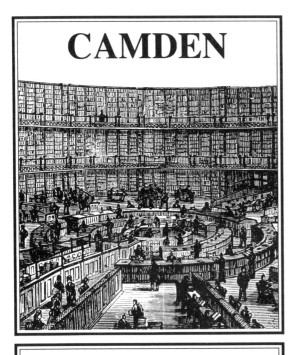

CAMDEN

BLOOMSBURY II

CAMDEN

From the Russell Square underground station, turn left towards Russell Square, and then right into Woburn Place. Within a couple of minutes' walk (passing Coram Street on the right) at the next junction, on the left, will be found the southern end of Tavistock Square.

Here the Tavistock Hotel covers the site of a former house, bombed out during the war, occupied by the Woolfs, Virginia (1882-1910) and Leonard (1880-1969), from 1924-39. It was the address too for the Hogarth Press which they had started in 1919 with hand-printed books made in the kitchen of Hogarth House in Richmond.

Continuing past the Hotel you will emerge at the south-east corner of Gordon Square, alongside the building housing the Percival David Collection of Chinese ceramics from the tenth to the eighteenth centuries.

Just up from this house, heading north along this side of the square, stands No 51, marked with a blue plaque to Lytton Strachey (1880-1932). Strachey's most famous works, designed to a method which largely revolutionised the art of biography, were: *Eminent Victorians* (1918) and a *Life of Queen Victoria* (1921), the latter of which he wrote whilst at this address.

Strachey himself became the subject of a two-volume biography with the publication in 1967 and 1968 of Michael Holroyd's brilliant and comprehensive *Lytton Strachey*. This work, which may be supplemented by Quentin Bell's *Virginia Woolf* (1972), provides the essential reading for those who wish to follow the liaisons – the shifting heterosexual and homosexual pairings and the *ménages à trois* and *quatre* – of many of the principal characters, including Strachey, who constituted the Bloomsbury Group.

The leading members of this Group were: Virginia Stephen (see above) who later married Leonard Woolf (see above); Virginia's sister Vanessa who married Clive Bell, art and literary critic; Desmond MacCarthy, critic and journalist; James Strachey, psychologist, and brother of Lytton; John Maynard Keynes, economist; Roger Fry, artist and art critic; and Duncan Grant, artist. Among others associated with the Bloomsbury Group were: T. S. Eliot; E. M. Forster; and David Garnett, novelist, critic, editor, and biographer. Although Arthur Waley has been frequently associated with the Group, and although he was certainly known to most of them, David Garnett asserts flatly that Waley 'was never a member of the Group' (in *Great Friends*, 1979). Indeed he was considered 'a bore' by some of them, though acknowledged by Garnett to be one of the greatest scholars he had ever known.

It is here, Gordon Square, which provides a nexus for the history of the Group – as will be seen from the next door house, No 50, which displays a blue plaque carrying the legend: 'Here and in neighbouring houses during the first half of the twentieth century there lived several members of the Bloomsbury Group including Virginia Woolf, Clive Bell and the Stracheys'.

It should be remembered, as has been pointed out by Desmond MacCarthy, that by the time the Group had been dubbed and become known as such, it had ceased to exist. The Group, with neither programme nor manifesto, was in fact a meeting of friends – intellectuals, writers, and artists, which began around the children of Sir Leslie Stephen (1832-1904), editor of the massive *Dictionary of National Biography*. In the autumn of the year of

The east flank of Gordon Square, several houses along which are associated with various members of the Bloomsbury Group.

his death his daughters by his second marriage (Stephen's first wife having been the younger of William Makepeace Thackeray's daughters), Vanessa and Virginia, moved to 46 Gordon Square, just a little further along this flank of houses, from the family home in Hyde Park Gate. It was at this Gordon Square address, initiated by the sisters' brother Thoby, two years Virginia's senior, that began the gatherings of friends. In 1906 Thoby died suddenly of a mysterious illness, whilst on a trip to Greece. Two days later, in the words of Quentin Bell (Clive's son) Vanessa 'turned to Clive Bell for comfort and agreed to marry him'.

In 1907 Virginia Stephen, together with her surviving brother Adrian, moved from Gordon Square to Fitzroy Square, where they lived for the following four years, and where the parties of intellectuals continued to gather. Clive and Vanessa Bell, together with Duncan Grant, returned to No 46, where they took rooms, during the First World War. At a different period they lived at No 50 – the address too of Adrian Stephen following his marriage. From 1922, No 46 became the home of John Maynard Keynes and his wife, Lydia Lopokova.

Lydia Lopokova had earlier lived a few doors further along the row, at No 41, which she shared with James Strachey and his wife Alix. There too lived Ralph Partridge with Frances Marshall and Dora Carrington, the latter also the mistress of Lytton Strachey (though Strachey, in order to evade the ridicule he thought some members of the group would pour upon him for his relationship with a young woman, contrived to maintain his posture of homosexuality). Strachey became a conscientious objector during the First World War; and when being challenged in committee on these beliefs he was posed the question as to what he would do should a German soldier make an attempt to violate his sister. Strachey replied that he would endeavour to interpose his body between them.

At Nos 39 and 37 – where David Garnett resided for a while – Duncan Grant and Vanessa Bell lived at different times.

Before leaving Gordon Square and the formative influences which marked the development of Virginia Woolf, it is worth passing comment that for Virginia Woolf, London was itself a major stimulus. In her diary for 26 May 1926 – twenty years after leaving this square – she wrote:

> London is enchanting . . . One of these days I will write about London, and how it takes up the private life and carries it on, without any effort.

In 'Street Haunting' (collected in the posthumous *The Death of the Moth*) she did just that. London scenes feature regularly in the novels – in *The Years, Jacob's Room*, and *Mrs Dalloway*, for example; the last of these including Peter Walsh's walk from Bloomsbury to Westminster. Indeed the use of London in this novel provides not only a setting (or, rather, a series of settings) but an organisational contribution too. David Daiches has argued that, for him: '*Mrs Dalloway* is Virginia Woolf's London novel. Not only does it reveal her attitudes to London more continuously and sensitively than any other of her novels, but it is also a topographical London novel . . . Every scene is specifically located in London and the main characters move about in London in a manner that is both precisely indicated and important to the novel's structure and meaning'. Readers interested in following these movements can find them detailed by Daiches in his *Literary Landscapes of the British Isles* (1979).

* * *

Having walked the right-hand side of Gordon Square, and coming to its top (northern) end, turn right into Endsleigh Place. Just yards ahead, at the western corner of Tavistock Square, Endsleigh Street leads off to the left.

In the top floor rooms of No 7 Endsleigh Street lived Dorothy Richardson (1882-1957), novelist, between the years 1896 and 1906. Richardson's novels, twelve in all, published between 1915 and 1935, compose the single work *Pilgrimage*. Though little read for several decades, her works have always had their admirers – and their re-issue in 1979, together with the accelerating movement of feminism, has prompted a renewed interest. At the very least, Richardson's works have their place in the evolution of the twentieth century novel. For she was the first novelist to bring to fiction the 'stream of consciousness' technique for the revelation of the constantly-shifting impressions of sensibility, the flux of apprehension. The term itself, now fastened most securely to the method of much of James Joyce's work, derives in fact from William James's *Principles of Psychology* (1890), and was first borrowed by May Sinclair, herself a novelist, in a 1918 review of the early volumes of Dorothy Richardson's sequence. And one of the best, if not still the most convincing, apologies for such a mode of fictional realisation followed shortly afterwards in Virginia Woolf's essay on 'Modern Fiction' (collected in *The Common Reader*, 1923).

* * *

Past the turning into Endsleigh Street, Tavistock Square itself opens up. Immediately ahead, in the far corner of the square, will be seen Tavistock House (1938), the home of the British Medical Association. It covers the site of the former Tavistock House (1803-1901). Set into the wall facing the square is mounted a plaque as a reminder that Charles Dickens (see above) lived in a part of the old House between the years 1851-60.

Whilst living here he wrote *Bleak House, Little*

Tavistock House. Hans Christian Andersen, once a house guest of Dickens, wrote of it: 'A large garden with a grass plot and high trees stretches behind the house, and gives it a countrified look in the midst of this coal and gas steaming London . . .'

Charles Dickens, from a Daguerrotype made the year after Dickens moved into Tavistock House.

Dorrit, *Hard Times*, *A Tale of Two Cities*, and a part of *Great Expectations*. In the garden of the House he had built a theatre, taking part himself in the productions staged there (and see entry for Dickens House, Bloomsbury I).

Indeed Dickens's passion for the theatre increasingly occupied him – and that sense of theatricality was one of the prime reasons which made the readings of his work such popular events. Whilst at Tavistock, engaged in rehearsing Wilkie Collins's melodrama *The Frozen Deep*, Dickens met and fell in love with the young actress Ellen Ternan. Dickens and his wife, Catherine, who was not wholly at ease in the society and the activities which engaged her husband, later separated.

***

At this corner of the square, Upper Woburn Place leads off to the left. Fifty yards along here, on the right-hand side, will be found the small entranceway to Woburn Walk. Formerly known as Woburn Buildings, this narrow file of a shopping parade (as originally designed in 1822) retains a bright and clean appearance, and has very evidently been well preserved.

Known locally as 'the toff what lives in the Buildings' – both for his habit of dress and because he was the only one among his neighbours to receive letters – W. B. Yeats (1865-1939) occupied No 5, which is on the left-hand side of the Walk as you enter. Yeats lived here from 1895 until 1919, at first on the second floor only; the ground floor being occupied by a cobbler, whilst on the first floor lived the family of a workman. The attic was occupied by a peddlar. In order to save money on the costs of eating out, Yeats took on the attic room when it became vacant, so that he could turn it into a small kitchen.

In those early days, when Yeats's income from his writing was small, his daily habit was to write until the late afternoon, when he would often go off for long walks, his striding figure draped in a cloak. Or, most frequently on a Monday evening, he would receive friends and entertain them in his rooms.

In the spring of 1889 Yeats had met and fallen in love with Maud Gonne. To Yeats she was both vision and inspiration, the ideal to whom he could make his poetic obeisances – a woman and a myth, his Helen. His first impressions of her conferred the status of goddess:

> I had never thought to see in a living woman so great beauty. It belonged to famous pictures, to poetry, to some legendary past. A complexion like the bloom of apples and yet the face and body had the beauty of lineaments which Blake calls the highest beauty because it changes least from youth to age, and stature so great that she seemed of a divine race. Her movements were works of grace and I understood at last why the poets of antiquity, where we could but speak of face and form, sing, serving some lady, that she seems like a goddess.

Two years after their meeting Yeats asked Maud Gonne to marry him. She refused. He repeated his proposal at intervals, but was always turned down – told that they would never marry but would always remain friends.

Maud Gonne had given herself with 'passionate intensity' to the cause of Irish independence, and partly to demonstrate that he too had a part to contribute to that movement – and in part too as a fabled warning of the dangers to the soul of fanatical engagement with political activity – Yeats had written the play *The Countess Kathleen* (published 1892, but revised many times over a period of thirty years).

Later Yeats was to give more direct expression to his sense of Maud Gonne's betrayal of self in the

The south side of Woburn Walk as it appears today. At No 2 on this side lived Dorothy Richardson. On the opposite side, at No 5, lived Yeats, whom Richardson often saw working by candlelight.

fanatical dedication to her cause – the 'opinionated mind' that barters 'every good . . . For an old bellows full of angry wind'. ('A Prayer For My Daughter'. See also, for example, 'Why Should Not Old Men Be Mad?')

Despite this long and unrequited passion for Maud Gonne, Yeats moved in to this home in the Buildings with a mistress, Olivia Shakespear (d.1938), herself a novelist. In the version of his *Autobiography* which he did not publish in its first form throughout his own lifetime, Yeats referred to her as 'Diana Vernon'. On first seeing her, he thought her face to have 'a perfect Greek regularity', and her whole impression to be one of 'an incomparable distinction'.

Olivia Shakespear remained the most constant of his women friends, perhaps too the wisest and gentlest of them. To her, when approaching his sixties, Yeats composed the beautiful poem 'After Long Silence':

Speech after long silence; it is right,
All other lovers being estranged or dead,
Unfriendly lamplight hid under its shade,
The curtains drawn upon unfriendly night,
That we descant and yet again descant
Upon the supreme theme of Art and Song:
Bodily decrepitude is wisdom; young
We loved each other and were ignorant.

There is an irony in the fact that when Yeats moved out of Woburn Walk, Maud Gonne herself came to live there – in the very house the poet had vacated.

For part of the time while Yeats was resident in Woburn Walk, there lived opposite to him, in one of the attic rooms, Dorothy Richardson (see above). She moved to the Walk from Endsleigh Street in 1906.

* * *

From Woburn Walk, retrace your steps to Upper Woburn Place and there turn to the right. A short distance ahead Endsleigh Gardens opens to the left and, within a minute or so, comes to a junction with Gordon Street. Directly ahead is Gower Place.

In Gower Place, at what was No 44, lived William Godwin (1756-1836) between the years 1827-33. A political philosopher, and atheist, Godwin also produced two novels (*Adventures of Caleb Williams* and *St Leon*) which embodied his views in fictional form.

At its furthest end Gower Place meets with Gower Street, running away to the left – a long, straight thoroughfare which will lead back to the south and the British Museum.

Very soon into Gower Street you will pas University College Hospital to the right; and some little distance further on, to the left, you will come to the extensive University College building. One of the sponsors of the College was Jeremy Bentham (1748-1832), political and ethical philosopher. Bentham bequeathed to the College his own body. And the somewhat bizarre appearance of his fully clothed skeleton, kept in a cabinet, will be shown to visitors upon request.

Set into the façade of University College's grey walls may be seen the blue plaque to Charles Darwin (1809-1882). To a house formerly on this site Darwin moved upon marriage to his cousin Emma Wedgwood. Here they resided between the years 1839 and 1842, during which time Darwin wrote his book on *Coral Reefs*. Seventeen years after this date appeared his great *On the Origin of Species . . .*, a work whose principal theory, though not uniquely belonging to Darwin, articulated most fully the theory of natural selection, and whose appearance generated both intense controversy and a changed climate of intellectual thought.

Just beyond this location, and on the opposite side of the street, is No 95, the home for more than twenty years of the literary critic and distinguished scholar W. P. Ker (1855-1923), some of whose works – such as those on the Epic and on Medieval Literature – remain classics in their fields.

Forty yards or so beyond Torrington Street, and also on the right-hand side of Gower Street, will be seen No 73 where D. H. Lawrence (1885-1930) spent a few days on his last visit to England, in 1925.

On the left-hand side of the street you will pass the Royal Academy of Dramatic Art. Founded by Sir Herbert Beerbohm Tree (1853-1917) in 1904, its first few months of operation took place actually in the dome of His Majesty's Theatre (now Her Majesty's Theatre, Haymarket). Later that same year it moved to Gower Street, and was granted its royal charter by George V in 1920.

Continuing along Gower Street, and passing Chenies Street which leads off to the right, you will come to the short Keppel Street, on the left. In a house which stood in this street was born Anthony Trollope (1815-82), novelist. And in passing it might be mentioned that John Constable, artist of the English landscape, lived for four years from 1817 in this street.

Opposite Keppel Street lies Store Street. Somewhere along here lived Mary Wollstonecraft (1759-97), during which time she wrote her *Vindication of the Rights of Women* (1792). She became the wife of William Godwin (see above), and died at the birth of their daughter, Mary – who became Percy Bysshe Shelley's second wife.

Beyond this junction, at No 14 on the left, lived Sir Anthony Hope Hawkins (1863-1933), the novelist and dramatist Anthony Hope, for four years (1921-5).

Two doors further on, at No 10, lived Lady Ottoline Morrell (1873-1938), here commemorated with a blue plaque inscribed: 'Literary hostess and patron of the arts'. Around Lady Ottoline, throughout the 1920s and 30s at this house – to which she had moved from Bedford Square – gathered many of the literary, artistic, and intellectual people of the day. She and her husband, the Liberal MP Philip Morrell, also did much entertaining at Garsington Manor, near Oxford – accounts of which, and the people invited on these occasions, will be found in *Ottoline at Garsington* (see Bibliography). She was, for example, a friend to many of the Bloomsbury Group (and lover to some), as well as being a regular correspondent with D. H. Lawrence. With Lawrence, Lady Ottoline on first meeting was able to share something of the experiences which they held in common; she having spent her childhood at Welbeck Abbey in Nottinghamshire.

Lady Ottoline was unconventional. A tall woman with red hair, and with facial features described by Augustus John as 'prognathous jaw and bold baronial nose', she nonetheless could express a majestic poise. As in dress and appearance, so in her living she ignored the restrictions of conventional society.

She was a generous patron, nonetheless, though her personal manner itself became the model for fictional embodiment: in Aldous Huxley's *Crome Yellow*, and in D. H. Lawrence's *Women in Love*. In the latter she is presented as Hermione Roddice, with a sing-song voice and a darting, butterfly habit of thought – a woman pursuing a tortuous, and unwanted, relationship with Rupert Birkin (himself a projection of Lawrence). Lady Ottoline was greatly offended at this portraiture of her, and was dissuaded from prosecuting Lawrence for libel only at the insistence of several of her friends.

* * *

On the other side of the road, at No 7, lived John Everett Millais (1829-96), artist – at the time when, with Rossetti, Holman Hunt and others, he helped to found the Pre-Raphaelite Brotherhood; an aesthetic movement whose consequences affected literature as well as art.

Two doors further on, at No 3, lived for a time Katherine Mansfield (1888-1923) – in the judgement of many one of the very finest of short-story writers – together with her lover, later her husband, John Middleton Murry (1889-1957), critic and biographer. Their few months here date from the end of September 1916 until February of the following year. They had lived for several years in straightened circumstances; so much so that even D. H. Lawrence – himself nearly always low on finance – offered at one time to lend them money! Lawrence's relationship with Murry was tetchy, often dismissive, sometimes hostile, and frequently accusative – usually of

Murry's lack of 'backbone' as Lawrence saw his character. Four years before the Murrys were living in Gower Street Lawrence had written a long letter from Italy analysing Murry and his relationship with Katherine, and including phrases such as 'you don't know what you are' and 'be a man for yourself'. In the year following Katherine's death, Lawrence bluntly exploded to Murry: 'You know I don't care a single straw for what you think of me. Realise that, once and for all. But when you get to twisting, I dislike you . . .' (Letter, 7 February 1924, from Baden-Baden, Germany).

In the same letter Lawrence refers to 'Brett'. The Honorable Dorothy, daughter of a Viscount, was a former student at the Slade School of Art – and in later times, following the death of Katherine Mansfield, she became the lover for a while of Middleton Murry. She was also, however, one of the most constant and supportive of Lawrence's friends; indeed it is clear she was in love with him. Later she recorded their friendship in a set of reminiscences. Brett was perhaps the most influential of those who encouraged Lawrence to turn to painting as a further expression of his creativity – especially when in the Americas. But at the time the Murrys were living in Gower Street, Brett was living there too. Indeed she, technically, was the tenant for the nine months from October 1916, and the other occupants (the Murrys and Dora Carrington) were her lodgers.

The house was in fact owned by the economist John Maynard Keynes, and in the time of its occupancy by Brett and her lodgers it became known as The Ark because – as Antony Alpers succinctly expresses the matter – 'its animals went in two by two'. The Murrys occupied the ground floor, Brett had the first floor, and Carrington occupied the attics. Keynes's housekeeper stayed on in the basement rooms.

* * *

Beyond this point, and within a minute or so (passing Bedford Square on the right), you will come to the junction with Great Russell Street. To the left is the main entrance to the British Museum, where this tour ends. (The Museum is open 10.00 to 5.00, Monday to Friday; 2.30 to 6.00, Sundays; closed Christmas, New Year's Day, Good Friday, and the first Monday in May.)

The inception of the British Museum dates from 1753 and the will of Sir Hans Sloane, in which he suggested that the nation should purchase his collection of works of art and antiquities – at a price substantially below that which he had paid in their collecting. The offer was accepted, and the monies required were raised by public lottery. Montagu House was purchased, and in 1759 it first opened to the public. Through time many more bequests and purchases augmented its collections. Notable among these were the Elgin marbles – brought back from the Parthenon and from Erechtheum by Lord Elgin – and the library of George III, containing more than 120,000 volumes. The space available at Montagu House became woefully inadequate for the museum's collections. In 1823, therefore, an extensive building programme was put in hand; in 1842 the old Montagu House was demolished, to be replaced with the present Greek portico and façade. A decade later work on the Reading Room began by converting the open courtyard to this purpose. In 1939 the Sutton Hoo treasure hoard found in the burial-ship of a 7th century Anglo-Saxon king was transferred to the museum.

Clearly many hours, and many visits, can well be spent exploring the museum's displays: of antiquities from prehistoric and Romano-British times, as also from Egypt, Greece, Rome, and Western Asia. On the Upper Floor there are, in addition, medieval, Renaissance, and modern collections on view.

In the limited space available here it is possible only to pick out a few items of interest. The Sutton Hoo Collection, for example – from which scholars have been able to adduce further understandings of *Boewulf* – is to be found on the Upper Floor (room 41). The Elgin marbles are housed on the Ground Floor (room 8). These John Keats first visited, together with the painter Benjamin Robert Haydon (who had campaigned on behalf of their acquisition by the state) on Sunday 2 March 1817. Some part of the effect they had upon him was later recalled in the wider scenes of classical Greek life in the 'Ode On a Grecian Urn', though Keats's most immediate responses were in the sonnets written to Haydon, and in 'On Seeing the Elgin Marbles' – the opening to which contains a wonderful image of the poet:

> My spirit is too weak – mortality
>   Weighs heavily on me like unwilling sleep,
>   And each imagin'd pinnacle and steep
> Of godlike hardship, tells me I must die
> Like a sick Eagle looking at the sky.

On the Ground Floor of the Museum are dis-

Front of Montagu House, the first British Museum.

played many exhibits from the British Library (to the right on entering, rooms 29-31). Among the many manuscript books on display is the *Lindisfarne Gospels*, from the end of the 7th century – a beautiful and brightly illuminated book. Tenth century Anglo-Saxon glosses added to the manuscript provide the earliest known translation of the Gospels into any form of the English language.

Dating from about 1000 AD may be seen the *only* known copy of the Anglo-Saxon epic poem *Boewulf*. The story of Boewulf the Goth who slew the monster Grendel, and Grendel's mother, and later died in a fight with a fire-dragon, dates from three or four centuries prior to this copying-out.

The display copy of Langland's *Vision of Piers Plowman* dates from 1390-1400, the approximate date of the manuscript also of *Sir Gawain and the Green Knight*, this latter a unique copy.

Among the printed books many visitors will want to see is the folio of Chaucer's *Canterbury Tales*, printed by William Caxton, probably at the end of 1476-7. Caxton, having learned the art of moveable-type printing on the continent, returned to England and set up his own printing press in the grounds of Westminster Abbey. Analysis of this edition of Chaucer's great work suggests that this was the first major work to be printed in England.

Dating from 1623 is the First Folio of Shakespeare's plays. This collection, put together by his friends, Heminge and Condell, fellows of the same company of actors, added a further 18 plays to Shakespeare's name. And among these are some of the most famous, and the greatest, of his plays, including: *The Tempest, Measure for Measure, A Winter's Tale, Antony and Cleopatra, Julius Caesar,* and *Macbeth*.

On view in a series of cabinet exhibitions are letters and other autograph materials of many of the most famous of English literary names. There are letters of Spenser, Donne, Marvell, and Swift. Among the wealth of autograph materials are the following: Raleigh's notebook, showing a fair copy

The Reading Room of the British Museum which, in 1973, became part of the British Library. The venue for study by scores of authors (including Marx, Dickens, Shaw and Hardy), the Library is to move in 1991 to a new building close to King's Cross.

version of his poems to Cynthia (Elizabeth I); Bacon's memorandum book; Ben Jonson's manuscript of *The Masque of Queens*, 1608; Massinger's prompt-copy of *Believe as You List*, 1631; a commonplace book of Milton; a notebook of Sir Thomas Browne containing drafts of *Hydriotaphia*.

Among the autograph copies, mostly fair copies, of poems are pieces of the following; Dryden, Gray, Shelley, Wordsworth, Coleridge, Elizabeth Barrett Browning, Emily Brontë, Keats. Autograph manuscripts of prose works include these authors: Defoe, Sterne, Charlotte Brontë, Trollope, George Eliot, Dickens.

Finally, two exhibits from modern times will be mentioned: a notebook of Philip Larkin – pencil with ink corrections of a poem published in *The North Ship*, 1945; and a notebook of James Joyce which may have a particular fascination for some – showing pencil workings for *Finnegan's Wake*, and red crossings.

* * *

From the Museum the nearest underground stations are about equidistant. Directly facing the exit Museum Street leads to the junction with New Oxford Street. To the right is Tottenham Court Road station; to the left – along New Oxford Street leading into High Holborn – is Holborn station. Both are just a couple of minutes' walk away.

HAMPSTEAD

CAMDEN

Hampstead, in the words of one of its historians, 'has become almost the archetype of a high-class residential district'. It is an accurate impression of its character which will remain with the visitor – as will the geography of its location which rises, with many dips and folds, towards the heights of the Heath.

In prehistoric times a dense forest with deer, boar and wild cattle, the remains of the Heath's tribal occupation is evidenced in the barrow sited on Parliament Hill – a second barrow on Primrose Hill having been flattened.

Evidence for the Roman occupation of the area rests upon the discovery, in 1774, of a large sepulchral urn – which in turn has lead to the conjecture that Hampstead was on the original Roman route from London to St Albans. In all probability such a route was a temporary measure only, replaced with the construction of Watling Street (Edgware Road).

In medieval times Hampstead was first monastic, then manorial, agricultural land. Only from the seventeenth century onwards did Hampstead develop to any degree its residential status as a small satellite town a few miles from the centre of London. The great surge to its enlargement was the discovery and exploitation of Hampstead's mineral springs. Hampstead's elevation to the status of a fashionable London spa town was marked by the building of the Assembly Room (including pump room and ballroom), which opened in 1701 and was sited on the south side of Well Walk. The chalybeate waters were also bottled (from the spring in Flask Walk), taken to London, and sold from shops in Fleet Street, Ludgate Hill, and elsewhere.

Such a congregation of people inevitably attracted other visitors: the gamester, trickster, thief, and what one contemporary observer referred to as 'loose women in vampt-up old clothes'. The boom period when Hampstead traded in its mineral waters did not, however, last long – probably not much more than twenty years. A subsequent attempt, later in the eighteenth century, to revive the customs and the trade met with some success. A second spa was opened, near to Burgh House in West End Square (at the southern end of Well Walk). Among those who visited were Henry Fielding, and Dr Johnson in the company of David Garrick and Fanny Burney. The heroine of Burney's *Evelina* (1778) refused to grant to 'inelegant and low bred partners' the favour of 'hopping a dance with her' at the spa. As was the fate of its first opening as a spa town, so on the latter occasion Hampstead soon attracted also the vulgar, raffish, and criminal visitor.

Nonetheless, there had been very substantial development of Hampstead in the years of its greatest success as a spa town, as Daniel Defoe noted in his *Tour Through the Whole Island of Great Britain* (1724):

> Hampstead indeed is risen from a little Country Village, to a City, not upon the Credit only of the Waters, Though 'tis apparent, its growing Greatness began there; but Company increasing gradually and the People liking both the Place and the Diversions together; it grew suddenly Populous, and the Concourse of People was Incredible. This consequently raised the Rate of Lodgings, and that increased Buildings, till the Town grew up from a little Village, to a Magnitude equal to some Cities; nor could the uneven Surface, inconvenient for Building, uncompact, and unpleasant, check the humour of the Town, for even on the very steep of the Hill, where there's no walking

Twenty Yards together, without Tugging up a Hill, or Straddling down a Hill, yet 'tis all one, the Buildings encreased to that degree, that the Town almost Spreads the whole side of the Hill.

Not until the early decades of the nineteenth century did Hampstead begin to accumulate its literary associations: first with the arrival of Joanna Baillie (see below) and her literary salon, and secondly with the group of poets brought together by Leigh Hunt.

Hunt (1784-1859) first lived in a cottage at West End in 1812, at a time when he was editing both the *Examiner* and the *Reflector*. For remarks made in the first of these periodicals against the person and character of the Prince Regent he was sentenced to two years' imprisonment in 1813. Shortly after his release from gaol he again took up residence in Hampstead, this time in the Vale of Health (see below). Hunt's circle included Lamb, Byron, Moore, Hazlitt, Shelley, and Keats – the last two of whom he introduced to each other. By all of these he was visited in the Vale of Health.

Through Hunt, directly, and through those whom he attracted to him, the heathland began to acquire a romantic sense of unspoiled nature – its wildness complemented by the character of the village itself. One of Hunt's own sonnets delineates the sensibility of theme:

> A steeple issuing from a leafy rise,
> With farmy fields in front and sloping green,
> Dear Hampstead, is thy southern face serene,
> Silently smiling on approaching eyes,
> Within, thine ever-shifting looks surprise,
> Streets, hills and dells, trees overhead now seen,
> Now down below, with smoking roofs between, –
> A village, revelling in varieties.
> Then northward what a range – with heath and pond
> Nature's own ground; woods that let mansions through,
> And cottaged vales with billowy fields beyond,
> And clumps of darkening pines, and prospects blue,
> And that clear path through all, where daily meet
> Cool cheeks, and brilliant eyes, and morn-elastic feet.

**

The design of the following tour necessarily involves a steady climb upwards to the north and the high heathland, followed by a downward return – but both with many dips and rises in between.

From Belsize underground station turn to the right and begin the ascent up Haverstock Hill, which

Frances ('Fanny') Burney: portrait of c 1784/5.
National Portrait Gallery, London

becomes Rosslyn Hill. After some minutes, on the right-hand side, will be seen the opening into Pond Street.

About one hundred and fifty yards down Pond Street, on the left-hand side, stands No 31, marked with a plaque as the former residence of Sir Julian Huxley (1887-1975). Brother to Aldous Huxley, the novelist, and grandson of the distinguished Victorian T. H. Huxley, Sir Julian was himself an eminent biologist and populariser of the science.

***

Returning to Rosslyn Hill and a little further up its length, the horseshoe of Hampstead Hill Gardens opens on the right.

Here, just into the Gardens and on the left-hand side, will be found the wooden gate entrance (carrying a small sign 'No 1 EMPSON') to the Studio House.

William Empson (b.1906) established his first reputation as a critic with the stimulating, but on occasion perverse, *Seven Types of Ambiguity* (1930);

followed by *Some Versions of Pastoral* (1935). A later noted work of criticism is *Milton's God* (1961).

Empson's reputation as a poet, whose total output has not been extensive, was largely implicated in the so-dubbed 'Movement' of English poets in the 1950s. For Empson's own poetry provides a model for a greater taughtness of expression; a compression, at times ellipsis, which – together with a strict control of poetic structures – leads to a density of organisation. The complexity resulting from such procedures is achieved often at the expense of the lyrical voice, though the intellectual demands of many of the pieces certainly illustrate what Empson himself referred to as the 'puzzle interest' of poetry.

***

Return to Rosslyn Hill and turn right. The next turning to the right off Rosslyn Hill is Downshire Hill, and something over a hundred yards down this hill, on the left-hand side, will be found No 7.

Here lived Edwin Muir (1887-1959). Muir's total contribution to literature was considerable: poet, critic, and novelist in his own right, together with his wife Willa he was responsible for introducing, in translation, the works of Franz Kafka to the English-speaking world.

Muir's own poetic reputation seems now to have settled around a score or so of his most achieved poems, much-anthologized, which embrace those of a 'visionary' or 'parable' nature; and would include such splendid pieces as 'The Horses' and 'The Combat'. *An Autobiography* (first published in its final form in 1954) is an extraordinary chronology of Muir's own life; from his childhood in the Orkneys, through his passage of time in Glasgow and Fairport, to his extensive travels through and residences on the continent of Europe. The geography of his life-travel is important because, in the words of one commentator, the places visited 'mark the stations of an inner journey'.

***

Retracing one's steps to Rosslyn Hill and again turning to the right one will enter, some distance on, Hampstead High Street. Just beyond Gayton Road, which leads off to the right, there will be seen a narrow opening on the opposite side of the High Street. This is Perrin's Court which in a few yards comes to its junction with Heath Street. And here, just a little to the right and opening up on the opposite side of Heath Street, will be seen Church Row – whose houses, dating from the 1720s, remain largely unspoiled.

Just into Church Row, on the left, stands No 26 – the home in the years 1913-14 of Lord Alfred Douglas (1870-1945). Douglas, a writer of minor verse, is remembered largely for his association with Oscar Wilde. For it was their friendship which provoked Lord Douglas's father, the Marquis of Queensberry, to leave the famous note which lead to Wilde's imprisonment (see section: Charterhouse and Smithfield).

A further fifty yards into Church Row, and on the same side of the street, is No 17. H. G. Wells (1866-1946) lived at this address from 1909 to 1914. By the time Wells took up occupancy at this house he had already a large reputation as a writer of novels of fantasy through such works as: *The Time Machine* (1895), *The Invisible Man* (1897), and *The War of the Worlds* (1898). He had also published works of the social character of *Kipps* (1905) and, just before taking up residence in Church Row, one of his finest works *Tono-Bungay* (1909). Among other works which appeared whilst he was at Hampstead, Wells published *Ann Veronica* (1909), and the gently humorous *History of Mr Polly* (1910).

Three other novelists have lived at different times in Church Row: Wilkie Collins (1824-89), author of *The Woman in White* and *The Moonstone* among other works; George du Maurier (1834-96), before taking up lengthy residence at New Grove House (see later entry); and Sir Compton Mackenzie (1883-1972), whose most endearing works remain the early *Sinister Street*, which established his reputation, and the broadly humorous *Whisky Galore*

***

At the lower end of Church Row stands St John's, the parish church of Hampstead, dating from 1744-7 with nineteenth century additions. In the north aisle of the church may be seen a bust (by Anne Whitney) of John Keats, donated in 1894 by American admirers of his work. There is also a memorial to Joanna Baillie (1762-1851: see later entry).

In this church was married Coventry Patmore (1823-96), the Victorian celebrant of married love, whose *Angel in the House* gives a mystical sense of the achievement of love amidst the commonplace of everyday domesticity.

In the south-east corner of the churchyard may be found the grave of John Constable, many of whose paintings depict the landscapes of Hampstead – and

Church Row, described by Thackeray's daughter as 'an avenue of Dutch red-faced houses, leading demurely to the old church tower that stands guarding its graves in the flowery churchyard'.

some of whose views of the Heath helped to endow it with its nineteenth century romanticism.

On the opposite (north) side of the Row lie the grounds of the newer cemetery. In the right-hand corner of the grounds as you face the cemetery, just beyond the railings and clearly visible from the pavement, are the graves of George du Maurier (see above), and of Sir Herbert Beerbohm Tree (1853-1917), actor-manager and founder of the Royal Academy of Dramatic Art. Close to the west side of the cemetery may be found the grave of Sir Walter Besant (1836-1901), novelist, co-founder of the Society of Authors, social campaigner, and a notable historian of London.

* * *

Fifty yards beyond the cemetery Frognal Gardens emerges to the right. At the top of the rise where Frognal Gardens turns sharp left there will be seen a long driveway leading to No 18 – formerly the home of Sir Walter Besant (see above) who lived at this place from 1895 until his death. From the road, the blue plaque to his memory may just be sighted on the facing flank of the house.

Shortly beyond this residence, Frognal Gardens meets Frognal. At this junction turn to the right. In something under a hundred yards up this slope, on the right, there is a narrow opening to Mount Vernon – the sign to which, however, faces in the opposite direction to your approach.

The house immediately to the right of this entranceway, No 110 Frognal (once a tavern: *The Three Pigeons*) was the home, in the years 1945-51, of E. V. Knox (1881-1971), editor of *Punch* for seventeen years from 1932. His own humorous articles and parodies were published under the pen-name of 'Evoe'; many of such pieces re-printed in book-form and carrying titles such as *Parodies Regained*. A commemorative plaque to Knox is carried on the side of the house.

The entranceway beside this house leads to steps up a fairly sharp incline to Mount Vernon itself. At the top of the steps will be seen a row of houses leading off to the left. At the near corner of this row stands Abernethy House. In 1874 Robert Louis

Stevenson (1850-94) lodged here, together with his friend Sir Sidney Colvin (1845-1927). At the time of their brief occupancy here Stevenson, though ambitious for a literary reputation, had published very little. His first paid piece of work ('Roads') had been taken up directly through the influence of Colvin, who knew the editor of the magazine. Colvin was himself by this time Slade Professor of Fine Art at Cambridge, and it was he who had proposed Stevenson for membership of the Savile Club, his election to which dates from their months at Abernethy House. Colvin was later to be editor of Stevenson's collected works and letters; and produced too a biography of the writer.

Further along the row of houses is No 3 Mount Vernon – where lived Coventry Patmore (see above).

* * *

Beyond the iron railings at the end of this row of houses will be found a walkway which swings off and down to the left. It emerges more or less opposite Holly Mount, at a nearby conjunction of streets, with Holly Hill to the right and Holly Bush Hill to the left.

A few yards to the left at this point, on the corner of Holly Bush Hill, is the distinctive house built in 1797 (and restored in 1957) for the portrait painter George Romney (1734-1802). The year following its completion Romney moved back to Kendal, Westmoreland, where he spent the last few years of his life.

To the left of this junction (where there is a small triangular green) and at the foot of Windmill Hill stands Bolton House, set back from the road in its own grounds. The house was formerly the residence of Joanna Baillie (b.1762) where she lived from 1806 until the year of her death in 1851. Joanna Baillie was in her time a successful dramatist, known and admired for her collections of *Plays on the Passions* – in one of which Mrs Siddons acted at Drury Lane.

Across a span of something like fifty years Joanna Baillie became acquainted with many of the literary figures of the decades. Among regular guests at the salon which she held at Bolton House were Sir Walter Scott, a close friend, and William Wordsworth, both of whom enjoyed her hospitality and her lively and informed conversation. Another regular guest was Maria Edgeworth, whose own writings were much admired by the fellow novelist Scott.

Henry Crabb Robinson, who made a point of getting to know almost every person of any distinction, wrote of Baillie in his diary (on an occasion when he and Wordsworth walked together to her Hampstead home):

> She is small in figure, and her gait is mean and shuffling; but her manners are those of a well-bred lady. She has none of the unpleasant airs too common of literary ladies, even her conversation is pleasant!

* * *

From the Baillie house, which is clearly marked with a commemorative plaque, retrace a few steps to Hampstead Grove – which leads off directly north from the George Romney house.

Within a couple of minutes' walk you will arrive at No 28 Hampstead Grove, sited on the right-hand side. New Grove House was the home of George du Maurier (see above). Du Maurier, cartoonist and writer for *Punch*, lived here for the last twenty-one years of his life, and here composed his three novels from his late fifties on – the last of which was published very soon after his death. Of these three works it is *Trilby* (1894) which attracted the largest readership, because of du Maurier's invention therein of Svengali, the musician with hypnotic powers.

Just beyond the du Maurier house, and on the left, will be seen Admiral's Walk – at the foot of which slope stands the Admiral's House, dating from 1700. The house has the notable feature of a quarterdeck on the roof, an addition of one of its owners at the end of the eighteenth century. The tradition that Admiral Barton, in George IV's time, from that quarterdeck fired salutes on special occasions, though a charming explanation for the house's name, is erroneous. The house, nonetheless, provided P. L. Travers with the model on which to make Admiral Boom's house in *Mary Poppins* (1934).

Alongside Admiral's House stands Grove Lodge, dating from early in the eighteenth century. Here, from 1918 until his death in 1933, lived John Galsworthy (b.1867), novelist and playwright.

Galsworthy and his wife, Ada, did not live continuously at Grove Lodge throughout this period, however. Apart from several winters spent in the USA and on the continent of Europe, a great deal of the Galsworthys' time was spent at their country house at Bury, near Pulborough, in Sussex. It was there that they did a great deal of their entertaining, for they found Grove Lodge to be so small that the dining room would seat only six together at a time. And the back yard of the dwelling the Galsworthys built over in order to create a sitting room large enough to house Ada's grand piano. The attic study, however, proved a congenial place in which Galsworthy could pursue his writing.

Four years after taking up the occupancy of Grove Lodge Galsworthy's *The Forsyte Saga*, the family history on which its author's literary reputation now mainly rests, was published as a single work. Yet the life of Galsworthy is also significant as an exemplum of kindliness and campaigning, of duty and of consideration, of essential humanitarian virtues. A year or two before his death he wrote in a letter of his own sustaining 'creed':

> I am not a churchman, nor even, I suppose, properly speaking a Christian . . . You probably know the saying: God is the helping of man by man. That, I think, is the only religion which has any chance now of making headway; and being essentially practical, the only faith which will steady, comfort and uplift us all again.

* * *

George du Maurier pictured in the 1880s during his residence at Hampstead Grove.

From Grove Lodge return to Hampstead Grove, turning to the left. Within a couple of minutes' walk directly ahead you will emerge at Whitestone Pond – which takes its name from the nearby old white milestone – and the highest point of Hampstead Heath (440 feet, marked by the flagstaff just ahead). On his walks across the heath to visit Leigh Hunt in the Vale of Health, Percy Bysshe Shelley (1792-1822) would sometimes pause to sail paper boats for the children playing there – an example, perhaps, of one of his more endearing traits.

A little way ahead, past the Pond, Jack Straw's Castle stands on the left side of North End Way. The original old coaching inn which occupied the site was named after one of the leaders of the Peasants' Revolt of 1381 who took refuge at the inn, from which he was taken and executed by Richard II's men.

In the nineteenth century Jack Straw's Castle was frequented by the novelists Thackeray and Wilkie Collins. Charles Dickens was another regular visitor. In a letter to his friend and biographer John Forster, Dickens wrote:

> You don't feel disposed, do you, to muffle yourself up and start off with me for a good brisk walk over Hampstead Heath? . . . I know a good 'ouse where we can have a red hot chop for dinner, and a glass of good wine.

This initial invitation led 'to our first experience of Jack Straw's Castle', adds Forster, 'memorable for many happy meetings in coming years'.

The American writer Washington Irving (1783-1859) also frequented the inn. In his *Tales of a Traveller* (1824), the 'Poor-Devil Author' narrates his history, and comes to this point:

> I had frequently in my ramblings, loitered about Hampstead Hill, which is a kind of Parnassus of the metropolis. At such times I occasionally took my dinner at Jack Straw's Castle. It is a country inn so named: the very spot where that notorious rebel and his followers held their council of war. It is a favourite resort of citizens when rurally inclined, as it commands fine fresh air, and a good view of the city. I sat one day in the public rooms of this inn, ruminating over a beefsteak and a pint of port, when my imagination kindled . . .

Here, too, the naïf author met 'the man in green'

who befriends him, bolsters his imagination further, only to deceive him.

Badly damaged by bombing in the 2nd World War, the inn was re-built in 1963-4 to its eighteenth century design.

* * *

More or less opposite Whitestone Pond, on the far side of Heath Street, East Heath Road runs away downhill along the edge of the Heath. At the right-hand junction of Heath Street with East Heath Road formerly stood the Upper Flask Inn (the site now occupied by Queen Mary's Maternity Hospital). Here the members of the Kit-Kat Club held regular meetings.

Founded by Jacob Tonson, the bookseller, in 1700, the Club reputedly took its name from Christopher Katt, a pastry cook, whose mutton pies were known as Kit-cats (as reported in the *Spectator*, No ix). From its first meetings at Katt's house close to Temple Bar and then at Tonson's house at Barn Elms, the Club held many of its summer meetings at this Hampstead location. The Kit-Kat Club came to an end in 1720.

The Club, a collection of influential Whigs, was dedicated to the purpose of ensuring a Protestant successor to William III. Its members included the dramatists Sir John Vanbrugh (who thought the Kit-Kat the best club of all) and William Congreve; the essayists Sir Richard Steele and Joseph Addison; the Duke of Marlborough and Sir Robert Walpole. Sir Godfrey Kneller made forty-two portraits of the Club's members, some of which are on display at the National Portrait Gallery.

The Upper Flask Inn also provided Samuel Richardson with a setting for several of the scenes in his novel *Clarissa Harlowe* (1747-8), the heroine taking refuge in Hampstead to avoid the advances of Lovelace.

* * *

About a hundred-and-fifty yards down East Heath Road, the Vale of Health opens up on the left at an acute angle. And at the foot of the slope clusters a collection of terraced houses, somewhat randomly arranged. On the left, arrived at the first of these homes, there is on display, however, a plan of this distribution to help the visitor.

The Vale of Health acquired its unusual name by the very first years of the nineteenth century. Until 1777 the low-lying dip of the land had been occupied by a malarial marsh; its draining made, obviously, a great change to the area – and its re-naming was doubtless intended to attract residents to the houses developed there.

In the Vale, Leigh Hunt (see above) took a cottage upon his release from prison, and here received his visitors. A drawing of Vale Lodge – his probable residence – is also on display in the Keats House (see later entry).

At No 3 the Villas on the Heath, a short row leading off to the left of the approach road to the Vale, the Indian poet Rabindranath Tagore (1861-1941) stayed in 1912. Deeply religious, and with a close affinity to nature, many of his poems are available in English translations of Tagore's Bengali originals.

In the ground floor flat of No 1 Byron Villas, beyond and just around the corner, to the right, from the Tagore house, D. H. Lawrence (1885-1930) lived for several months from the late summer of 1915. By this time he was married to Frieda (von Richthofen of an aristocratic Silesian family), with whom he had previously eloped to Germany in May 1912 – she having left her husband, Ernest Weekley, a philologist and Professor at Nottingham University.

Lawrence's decision to take the rooms in the Vale of Health prompted a move from Katherine Mansfield and John Middleton Murry (see later entry) to St John's Wood. There, at No 5 Acacia Road, they would be within a comfortable distance of the Lawrences without feeling too close. With Mansfield and Murry, Lawrence was planning to collaborate on a new periodical to be called *The Signature*. The venture failed, only three issues emerging – though Lawrence's contribution to the periodical did find an eventual form in the story 'The Man Who Died'. Other visitors to the Lawrences at the Vale of Health included W. B Yeats, Ezra Pound, and Aldous Huxley.

Lawrence's stay in the Vale of Health followed on a recent disengagement from Bertrand Russell. Together they had planned to deliver a series of lectures on the 'Philosophy of Social Reconstruction'. For Lawrence the 1st World War brought both anger and agony, and he could see that the manner in which the war was conducted would determine the fashion in which the after-peace would be wrought, and the quality of life issuing from that. Hence his interest in the philosophical venture, and the many impassioned letters of the time – his railing against the present and his fervent hopes for the future.

During their brief residence here the Lawrences witnessed, from the heights of the Heath, the first concerted Zeppelin attack upon London on the night of 8 September 1915. Recorded in his letters, the incident was later incorporated into his novel *Kangaroo* (1923):

> At night all the great beams of the searchlights, in great straight bars, feeling across the London sky, feeling the clouds, feeling the body of the dark overhead. And then Zeppelin raids: the awful noise and the excitement. One evening . . . across the Heath . . . there, in the sky, like some god vision, a Zeppelin, and the searchlights catching it, so that it gleamed like a manifestation in the heavens, then losing it, so that only the strange drumming came down out of the sky where the searchlights tangled their feelers. There it was again, high, high, high, tiny, pale, as one might imagine the Holy Ghost, far, far above. And the crashes of guns, and the awful hoarseness of shells bursting in the city. Then gradually, quiet. And from Parliament Hill, a great red glow below, near St Paul's. Something ablaze in the city . . .

Lawrence's mood whilst at Hampstead darkened also with the responses to *The Rainbow* and the following consequences. The novel, released at the end of September, was greeted by reviews which utterly condemned the work as vicious and obscene – leading to a prosecution of its publishers, who had not informed Lawrence of the impending proceedings. The action was undefended, the remaining copies of the work were destroyed, and thus the whole opprobrium for the work fell upon Lawrence himself. Towards the end of the year Lawrence and Frieda removed to Cornwall, and soon into the following year he was writing of 'this England, which nauseates my soul, nauseates my spirit and my body . . .'

* * *

Returning to East Heath from the Vale of Health and turning to the left, just beyond the junction on the far side of the road will be seen No 17. It is marked with a blue plaque to Katherine Mansfield (1888-1923) and John Middleton Murry (1889-1957). They called the house 'The Elephant' – because of its largeness and greyness. It was the Murrys' first own house in which they lived from August 1918 (having formally married earlier that year) until the autumn of 1920, though Katherine Mansfield had to make frequent sojourns elsewhere during this period

D. H. Lawrence: portrait of 1925 by the Hon Dorothy Brett. National Portrait Gallery, London

for health reasons – to provide recuperative periods against her consumption.

When the Lawrences had stayed in a previous year in the Vale of Health, they and the Murrys had spent much time together – on occasions, for example, taking picnics together on the Heath. Later, Mansfield and Murry followed the Lawrences to Cornwall, where the complex tangle of their relationships became even more tortuous – and strained, with the first rifts of estrangement. This, in turn, led to the hectoring, annihilating tone which Lawrence would later adopt in his accusations against Murry, and his attacks upon Murry's treatment of Mansfield. Paradoxically, despite these contrary impulses and natures, there remained at the least a need for *some* kind of relationship; and Mansfield at least always found attractive Lawrence's energy for life.

* * *

Beyond the Murrys' house, and some distance down East Heath Road, Well Walk opens on the right. On the right-hand side of the Walk there may be seen

Keats House.

the Victorian fountain marking the spot whence flowed formerly the chalybeate springs which made for Hampstead's early reputation, encouraging the development of fashionable residences.

On the left-hand side of the Walk stands No 40, marked with a plaque, where lived John Constable (1776-1837), some of whose paintings feature, or originated at, the nearby Heath. Constable lived at this house from 1826, the same house which was later occupied for the last twenty years of his life by T. Sturge Moore (1870-1944), artist and poet.

At a site which was close to, or adjoined, the present Wells Tavern, once stood the house (then No 1) in which John Keats (1795-1821) and his brothers, George and Tom, took lodgings with the Bentleys from June 1817 until the following year – in which George emigrated to America and Tom died. Bentley, the local postman, proved a friendly landlord; Mrs Bentley was attentive and motherly – though the Bentley's children contrived to make the house feel even more cramped.

Here John Keats nursed his younger brother Tom throughout his consumptive illness; and despite his own situation pressed on with the composition of *Hyperion*.

Beyond the junction with Christchurch Hill, on the left-hand side of the Walk, will be seen No 27, the home for some years throughout the 1940s of J. B. Priestley (1894-1984), novelist and playwright.

Fifty yards further on, again on the left, you will come to No 14, a red brick-fronted house. It bears a plaque to Marie Stopes (1880-1958) advocate of family planning, campaigner for sex education and for frankness in the discussion of sexual matters: to which her own *Married Love* (1918) was one of the first contributions. Marie Stopes later made for herself a second, but smaller, reputation for her poetry and plays.

Another resident of Well Walk in the second decade of the present century was John Masefield (1878-1967), whose home was demolished in 1948 to make way for a council development of flats. Whilst living here Masefield composed one of his most successful long narrative poems, *Dauber*.

For those who may wish to visit Hampstead Museum of Local History, they will find it sited at the far end of Well Walk, where New End Square leads off to the right. Here is located Burgh House, of about 1702 (altered mid-nineteenth century, restored 1977). Admission is free (open: Wednesdays-

Sundays, 12.00 to 5.00pm; Bank Holidays, 2.00 to 5.00pm). Meetings and concerts are also held at the House.

For several years in the 1930s Burgh House was rented by Rudyard Kipling's daughter. Kipling visited Hampstead, and Burgh House, on many occasions – the house and garden providing for him a source of delight.

***

From Well Walk return to East Heath Road, turning to the right, and following the hill downwards. A few minutes' walk away Keats Grove opens on the right. Alternatively, having visited Burgh House, follow Willow Road downhill until it becomes South End Road, with Keats Grove very soon turning off to its right.

Fifty yards into Keats Grove, on the left, will be found Keats House, originally named Wentworth Place. Wentworth Place, a pair of semi-detached houses set in a common garden, was built in 1815-16 for Charles Armitage Brown (1786-1842) and Charles Wentworth Dilke (1789-1864). Dilke and his family lived in the larger of the two houses, Brown in the other.

At the time when John Keats (see above) was living in Well Walk, Dilke and his wife, Maria, were living near Pond Street, further still down the hill, at the bottom of the Heath. Through his friend and fellow poet, J. H. Reynolds, Keats had been introduced to Dilke, the two of them soon becoming 'capital Friends'. Dilke, a civil servant in the Navy Pay Office, was also a literary man; he had edited volumes of *Old English Plays* – which were to become sustained and devoted reading for Keats. Charles Brown, the son of a broker, was a Scot, and a bachelor. A legacy had left him with an adequate income, so that he had retired early from active business. He had, however, written a musical play performed at Drury Lane – for which he had obtained a silver ticket, that is, free admission for life. With this, and his own enthusiasm for drama he was to be signally influential in developing Keats's interest in theatre. Keats first met Brown in late August 1817, Brown returning from his summer in Scotland, having let out his part of Wentworth House during his absence to Mrs Brawne, a widow, and her daughters.

Shortly after his nineteenth birthday Tom Keats died in the early hours of the first day of December. Charles Brown records that he 'was awakened in bed by a pressure on [his] hand' by John Keats shortly after Tom's death. Brown's recollection continues: '. . . at last, my thoughts returning from the dead to the living I said, "Have you nothing more to do with those lodgings and alone, too. Had you better not live with me?" He pressed my hand warmly and replied, "I think that would be better". From that moment he was my inmate.' In fact he, Keats, became Brown's paying lodger.

The date of Keats's first meeting with Fanny Brawne is uncertain, though the strongest probability would locate this encounter in the month of November, at the home of the Dilkes'. The Brawnes were paying a visit to Wentworth, having moved in late September to Elm Cottage, further up Downshire Hill, upon Brown's return from Scotland.

In the first part of December Keats, in company with Brown, was visiting the Brawnes at Elm Cottage – and it is clear, despite the teasing and mock-fighting with each other, that Fanny and Keats were very strongly attracted to each other. At first, to describe the character of the eighteen year-old Fanny and her mixture of assurance, immaturity, the contrariness of her defensiveness and cutting repartee, Keats was driven to the epithet '*Minx*' to suggest her behaviour to him. Alongside this response his letters of the time show another view of her; a physical beauty and attractiveness which Keats undoubtedly had in mind when he later drafted into *Otho the Great* (V,v) this speech of Ludolph's:

> Deep blue eyes – semi-shaded in white lids,
> Finish'd with lashes fine for more soft shade,
> Completed by her twin-arch'd ebon brows –
> White temples of exactest elegance,
> Of even mould, felicitous and smooth –
> Cheeks fashion'd tenderly on either side,
> So perfect, so divine, that our poor eyes
> Are dazzled with the sweet proportioning,
> And wonder that 'tis so, . . .

In April of 1819 the Brawnes moved into Dilke's half of Wentworth Place, Dilke having decided to go to Westminster where his son was to attend school. In the weeks which followed, promoted by the almost daily encounters between them, it is evident that the relationship between Keats and Fanny deepened into some form of an understanding, though not a formal engagement. Keats's own health was now suspect, a cause for concern being the persistent sore throat which had developed

John Keats (1819): the miniature, on ivory, by Joseph Severn. National Portrait Gallery, London

and produced an intense fertility of composition. In under four weeks from the end of April Keats wrote the four famous *Odes: on Indolence, on Melancholy, to a Nightingale, on a Grecian Urn*. In some ways sharing the same pre-occupations of themes, a sensibility which interpenetrates each of them, the precise order of composition probably cannot be finally established; and indeed it is possible that Keats might have worked on more than one of them simultaneously. Of the *Ode to a Nightingale* Brown recorded that Keats drafted it one morning whilst sitting under a plum tree in the garden at Wentworth – the immediate geography of the setting extended and transformed, in the poem, to a more literary conception and treatment. Mutability, decay, death, the soul-maker's journey through the darkness of life, contrast with the nightingale's song of pure nature, a song repeating through the generations of man:

> Darkling I listen; and for many a time
>   I have been half in love with easeful Death,
> Call'd him soft names in many a mused rhyme,
>   To take into the air my quiet breath;
> Now more than ever seems it rich to die,
>   To cease upon the midnight with no pain,
> While though art pouring forth thy soul abroad
>   In such ecstasy!
> Still wouldst thou sing, and I have ears in vain –
>   To thy high requiem become a sod.

throughout the winter. In the same month of April Keats, who just days before had completed 'La Belle Dame Sans Merci', encountered Samuel Taylor Coleridge, also out walking the Heath. In *Table Talk* (1832) Coleridge recorded retrospectively the meeting. After a brief while with each other Keats returned to the older poet and said 'Let me carry away the memory, Coleridge, of having pressed your hand'. To which Coleridge added presciently (if his memory served accurately the moment): ' "There is death in that hand", I said when Keats was gone; yet this was, I believe, before the consumption showed itself distinctly.'

Nonetheless that early summer at Wentworth was to be the most concentratedly creative period of Keats's poetic career. The exceptionally fine spring weather and the presence of Fanny lifted his spirits,

In the autumn of 1819 Keats returned to Wentworth – Brown, as was his custom, having let out his part of the house for the summer period. Throughout that winter, which was especially severe, beset by anxieties about money and distracted by the near presence of Fanny and the impossibility of their marrying, Keats's health deteriorated. On the night of 3 February 1820 Keats returned from a visit to Town, having travelled on the outside of a stagecoach in order to save money. In a high fever he staggered back to Wentworth and collapsed into his bed.

Brown brought him spirits to revive him. Keats coughed, and Brown heard him say: 'That is blood from my mouth'. Brown's recollection continues: 'I went towards him; he was examining a single drop [of blood] upon the sheet. "Bring me the candle, Brown, and let me see this blood". After regarding it steadfastly, he looked up in my face with a calmness of countenance I can never forget and said, "I

Silhouette of Fanny Brawne.

know the colour of that blood; it is arterial blood. I cannot be deceived in that colour. That drop of blood is my death warrant. I must die".' Another much greater haemorrhage that same night confirmed Keats's own diagnosis.

In the weeks that followed Keats made a partial recovery, only to face the prospect of having to leave Wentworth Place again, Brown once more arranging to let his home for the summer period. Leigh Hunt came to his assistance, arranging lodgings for him close to his own accommodation in Kentish Town. But in August Keats returned to Hampstead, exhausted and weeping – arriving at Mrs Brawne's doorstep in the evening. Abandoning discretion Fanny's mother took in the sick man. With the Brawnes Keats stayed for the following month – the happiest period in his life he asserted. On 13 September 1820 Fanny wrote in her diary: 'Mr Keats left Hampstead'. After exchanging mementoes with Fanny, Keats left for Rome – where he died on 23 February the following year.

Wentworth Place, fully restored in 1974-5 and now known as Keats House, contains many memorabilia of Keats and his circle of contemporaries. (Open weekdays, 2.00pm-6.00pm; Sundays and Easter, Spring and Late Summer Bank Holidays, 2.00pm-5.00pm; Saturdays, 10.00am-1.00pm and 2.00-5.00pm.)

* * *

From Keats House turn left along Keats Grove until it joins with Downshire Hill where one turns left again, leading into Rosslyn Hill. A few minutes' walk down Rosslyn Hill (which becomes Haverstock Hill) will lead back to Belsize Park undergound station.

BIBLIOGRAPHY

The following works, which largely omit the literary titles referred to in the body of the text, are among those which have been consulted in the preparation of this book. They may be useful to readers who would like fuller information on particular times, locations, persons, and events referred to in the present work. Unless otherwise stated, it may be presumed that the publication is London, England.

* * *

I: London: Histories and Guides (including works which refer in part to London)
Baker, Timothy, *Medieval London*, Cassell 1970.
Banks, F.R., *The New Penguin Guide to London*, Penguin, 9th ed. 1986.
Barker, Felix, and Jackson, Peter, *London: 2000 Years of a City and its People*, Cassell 1974 and Macmillan 1983.
Borer, Mary Cathcart, *The City of London: a History*, Constable 1977.
Clarke Jennifer, *In Our Grandmothers' Footsteps*, Virago 1984.
Daiches, David, and Flower, John, *Literary Landscapes of the British Isles*, Paddington Press, New York and London 1979.
Dickens Fellowship, *The London of Charles Dickens*, Midas Books, Speldhurst 1979.
Eagle, Dorothy, and Carnell, Hilary, *The Oxford Literary Guide to the British Isles*, OUP 1980.
Fairfield, S., *The Streets of London*, Papermac 1983.
Farson, Daniel, *Soho in the Fifties*, Michael Joseph 1987.
Gray, Robert, *A History of London*, Hutchinson 1978.
Hall, Martin, *The Blue Plaque Guide to London Homes*, Queen Anne Press 1976.
Hartley, Rachel, *A Literary Guide to the City*, Queen Anne Press 1966.
Hibbert, Christopher, *London: The Biography of a City*, Penguin 1983.
Jenkins, Elizabeth, *The Princes in the Tower*, Hamish Hamilton 1978.
Lillywhite, Bryant, *London Coffee Houses*, Allen and Unwin 1963.
Loftie, W. J., *London City*, Leadenhall Press 1891 (facsimile edn., vol.I of *Victoria's London*, The Alderman Press 1984).
Mee, Arthur, *London: The City and Westminster*, revised edn., Hodder and Stoughton 1975.
Ogborn, M. E., *Staple Inn*, Institute of Actuaries 1964.
Ousby, Ian, *Blue Guide to Literary Great Britain and Ireland*, A & C Black 1985.
Sheldon, Harvey, and others, *Rescuing the Past in Southwark*, Southwark and Lambeth Archaeological Excavation Committee 1984.
Shepherd, Thomas H., *London in the Nineteenth Century* (1829), reprinted Frank Graham, Newcastle-upon-Tyne, n.d.
Stow, John, *Survey of London* (1598), Dent, corrected edn. 1955.
Summerson, John, *Georgian London*, Penguin 1978.
Thompson, F. M. L., *Hampstead: Building a Borough, 1650-1964*, Routledge and Kegan Paul 1974.
Weinreb, Ben, and Hibbert, Christopher, *The London Encyclopaedia*, Macmillan 1983.
Williams, George G., *Guide to Literary London*, Batsford 1973.

* * *

II: Reference: General and Literary
Baugh, Alec C., and Cable, Thomas, *A History of the English Language*, 3rd edn., Routledge and Kegan Paul 1978.
Bell, Quentin, *Bloomsbury*, Weidenfeld and Nicholson 1968.
Chambers, Sir E. K., *The Elizabethan Theatre*, 4 vols., OUP 1923.
Drabble, Margaret (ed.), *The Oxford Companion to English Literature*, 5th edn., OUP 1985.
Garnett, David, *Great Friends: Portraits of Seventeen Writers*, Macmillan 1979.
Gurr, Andrew, *The Shakespearian Stage, 1574-1642*, 2nd. edn., CUP 1980.
Gurr, Andrew, and Orwell, John, *Re-building Shakespeare's Globe*, Weidenfeld and Nicholson 1989.
Kermode, Frank, and Hollander, John (eds.), *The Oxford Anthology of English Literature*, 2 vols., OUP 1973.
Latter, D. A., 'Sight-Lines in a Conjectural Reconstruction of an Elizabethan Playhouse', *Shakespeare Survey,* Cambridge 1975.

Morton, Ann (ed.), *Men of Letters*, HMSO 1974.
Quennell, Peter, *A History of English Literature*, Weidenfeld and Nicholson 1973.
Rogers, Pat (ed.), *The Oxford Illustrated History of English Literature*, OUP 1987.
Sphere History of Literature in the English Language, (various eds.), Barrie and Jenkins 1970.
Stephen, Leslie, and Lee, Sidney, and others, *The Dictionary of National Biography*, OUP 1917 onwards.
Ward, A. W., and Waller, A.R., *The Cambridge History of English Literature*, 15 vols., CUP 1907-16.

* * *

III: Individual Authors

Ackroyd, Peter, *T. S. Eliot*, Hamish Hamilton 1984.
Aldington, Richard, *Portrait of a Genuis But . . .*, Heinemann 1950.
Alpers, Antony, *The Life of Katherine Mansfield*, Jonathan Cape 1980.
Beerbohm, Max, *Rossetti and his Circle*, Yale University Press, 1987.
Bell, Quentin, *Virginia Woolf: a Biography*, 2 vols., Hogarth 1972.
Bennett, Daphne, *Margot: a Life of the Countess of Oxford and Asquith*, Gollancz 1984.
Bentley, Phyllis, *The Brontës and their World*, Thames and Hudson 1969.
Bowle, John (ed.), *The Diary of John Evelyn*, Oxford 1985.
Brett, Dorothy, *Lawrence and Brett: A Friendship*, Santa Fe 1974.
Chambers, Sir E. K., *William Shakespeare: a Study of Facts and Problems*, 2 vols., OUP 1930.
Daiches, David, *James Boswell and his World*, Thomas and Hudson 1976.
Delaney, Paul, *D. H. Lawrence's Nightmare: The Writer and his Circle in the Years of the Great War*, Harvester Press, Sussex, 1979.
Donoghue, Denis (ed.), *Memoirs of W. B. Yeats*, Macmillan 1972.
Duffy, Maureen, *The Passionate Shepherdess: Aphra Behn 1640-89*, Jonathan Cape 1977.
Eliot, Valerie (ed.), *The Waste Land: a facsimile and transcript of the original drafts*, Faber and Faber 1971.
Ellman, Richard, *Oscar Wilde*, Hamish Hamilton 1987.
Evans, N. E., *Shakespeare in the Public Records*, HMSO 1985.
Forster, John, *The Life of Charles Dickens*, 2 vols, Dent 1969.
Foster, Margaret, *Elizabeth Barrett Browning*, Chatto and Windus 1988.
Gathorne-Hardy, Robert (ed.), *Ottoline at Garsington,* Faber and Faber 1974.
Gittings, Robert, *Young Thomas Hardy*, Penguin 1978.
Gittings, Robert, *John Keats*, Heinemann, corrected edn. 1970.
Gordon, Lyndall, *Eliot's Early Years*, OUP 1973.
Gordon, Lyndall, *Virginia Woolf: a Writer's Life* OUP 1984.
Greene, Graham, *Lord Rochester's Monkey*, Bodley Head 1974.
Hennessy, James Pope, *Anthony Trollope*, Jonathan Cape 1971.
Holroyd, Michael, *Lytton Strachey: A Critical Biography*, 2 vols., Oxford 1967, 1968.
Lathan, Robert, and Mathews, William, *The Diary of Samuel Pepys*, Bell and Hyman 1978.
Moore, Harry T., *The Collected Letters of D. H. Lawrence*, Heinemann 1962.
Ollard, Richard, *Pepys*, Hodder and Stoughton 1974.
Pearson, Hesketh, *The Life of Oscar Wilde*, Methuen, 1946, Penguin 1960.
Pottle, Frederick A. (ed.), *Boswell's London Journal 1762-1763*, Heinemann 1952.
Robinson, Kenneth, *Wilkie Collins*, Davis-Poynter 1974.
Rogers, Pat, *Henry Fielding*, Oxford 1979.
Sagar, Keith, *The Life of D. H. Lawrence*, Eyre Methuen 1980.
Schoenbaum, S., *William Shakespeare: A Documentary Life*, Clarendon, Oxford 1975.
Sencourt, Robert, *T. S. Eliot: A Memoir*, Garstone Press 1971.
Thomas, Donald, *Robert Browning: A Life Within Life*, Weidenfeld and Nicholson 1982.
Trollope, Anthony, *An Autobiography*, OUP 1980.
Walton, Izaak, *The Life of Dr John Donne* (1640) in *Izaak Walton's Lives*, Nelson n.d..
Wilson, A. N. *The Life of John Milton*, OUP 1984.
Winn, James Anderson, *John Dryden and his World*, Yale University Press 1987.
Yeats, W. B., *Autobiographies*, Macmillan 1955.

INDEX OF PERSONS

Abney, Sir Thomas, and Lady 54
Ackroyd, Peter 161
Addison, Joseph 16, 39, 42, 69, 124, 125, 160, 195
A.E. *see* Russell, George William
Ainsworth, Harrison 46
Akenside, Mark 113, 170-1
Aldington, Richard 175
Alleyn, Edward 55, 57, 93, 100
Andrewes, Bishop Launcelot 58, 91-2
Arbuthnot, John 133
Arne, Thomas 127, 129
Arnold, Matthew 17, 173
Arnold, Thomas 173
Arouet, Françoise Marie: *see* Voltaire
Ascham, Roger 47-8
Asquith, Herbert Henry 153, 172-3
Asquith, Margot 153, 172-3
Aubrey, John 91, 164
Auden, W. H. 109, 135
Austen, Cassandra 131
Austen, Jane 109, 129, 131, 174
Austen, Henry 129

Bacon, Sir Francis 17, 131, 158, 160
Baillie, Joanna 190, 191, 193
Bailly, Harry 88
Barham, R. H. 37
Barrie, Sir James M. 116, 123, 148, 150, 153, 179
Barrow, Thomas 134
Barry, James 131
Barry, Elizabeth 166
Beauclerk, Topham 116, 172
Beaumont, Francis 23, 26, 63, 91, 100, 105, 107-8, 121
Beckford, William 140, 157
Beerbohm, Max 36, 39
Behn, Mrs Aphra 109
Bell, Clive 180, 181
Bell, Quentin 180, 181
Bell, Vanessa 180, 181
Belloc, Hilaire 134, 160
'Bendo, Alexander': *see* Wilmot, John
Bennett, Arnold 158
Bentham, Jeremy 164, 183
Besant, Sir Walter 37, 192
Betterton, Thomas 166
Blake, William 36, 51, 54-5, 109, 117, 131, 134, 141-2
Blomfield, Sir Arthur 116
Bloodworth, Sir Thomas 74

Blunden, Edmund 160
Boleyn, Anne 79-80
Borrow, George 147, 148, 177, 178
Boswell, James 15, 16, 17, 19, 20, 22, 24, 33, 74, 104, 105, 116, 119, 120, 125, 126-7, 129, 131, 134, 151, 154
Boucher, Catherine 54
Bracegirdle, Anne 166
Brawne, Fanny 198-200
Bray, John 38
Brett, Dorothy 186
Bridges, Robert 159, 179
Brontë, Anne 66-8, 131
Brontë, Branwell 67, 131
Brontë, Charlotte 66-8, 131, 188
Brontë, Emily 66-8, 131, 188
Brooke, Rupert 160
Brown, Charles Armitage 198, 199, 200
Browne, H. K. ('Phiz') 140, 176
Browne, Sir Thomas 188
Browning, Elizabeth Barrett 144-5, 153, 154-5, 158, 188
Browning, Robert 108, 109, 145, 153, 154-5, 158, 173
Buchan, John 148
Bulwer-Lytton, Edward 147
Bunyan, John 17, 48, 51-2, 57, 58
Burbage, Cuthbert 31, 98
Burbage, James 30, 98
Burbage, Richard 30-1, 98
Burke, Edmund 134, 136, 151, 154
Burne-Jones, Sir Edward 159, 179
Burney, Dr Charles 20, 116, 133-4, 179
Burney, Frances ('Fanny') 116, 133-4, 140, 179, 189
Butler, Samuel 82, 129
Button, Daniel 125
Byron, Allegra 128
Byron, Lord George Gordon 109, 128, 147, 153, 158, 190

Cade, Jack 89
Campbell, Thomas 147, 153
Campion, Thomas 18, 105
Canaletto, Antonio 169
Carew, Thomas 18
Carlyle, Thomas 20
Carr, Robert, Viscount Rochester (later, Earl of Somerset) 81-2
Carrington, Dora 181, 186
Carroll, Lewis 109
Carte, Richard D'Oyly 117, 118
Cawarden, Sir Thomas 30
Caxton, William 61, 111, 187
Chamier, Anthony 136-7

203

Chapman, George 91, 128, 160
Charles, Duke of Orléans 78
Charles I, King 32, 35, 51, 96, 105, 149
Charles II, King 74, 75, 79, 82-3, 84, 109, 113, 121, 130, 135, 149
Chatterton, Thomas 161
Chaucer, Geoffrey 9, 61, 88-9, 90, 108, 118, 135, 187
Chaucer, Richard 63
Chesterfield, 4th Earl of: *see* Stanhope, Philip Dormer
Chesterton, G. K. 134
Chettle, Henry 55
Church, Richard 16, 165
Churchill, Sir Winston 106, 108, 131
Cibber, Colley 64, 121, 125, 128, 166, 170
Cleland, John 109, 118
Coleridge, Samuel Taylor 116, 127, 139, 164, 188, 199
Colet, John 38
Collins, William Wilkie 126, 145-6, 153, 154, 155, 191, 194
Colvin, Sir Sidney 193
Condell, Henry 31, 59, 187
Congreve, William 23, 69, 123, 130, 133, 166, 195
Conrad, Joseph 134, 152
Constable, John 185, 191-2, 197
Cooper, Anthony Ashley, 3rd Earl of Shaftesbury 119
Cornwall, Barry: *see* Proctor, Bryan Waller
Coverdale, Miles 61, 71-2
Cowley, Abraham 109
Cowper, William 24, 27-8, 109, 151, 173
Cox, Tom 119
Cranmer, Thomas 60
Crashaw, Richard 39
Cromwell, Oliver 58, 135
Cumberland, Richard 154, 171

Dance ('the Younger'), George 42, 43
Darwin, Charles 183
D'Avenant, William 23, 26, 82, 100, 131, 166
Davies, Thomas 124, 125, 129
Davies, W. H. 134, 160, 171, 172
Day, John 55
Defoe, Daniel 10, 17, 45, 52-3, 56, 57, 58, 65, 66, 188, 189-90
Dekker, Thomas 33, 81, 92, 100
Denham, Sir John 44-5, 164
Dickens, Charles 10, 16, 17, 19, 20, 27, 33, 41, 43, 46, 49, 60-1, 66, 70, 75, 77, 89, 108, 111, 114-5, 118, 119, 134, 137, 138, 140, 146, 152, 153, 157-8, 160, 162, 163-4, 165, 166, 167, 168, 170, 172, 175, 176-7, 182-3, 188, 194
Dilke, Charles Wentworth 198

Disraeli, Benjamin 49, 105, 106, 108, 130, 164
Dixon, Richard Watson 159
Dobrée, Bonamy 16
Donne, Anne (*neé* More) 35, 118, 119
Donne, Constance 57
Donne, John 18, 32, 35-6, 44, 62, 91, 118, 119, 165, 187
Doolittle, Hilda 175
Douglas, Lord Alfred 47, 191
Dowson, Ernest 20
Doyle, Sir Arthur Conan 20, 113, 144, 145, 146, 156-7
Drake, Sir Francis 28
Drayton, Michael 55, 109
Drinkwater, John 160
Droeshout, Martin 59
Drury, Sir Robert, and Lady 35
Dryden, John 10, 13, 26, 74, 82, 108, 109, 121, 124, 127, 135-6, 169, 188
Dudley, Lord Guildford 60
Dyer, John 109

Edgeworth, Maria 153, 193
Edward IV, King 77
Edward V, King 107
Edward VIII, King 107
Edward the Confessor, King 107
Egerton, Sir Thomas 35
Eliot, George 109, 188
Eliot, T. S. 15, 16, 20, 35, 47, 65, 69-70, 72, 91, 128, 131, 146, 153, 173, 180
Eliot, Valerie 70
Eliot, Vivienne 70
Elizabeth I, Queen 34, 47, 80, 109, 119, 149, 188
Empson, William 190-1
Epstein, Jacob 130, 131, 138
Essex, Earl of 80, 111, 119
Evans, Henry 30
Evelyn, John 24, 35, 42, 69, 83, 102, 114, 149

Farrant, Richard 30
Fielding, Henry 10, 29, 46, 66, 115, 119, 122-3, 126, 148-9, 189
Fielding, John 122
Fitzgerald, Edward 174
Fitzroy, Henry, Duke of Richmond 60
FitzStephen, William 41
Flecker, James Elroy 160
Fletcher, John 26, 63, 90-1, 100, 121
Ford, Ford Madox 134
Ford, John 23
Forster, E. M. 47, 174, 180
Forster, John 19, 146, 168, 194
Foxe, John 57-8

Fry, Roger 180
Fuller, Thomas 118, 164
Fuseli, Henry 169

Gainsborough, Thomas 59
Gallienne, Richard le 20, 49, 171
Galsworthy, Ada 193-4
Galsworthy, John 27, 116, 134, 164, 166, 193-4
Gardner, Helen 47
Garnett, David 180
Garrick, David 20, 116, 121, 123, 124, 126, 128, 130, 137, 166, 189
Gascoigne, George 160
Gaunt, John of 49, 118
Gay, John 13, 123, 125, 156, 166, 167
Grant, Duncan 174
Granville, George, Lord Lansdowne 119-20
Gray, Thomas 108, 188
Greville, Sir Fulke, Lord Brooke 161
Gibbon, Edward 20, 109, 152
Gibson, W. W. 138, 160
Gilbert, W. S. 129, 130, 137, 160
Godwin, Mary 142, 160, 164, 184
Godwin, William 142, 183, 184
Goldsmith, Oliver 20-1, 25, 26, 28, 29, 71, 109, 123, 126, 134, 160
Gonne, Maud 183
Gower, John 90
Grahame, Kenneth 65
Grant, Duncan 180
Granville, George, Lord Lansdowne 84
Granville-Barker, Harley 116
Gray, Thomas 68
Graves, Robert 160
Greene, George 26
Grey, Lady Jane 60
Grossmith, George 117, 118
Grossmith, George (Jnr) 152
Grossmith, Walter Weedon 117
Gwynn, Nell 83, 121, 131
Gyles, Nathaniel 30

Haggard, H. Rider 26
Hallam, Arthur Henry 23, 154
Hallam, Henry 154
Hardy, Thomas 109, 116-7, 131
Harley, Edward 52-3
Harley, Robert, Earl of Oxford 115
Hawkins, Sir Anthony Hope 173, 185
Hawksmoor, Nicholas 107
Hawthorne, Nathaniel 163
Haydon, Benjamin Robert 186
Hazlitt, William 15, 49, 63, 136, 138-9, 164, 172, 173, 190

H.D. *see* Doolittle, Hilda
Heine, Heinrich 113
Helwys, Sir Gervase 82
Heminge, John 31, 59, 187
Henry I, King 41, 127
Henry III, King 107, 118
Henry IV, King 41
Henry VI, King 89
Henry VIII, King 32, 34, 39, 47, 60, 79, 80, 87, 111
Henslowe, Philip 55, 57, 93, 100, 102
Herbert, George 45, 109
Herrick, Robert 61
Hodgson, Ralph 160
Hogarth, Mary 176, 177
Hogarth, William 16, 42, 127, 133, 158, 169, 175
Hogg, Thomas Jefferson 29, 142-3
Holbein, Hans 130
Hollar, Wenceslaus 73, 93, 99, 119
Hood, Thomas 38, 116
Hooke, Robert 74
Hope, Anthony: *see* Hawkins, Sir Anthony Hope
Hopkins, Gerard Manley 109, 159
Howard, Frances, Countess of Essex 81-2
Howard, Henry, Earl of Surrey 13, 32, 60, 77, 80, 84
Hughes, Thomas 23
Hulme, T. E. 138
Hume, David 115-6, 136
Hunt, Leigh 63, 173, 190, 194, 195, 200
Hunt, William Holman 159, 185
Hunter, Dr John 133, 152
Huxley, Aldous 175, 185, 190, 195
Huxley, Sir Julian 190

Ibsen, Henrik 137
Irving, Sir Henry 130
Irving, Washington 194-5

James, Henry 109, 131, 136
James I, King 23, 34, 80, 91, 100, 105
James II, King 84, 107, 136
James, the Pretender (son of James II) 84
James, William 182
Jerrold, Douglas 137
Johnson, Lionel 20, 160, 166
Johnson, Dr Samuel 10, 15, 16, 19, 20-2, 24, 34, 35, 38, 43, 44, 46, 48-9, 57, 68, 108, 109, 113, 116, 119, 120, 124, 125, 126, 128, 129, 131, 133, 134-5, 136-7, 151, 152, 160, 163, 166, 170, 172, 179, 188, 189
Jones, Inigo 102, 105, 118, 126, 127, 129, 130, 165
Jonson, Ben 16, 17, 31, 33, 41, 44, 59, 62, 63, 91, 100, 102, 105, 108, 118, 137, 161, 164
Joyce, James 131, 182, 188

Kean, Edmun 123, 124, 134

Kafka, Franz 191
Katt, Christopher 195
Keats, George 197
Keats, John 57, 63, 109, 110, 128, 131, 186, 188, 190, 191, 198-200
Keats, Tom 197
Kelly, Frances Maria 129
Kemble, Charles 136, 141
Kemble, Frances ('Fanny') 136, 141
Ker, W. P. 185
Keynes, John Maynard 174, 180, 181, 186
Killigrew, Thomas 121
Kipling, Rudyard 114, 115, 198
Kneller, Sir Godfrey 195
Knox, E. V. 192
Kyd, Thomas 70

Laforgue, Jules 20
Lamb, Charles 24, 26, 27, 42, 49, 63, 124, 129, 138, 150, 159, 160, 164, 172, 173, 190
Lamb, Mary 24, 26, 27, 49, 124, 138, 159, 172
Landor, Walter Savage 156, 173
Langland, William 187
Larkin, Philip 188
Lawrence, D. H. 47, 109, 160, 175, 185-6, 195-6
Lawrence, T. E. 37
Lean, David 37
Lear, Edward 148
Lee, Nathaniel 39, 120, 124
Lewis, Matthew ('Monk') 157
Lewis, Wyndham 179
Linley, Elizabeth 129, 149, 151, 158
Linley, Thomas 129
Locke, John 109
Lopokova, Lydia 180
Lovelace, Richard 13-14, 39, 107
Lucas, E. V. 178
Lucy, Helen 58
Lyly, John 42, 118

Macauley, Thomas Babington 160, 179
MacCarthy, Desmond 180
MacKenzie, Sir Compton 191
Macklin, Charles 124, 127, 129
Macready, William Charles 138
Malory, Sir Thomas 43-4
Manny, Sir Walter de 39
Mansfield, Katharine 185-6, 195, 196
Mare, Walter de la 36-7, 160
Marlowe, Christopher 44, 94, 100, 128
Marryat, Captain Frederick 152
Marsh, Edward 138, 160
Marshall, Frances 181
Marston, John 26

Marvell, Andrew 128, 130, 187
Marx, Karl 134, 138
Masefield, John 108, 134, 160, 176, 197
Massinger, Philip 90, 91, 188
Maughan, William Somerset 147
Maurier, George du 157, 171-2, 191, 192, 193
Melville, Herman 113
Meredith, George 178
Meynell, Alice 139, 148
Meynell, Wilfred 139, 148
Middleton, Thomas 61, 91, 100, 160
Mill, J. S. 152
Millais, John Everett 130, 159, 177, 185
Milne, A. A. 109
Milton, John 13, 17, 38, 55, 58, 61, 62, 109, 112, 127, 128, 131, 169, 188
Minshull, Elizabeth 55
Mist, Nathaniel 53
Mitford, Mary Russell 173
Monro, Harold 16, 171
Montagu, Basil 166
Montagu, Mrs Elizabeth 151, 152
Montagu, Lady Mary Wortley 127, 129, 141, 151, 153
Moore, George 26
Moore, Henry 63
Moore, Thomas 24, 147, 190
Moore, T. Sturge 197
More, Anne: *see* Donne, Anne
More, Sir Thomas 39, 57, 61, 72, 79, 84, 111, 130, 162, 164, 166
Morley, Frank 16
Morrell, Lady Ottoline 173, 185
Morrell, Philip 173, 185
Morris, William 159, 178, 179
Mozart, Wolfgang Amadeus 138, 139, 176
Muir, Edwin 191
Muir, Willa 191
Murphy, Arthur 139, 166
Murry, John Middleton 138, 185-6, 195, 196

Nashe, Thomas 33
Newby, Thomas 67-8
Newton, Sir Isaac 133
Nicolson, Sir Harold 26
Norton, Thomas 13, 26

Oates, Titus 83, 115
Oldcastle, Sir John 111, 127-8
Otway, Rhomas 120, 166
Overbury, Sir Thomas 81-2
Owen, Wilfrid 109

Partridge, Ralph 181
Patmore, Coventry 139, 191, 193

Peacock, Thomas Love 164
Pepys, Samuel 13, 16, 17, 38, 42, 61, 63, 74-5, 76, 77, 82, 83, 102, 107, 108, 112, 115, 119, 124, 131, 149-50, 160, 165
Pepys, Elizabeth (*née* St Michel) 63, 76, 112
Philips, Ambrose 125
Philips, Thomas 131
Piozzi, Gabriel 152
Pope, Alexander 69, 120, 121, 124, 125, 126, 129, 130, 131, 133, 141, 151, 170
Pound, Ezra 70, 138, 195
Powell, Mary 112
Priestley, J. B. 197
Prior, Matthew 108, 109, 133
Proctor, Bryan Waller 173, 174

Queensberry, Marquis of 46-7, 191
Quincey, Thomas de 24, 129, 139, 158

Radcliffe, Ann 49, 163
Rahere 41
Ralegh, Sir Walter 24, 63, 80-1, 105, 107, 110, 111, 112, 128, 160, 187
Read, Herbert 16
Reade, Charles 37, 124, 164
Reynolds, Sir Joshua 20, 35, 36, 116, 124, 126, 131, 133, 134, 169
Reynolds, J. H. 198
Rice, James 37
Rich, John 123, 166
Richard II, King 42, 194
Richardson, Dorothy 182, 183
Richardson, Samuel 10, 14-15, 20, 195
Robinson, Henry Crabb 173, 193
Rochester, Earl of: *see* Wilmot, John
Rogers, Samuel 27
Romney, George 193
Rossetti, Christina 171
Rossetti, Dante Gabriel 159, 168-9, 179
Rousseau, Jean-Jacques 115-6
Rowe, Nicholas 23
Rowley, William 55, 91
Rubens, Peter Paul 105
Ruskin, John 175
Russell, Bertrand 70, 159
Russell, George William 174

Sackville, Charles, 6th Earl of Dorset 168
Sackville, Thomas 13, 14, 26
Sackville-West, Victoria 26
Sassoon, Siegfried 160
Savage, Richard 33, 46, 48-9
Sayers, Dorothy L. 136, 175, 178
Schreiner, Olive 147

Scott, Sir Walter 193
Sedley, Sir Charles 119, 170
Shadwell, Thomas 23
Shaftesbury, Earl of: *see* Cooper, Anthony Ashley
Shakespear, Olivia 183
Shakespeare, Anne 17
Shakespeare, Edmund 59, 90, 91
Shakespeare, William 9, 10, 13, 17-18, 19, 28, 29, 30, 31, 34, 41, 49, 58-9, 63, 71, 77, 80, 82, 89, 91, 92, 98, 100, 103, 105, 109, 111, 119, 124, 128, 130, 131, 133, 134, 160, 161, 166, 187
Shaw, G. B. 117, 129-30
Shawe, Isabella 174
Shelley, Percy Bysshe 28, 63, 109, 128, 142-3, 150, 160, 164, 185, 188, 190, 194
Sheppard, Jack 45-6
Sheridan, Richard Brinsley 24, 65, 108, 121-2, 123, 126, 129, 134, 149, 151, 154, 158, 171
Sheridan, Thomas 129
Shirley, James 105, 128, 160
Sickert, Walter 131
Siddal, Elizabeth 168-9
Siddons, Mrs Sarah 124, 193
Sidney, Sir Philip 17, 160
Sinclair, May 182
Skelton, John 112
Sloane, Sir Hans 186
Sly, William 31
Smollett, Tobias 105, 140
Snow, C.P. 147
Soane, Sir John 169
Southampton, Earl of: *see* Wriothesley, Henry
Southey, Robert 109, 160
Southwell, Robert 45, 148-9
Spenser, Edmund 108, 119, 187
Stanhope, Philip Dormer, 4th Earl of Chesterfield 22, 170
Steele, Sir Richard 13, 16, 39, 42, 69, 114, 124, 125, 140, 171, 195
Stephen, Adrian 174, 181
Stephen, Sir Leslie 23, 180-1
Stephen, Thoby 181
Stephen, Vanessa: *see* Bell, Vanessa
Stephen, Virginia: *see* Woolf, Virginia
Sterne, Laurence 140, 188
Stevenson, Robert Louis 192-3
Stoddart, Sarah 49, 172
Stoker, Bram 130
Stopes, Marie 197
Stow, John 61
Strachey, James 180, 181
Strachey, Lytton 180, 181
Strang, William 131
Straw, Jack 194

Suckling, Sir John 160
Sullivan, Sir Arthur 137
Surrey, Earl of: see Howard, Henry
Sutton, Thomas 39
Swift, Jonathan 16, 66, 69, 115, 117, 125, 133, 187
Swinburne, Algernon Charles 145, 177-8
Swinnerton, Frank 178
Symons, Arthur 20

Tagore, Rabindranath 195
Tawney, R.H. 176
Tennyson, Lord Alfred 16, 20, 23, 27, 108, 154
Terry, Ellen 129
Thackeray, William Makepeace 24, 27, 29, 39, 41, 66-8, 109, 139, 151, 173, 1174, 194
Thomas, Dylan 45, 109
Thomas, Edward 134
Thompson, Francis 139, 148
Thorndike, Dame Sybil 92
Thrale, Mrs Hester Lynch Salusbury 120, 137, 152-3
Throckmorton, Elizabeth 80
Tonson, Jacob 135
Tottel, Richard 13, 80
Travers, P.L. 193
Tree, Sir Herbert Beerbohm 185, 192
Trollope, Anthony 146, 152, 153, 185, 188
Turner, J.M.W. 169
Twain, Mark 20
Tyler, Wat 42

Udall, Nicholas 109, 111
Ustinov, Peter 109

Vallon, Marie-Anne ('Annette') 104
Vanbrugh, Sir John 13, 64, 195
Veil, Thomas de 122
Verlaine, Paul 20
Villiers, George, 2nd Duke of Buckingham 82-3, 109, 113-4, 135
Violetti, Eva Maria 128, 130
Voltaire 130

Waley, Arthur 178, 181
Wallace, Edgar 119
Waller, Edmund 44, 166
Walpole, Horace 43, 49, 68, 105, 126, 140, 149, 150, 164

Walpole, Sir Robert 105, 117, 122, 195
Walsingham, Sir Francis 44
Walton, Izaak 18-19, 35
Walworth, William 42
Ward, Mrs Humphrey 173
Warwick, Countess of 125
Watson, Thomas 42
Watts, Isaac 51, 53-4
Watts-Duncan, Theodore 177
Webster, John 23, 81, 100
Weekley, Ernest 195
Wells, H.G. 158, 191
Wesley, Charles 38, 127, 128, 156, 158
Wesley, John 38, 39, 50, 127, 128
Westbrook, Harriet 128, 142, 150
Whittington, Richard 63
Wild, Jonathan 46, 149
Wilde, Oscar 20, 46-7, 48, 191
William I ('the Conqueror'), King 77, 107
William III, King 52, 135
Williams, George 14
Wilmot, John, Lord Rochester 83-4, 127
Wither, George 44-5, 83, 118, 164
Witt, Johannes de 93-4
Wodehouse, P.G. 152
Woffington, Peg 123, 137
Wollstonecraft, Mary 142, 185
Woodcock, Catharine 112
Woolf, Leonard 174, 175, 180
Woolf, Virginia 23, 70, 174, 175, 180, 181-2
Woolner, Thomas 152
Worde, Wynken de 61
Wordsworth, William 10, 42, 61-2, 104, 109, 161, 166, 173, 188, 193
Wordsworth, Dorothy 42, 104
Wotton, Sir Henry 98-9
Wren, Christopher 11, 13, 26, 34, 36, 47, 48, 61, 63, 64, 74, 119, 120, 121
Wriothesley, Henry, Earl of Southampton 9, 33, 80, 111
Wyatt, Sir Thomas 13, 33, 79-80
Wycherley, William 23, 26, 33, 124, 129
Wycliffe, John 118

Yorke, Dorothy 175
Yeats, W.B. 20, 174, 183-4, 195